THE NATIONAL QUESTION

'HE NATIONAL QUESTION

Selected Writings

Rosa Luxemburg

edited with an introduction by
Horace B. Davis

The National Question: Selected Writings
Rosa Luxemburg

First Published in India 2009
Reprinted 2014
Reprinted 2023

ISBN 978-93-5002-005-0

Published in agreement with Monthly Review Press, New York for publication and sale only in South Asia.

Published by
AAKAR BOOKS
28 E Pocket IV, Mayur Vihar Phase I
Delhi 110 091, India
www.aakarbooks.com

Printed at
D.K. Fine Art Press, Delhi

Contents

Foreword

English-speaking readers have not had in the past any access to Rosa Luxemburg's writings in Polish, so that a comparison of her ideas with Lenin's has been difficult. We here present her basic articles of 1908–1909, plus a selection of other writings which bear on the differences between the two. The final 1908–1909 article on the national question and autonomy (meaning the autonomy of Poland within a future democratized Russia) was not at issue and has been omitted. On the other hand, the "Theses" of the editors of *Gazeta Robotnicza,* presented to the Zimmerwald Conference and published in 1916, although not by Rosa Luxemburg, were answered at length by Lenin—in "Theses" of his own, and in the article "The Discussion on Self-Determination Summed Up" (1916). We have included the *Gazeta* theses as an Appendix.

Rosa Luxemburg's own reference notes appear at the bottoms of pages; the editor's are numbered and appear at the end of each selection.

The editor takes responsibility for the final form in which the translation appears, but the tough, early work of rendering Polish into English has been shared by a galaxy of collaborators. Translators have included Colleen Taylor, Sophia Miskiewicz, Ludwik Krzyzanowski, and very briefly Eugenia

Jarosiewicz, with extensive editing by Elzbieta Chodakowska. My collaborators on the German texts were Michel Vale and Cliff Gaddy. I owe all of them a deep debt of gratitude for trying, along with me, to preserve the verve and variety of the original and to avoid stultifying condensations. I have used with appreciation some background material contained in Jürgen Hentze's *Rosa Luxemburg: Internationalismus und Klassenkampf* (Luchterhand, 1971).

I also acknowledge the valued cooperation of the University Library at Warsaw and of Feliks Tych, long-time expert on Rosa Luxemburg, at the Institute of Party History.

H. B. D.

Introduction

The Right of National Self-Determination in Marxist Theory—Luxemburg vs. Lenin

It is perhaps little known that despite Lenin's attacks on her, the philosophical position so ably expounded by Rosa Luxemburg in her articles of 1908–1909 was never refuted; that it was, on the contrary, adopted by a substantial section of the Bolshevik Party, which fought Lenin on the issue, using Rosa Luxemburg's arguments–and eventually, in 1919, defeated him, so that the slogan of the right of self-determination was removed from the platform of the Communist Party of the Soviet Union (CPSU). Later, when the issue was no longer so acute, the slogan was revived and today represents part of the CPSU's stock in trade. But the basic arguments in its favor are precisely those which were successfully opposed by Rosa Luxemburg and her partisans. The Soviet leadership is working with a blunted tool.

Julius K. Nyerere, President of Tanzania and one of the more subtle theorists of the new nationalism in Africa, has suggested that overemphasis on the slogan of "self-determination" in the campaign for decolonization may make the eventual attainment of socialism more difficult. He says:

> Everyone wants to be free, and the task of the nationalist is simply to rouse the people to a confidence in their own power of protest. But to build the real freedom which socialism represents is a very different thing. It

> demands a positive understanding and positive actions, not simply a rejection of colonialism and a willingness to cooperate in noncooperation.[1]

It might come as a surprise to Nyerere to learn that just this difficulty with the slogan was pointed out by Rosa Luxemburg sixty years earlier. Surely Marxism has been remiss in neglecting the theory of nationalism for so long.

Western scholars who are aware of this situation have been hampered in their efforts to evaluate the "Great Debate" by the fact that only one side—Lenin's—has been available to them. Lenin, as is known, was an ardent polemicist, and he was not one to present fully an argument of his opponent's which he was unable to answer to his own satisfaction. Thus, some of Luxemburg's most telling points have been neglected or received secondhand, often from the very person engaged in "refuting" them.

We do not intend to imply that either of the antagonists "won" the debate. Certainly Rosa Luxemburg did not. Her estimates of the tendencies of the time were on the whole less accurate than Lenin's, which is one reason for the neglect her views have suffered. She underestimated the force of the nationalist drive (while perfectly appreciating the reasons for it), and her theory was thus unable to cope with the centrifugal tendencies in the modern multinational state. Like Lenin, she wrote for a European audience, so that her presentation lacks generality. But her statement of the case *against* the theory of national self-determination is as relevant today as when it was written in 1908. Indeed, it has never been surpassed in Marxist theory, if at all. The name of Marx is always likely to be drawn into a debate between Marxists, and the present case is no exception. Although Marx was not interested in the principle of self-determination as such,[2] he was still prepared to employ the slogan on occasion.

In 1867 an "Instruction to Delegates" (to the General Council of the First International) included a passage on the "necessity to annihilate the Russian influence on Europe by the application of *the right of peoples to dispose of themselves* and to reconstruct a Poland on a democratic and social basis."[3] This passage was adopted by the General Council and became part of the policy of the First International. Marx probably did not write it but was willing to accept it, although a pamphlet edited by him containing the resolutions of the International Workingmen's Association (IWMA) Congresses of 1866 and 1868 does not include the passage in question.[4]

The differences between Rosa Luxemburg and Lenin may be summarized under several headings as follows:

1. Lenin strongly emphasized the right of self-determination of nations. Rosa Luxemburg said that there was no such right, and putting forward this slogan when the terms were not defined carefully could mean not a contribution to solving the problem but a means of avoiding it.

Luxemburg's point was sound then and it is sound today, but she overstated it. There is a *moral* right of self-determination, when the terms are defined; and she should have so indicated. Her opposition to national oppression shows that she recognized the principle.

2. Lenin emphasized the role of the bourgeoisie in building modern nations. Luxemburg said that there were circumstances when the role of the bourgeoisie in nation-building was minimal, and she was correct, not only with regard to Poland but in relation to precapitalist economic formations, colonies, and so on.

3. Luxemburg allowed a place for federation and autonomy. Lenin's position on federalism was ambiguous. He at first opposed it, then later adopted it for the Soviet Union, at least nominally. Luxemburg's thinking was more flexible on this point, and her criticism of Lenin is receiving renewed attention today. But autonomy may mean little in an undemocratic state.

4. Rosa Luxemburg and her followers interpreted self-determination as meaning the self-determination of the working class. Lenin correctly opposed this formulation, but his statement of the case against it failed to carry conviction and he was overridden by the 1919 CPSU Congress, as we shall see.

5. Rosa Luxemburg opposed nationalism as leading to fragmentation. Lenin stressed the advantages of large national units, but at the same time appreciated the strength of the tendency to fragmentation, to which he was not entirely unsympathetic. Lenin was correct, as anyone today would have to concede.

Our main concern is with the first point above, the question of whether there is a *right* to self-determination of nations. In discussing this and the other points, we shall attempt to show that nationality theory, which heretofore has been treated as lying outside Marxist theory or only distantly related to it, is in fact a central part of Marxist theory; indeed, without a correct nationality theory Marxism cannot solve the most pressing problems of the world today. Hence the importance of a restudy of the whole debate, and especially of Rosa Luxemburg's contributions to it, which have been neglected for so many years.

The Historical Setting

Rosa Luxemburg was born and went to school in what was then Russian Poland. She came of middle-class Jewish parents. She early showed an interest in the revolutionary movement and attracted so much attention from the authorities that she found it advisable to leave Russia. She went first to Switzerland and then to Germany, where she completed her studies while continuing active in the social-democratic movement. She studied Polish history, and was later able to correct Lenin in his exclusive emphasis on the bourgeoisie as the creator of nationalism; for in Poland the nationalist movement was led for many years by the landed nobility (*schlachta*).[5] She always retained her interest in Poland; she worked among the Poles in East Prussia and was the German Social Democratic Party's expert on Poland. At the same time she participated—at a distance most of the time—in the social-democratic movement in Russia, where she usually sympathized with the Bolshevik position. Lenin, although he disagreed with her on a number of points, always had the highest opinion of her ability and sincerity.

The whole 1893-1914 period was characterized by a debate between two parties in Poland on the subject of national self-determination. The Polish Socialist Party (Polska Partia Socialistyczma—PPS) favored the reconstitution of Poland, and its branch parties in each of the partition states (Germany, Austria, and Russia) campaigned among the workers, the peasants, and the middle class on this strictly nationalist basis, hardly mentioning socialism. The Social Democratic Party of Poland—later, after the inclusion of Lithuania in 1899, known as the SDKPiL—was founded by Rosa Luxemburg and others in 1893, and continued an earlier Marxist tradition in opposing self-determination for Poland.

First one and then the other of the parties seemed to have the ear of the workers. The International Socialist Congress at London (1896) heard both sides present their cases and decided, in effect, not to interfere. The SDKPiL seemed to have only a small following in 1903, but when the First Russian Revolution broke out in 1905 the workers in Russian Poland flocked into the SDKPiL and made common cause with the Russian workers. Barricades were erected and there was street fighting in several Polish cities. The PPS split: one faction gravitated toward the position of the SDKPiL and eventually (in December 1918) merged with it; a smaller group, led by Pilsudski, survived and eventually, after the war, took over the leadership in the newly reconstituted country of Poland.

Rosa Luxemburg's position on nationalism was that it was a movement in which the working class had only an indirect interest. She always maintained that the best and quickest way for workers to get rid of the bane of national domination was to bring about the international socialist revolution. In 1903, partisans of Rosa Luxemburg's point of view appeared at the Congress of the Russian Social Democratic Labor Party (RSDLP) and urged that the Congress make no endorsement of self-determination. The RSDLP did come out for self-determination of nations, whereupon the Polish delegates left. Both Bolsheviks and Mensheviks favored self-determination.

The Poles again appeared at the 1906 Congress of the Russian Party, and this time did not press their opposition to self-determination, though they still held the same position as in 1903. They cooperated with Lenin at this Congress, thus indicating the extent of the similarity between their views and his. But the basic philosophical question remained unresolved.

Rosa Luxemburg set forth her position in detail in a series of articles, "The National Question and Autonomy," which were published in 1908–1909 in her Cracow magazine, *Przeglad Sozialdemokratyczny*. Other Marxists also contributed to the discussion, and Lenin commissioned Stalin to write a pamphlet on the subject of nationalism. This appeared early in 1913, and was devoted chiefly to a refutation of the views of Karl Renner and Otto Bauer on national-cultural autonomy.[6]

However, no one had really answered Rosa Luxemburg, and Lenin himself undertook this task. "On the Right of Nations to Self-Determination," written at the beginning of 1914, was directed specifically against her.

The "Right" of Self-Determination

It is non-Marxist, said Rosa Luxemburg, to talk in terms of absolute rights, or indeed of rights at all, since the dialectic does not recognize the existence of rights in general; the "rights" and "wrongs" of a given situation must be arrived at by an analysis of the given historical circumstances.

Lenin as a Marxist had absolutely no answer to this contention, since he had often expounded this very point. He said both before and after 1908 that the interests of the proletarian revolution were paramount, and he was prepared to sacrifice the right of self-determination to the cause of the revolution at any time. He was also not in favor of self-determination in the abstract, for this might lead to unacceptable conclusions.

Luxemburg denied that there was any "right" to freedom from oppression. Such questions, she maintained, are questions of power and are settled as such. She said that telling the workers that they had the "right" to self-determination was like telling them that they had the right to eat off gold plates.

In a class society, to speak of self-determination for the "people" would ordinarily mean the self-determination of the ruling class; the workers would be left in a subordinate position as before. This was why in her discussions, with Poland very much in mind, she gravitated toward the position that self-determination was the self-determination of the *working* class. This, as we shall see, was a slogan that was used in the Russian Revolution.

Since Luxemburg was specifically opposed to the right of self-determination, it might be supposed that she would also have objected to any special consideration being shown to the minor nationalities as such. But that would not be correct at all. She had a strong feeling for the autonomy of Poland, the smaller nationality in which she was most interested. It is only necessary to read the sixth and last article of the 1908–1909 series in order fully to appreciate how hard she was prepared to work to come up with a plan which, while not based on any general principle of self-determination, still would guarantee the requisite degree of self-government and cultural autonomy to her people. Lenin complained that she limited her demands for autonomy to Poland alone, but that did not necessarily follow. In the dialectical method Lenin himself advocated, each case has to be considered on its merits, and it is necessary to start somewhere.

Luxemburg took occasion to state why she thought Lithuania and Georgia would *not* be suitable territories in which to apply the principle of autonomy. The reason was quite simply that they were too small—even Georgia with its 1.2 million people was not in her estimation a viable unit. Lenin, by contrast, mentioned a figure as small as 50,000, and indeed some of the nationalities in the Soviet Union are not much larger than that.[7] Since Lenin was prepared to go in for mini-nations, he was also prepared to carve up the administrative units of the old Russian empire where these included more than one nationality.

But did Lenin not realize that a nation with only 50,000 people would not be capable of defending itself, or of developing an internal market large enough to bring the advantages of large-scale production? How could such microscopic nations survive at all? Luxemburg, following in the footsteps of Marx and Engels, emphasized the tendency to form larger and larger national units. Her solution to the problem of popular control was in the Marxist tradition: to have the proletariat of the advanced nations, making common cause with the minor nationalities, overthrow capitalism and bring freedom to the smaller nationalities and to the colonies from the center, under a socialist government. Pending such a solution, it was Luxemburg's view that the smaller nationalities would do better within the larger (imperialist) country. She even criticized Marx for having advocated the independence of Poland. She contended that such a move would have the effect of solidifying the control of the gentry (and, later, the bourgeoisie), and would be of little value to the peasants and workers, who should make common cause with the workers and peasants of the larger country in which they found themselves.

This was indeed a major difference between Lenin and Luxemburg, but it was a difference more of judgment on the practical application of the theory than of theory or method as such. Lenin's attempts to label Luxemburg's theory "abstract" and "metaphysical" come down largely to matters of definition. Lenin asked Luxemburg, rhetorically, why she did not define the nation in accordance with Kautsky's historical-economic analysis and take specific exception to Otto Bauer's psychological definition. Here Lenin was on dangerous ground. In the first place, Stalin, with Lenin's apparent blessing, had just published an article containing a definition of the nation which was based partly on Bauer's "psychological" one. And in the second place, Kautsky, writing incessantly on the nation, had come to define nationality in terms of language, a definition so defective that Lenin himself was presently obliged to attack it. Lenin saved himself the trouble of defining a nation, but that did not give him the license to impose definitions arbitrarily on others. (Incidentally, Kautsky, who had been criticized by Luxemburg for emphasizing the fissiparous tendencies of contemporary capitalism, after the First World War came to the belief that peace could be best assured by a cartel of the leading capitalist nations!)

In calling for the "right of self-determination of nations" Lenin was endorsing the idea that nations have rights. Luxemburg denied this absolutely; if she was prepared to talk about rights at all, it would be exclusively in terms of the rights of the working class.

Since Lenin was fully aware of the economic advantages of large states—he intended to make a single economic unit of the socialist society of the future, which would be not only as large as the empire of the Tsar but much larger—and since he looked on the "right of self-determination of nations" as a qualified right, subordinate to the aims of the socialist revolution, was he then not seeking to deceive the smaller nationalities about the nature of this "self-determination"? Luxemburg maintained, in effect, that he was, and she proceeded to argue that in a contest involving nationality, the ruling class held all the trump cards. At any given time—short of socialism—any "democratic" determination of the wishes of the "people," even of the proletariat, might be expected to show a majority for the bourgeoisie.

This was a fundamental criticism of Lenin's position. Since Lenin advocated self-determination only up to a point, those who wished for self-determination beyond that point—those who were not interested in social revolution (except to combat it)—would of course charge Lenin with hypocrisy; and this was done, both at the time and later. Luxemburg's position was not any more palatable to the conservatives, but she did escape from the charge of hypocrisy.

By way of defining his position on the separation of small nations from larger, Lenin wrote:

> Never in favor of petty states, or the splitting up of states in general, or the principle of federation, Marx considered the separation of an oppressed nation to be a step towards federation, and consequently, not towards a split, but towards concentration, both political and economic, but concentration on the basis of democracy.[8]

The differences between Luxemburg and Lenin were partly due to a difference in the set of "facts" with which they were operating. This difference emerges most clearly in the discussion of Norway's secession from Sweden in 1905. It is indeed difficult to believe, after reading the two accounts, that the authors are referring to the same incident. Luxemburg's proposition that Sweden was prepared to let Norway go was one that Lenin could not refute. Lenin is less than forthright when he asks Luxemburg: Does the recognition of the equality of nations include the recognition of the right of secession? In the first place, there was no agreed definition of a nation, as already noted. But in the second place, the "right" of secession was a term Luxemburg would have immediately rejected, for the same reason that she rejected the "right" of self-determination.[9]

Lenin did not really anticipate that the "right" of secession would be exercised, but he was prepared to have a small nation secede from Russia (the Soviet Union) because he fully expected that the economic advantages of belonging to a larger economic unit, plus, for the workers, the advantage of belonging to a workers' state, would bring any such seceding nation back again.

Luxemburg was opposed on principle to the creation of new, small, and as she saw it, nonviable states, even when it could be shown that all classes, including the workers, were in favor. Lenin saw as clearly as she the economic forces that were driving toward creation of larger and larger states. But he saw what she did not see (or chose to overlook), that the contrary forces, making for smaller states, were powerful too and in the short run perhaps determining. Further—and this was the crucial point—Lenin opposed *overruling* the nationalists even when he did not agree with them. They should be brought to see the error of their ways, while at the same time being allowed full *cultural* freedom for their respective nationalities.

Luxemburg was confronted with a particular situation in Poland (which was not necessarily typical, as Lenin pointed out). The Poles in Austria already enjoyed *de facto* autonomy and considerable democratic rights, and the Polish workers there had little to gain and possibly much to lose from being put into a reconstituted Poland dominated by bourgeoisie and landowners. Much the same could be said of the Poles in East Prussia with whom Rosa Luxemburg worked, and in Russia it was plain that the days of tsarist absolutism were numbered, so that the Poles in "Kingdom Poland" could reasonably hope for autonomy and/or democracy within the foreseeable future.

It was the analysis of the concrete situation that divided Luxemburg and Lenin, not the method of analysis or the starting point, both of which were nearly identical. Lenin, as a Russian internationalist, was fighting against Great Russian chauvinism. Luxemburg, as a Polish (German) internationalist, was fighting against Polish social patriotism (chauvinism). Paradoxically, they arrived at exactly contrary positions on self-determination. But Lowy finds that Lenin's position was superior in that it applied elsewhere too; it recognized the constructive aspects of nationalist movements in a way that Luxemburg's did not.[10]

Is "freedom from national oppression" (a freedom which Luxemburg favored) the same as "self-determination of nations"? Her strong and continuing objections to the latter phrase make it seem as if she thought there was a difference. But if so, what? Or was she merely opposed to the idea that self-determination was a *right?*

Phrases like "national liberation" and "freedom from national oppression" are, to be sure, vague and general, but less so than "national self-determination." In either case, we have to define what the nation is supposed to include—that is, its territorial boundaries. There is also the question of who is to do the determining, or, alternatively, just what the nation is supposed to be liberated from. But the phrase self-determination is hopelessly vague on the question whether what is meant is independence or some status short of independence. The anticolonial movements of recent years have been in favor of independence, and when they called themselves "national liberation" movements no one has doubted what was meant.

Freedom from Oppression as a Moral Right

Perhaps Social Democrats do not have the duty to protest against national oppression. Rosa Luxemburg said that on the contrary, Social Democrats have the duty to raise such a protest, not because it is *national* oppression but simply because it is oppression. Luxemburg insisted that to be a socialist one had to protest against *all* kinds of oppression, and to this point Lenin had no real answer either.

When Luxemburg spoke of the *duty* of Marxists to protest against oppression, was she reintroducing, by the back door, the concept of morality and ethics which she had just thrown out the front door? Some have been misled by Marx's repeated attacks on "bourgeois" morality into thinking that Marxism recognizes no morality at all, that it is a philosophy of power pure and simple, one in which the "workers are always right." But the larger morality, for which Marx was contending, does not dispense with rights and duties; it redefines them, gives them a new content. So it is not a contradiction to speak in terms of socialist morality, and that is the concept that Luxemburg had in mind.

Did Lenin believe in the idea of (socialist) morality? Definitely. To the Young Communist League, in October 1920, he said: "Is there such a thing as communist morality? Of course there is."[11] Lenin continued, arguing that "our morality is subordinated to the class struggle of the proletariat. . . . Communist morality is the morality . . . which unites the working people against all exploitation."[12]

Let us pause a moment at the phrase "all exploitation." Against exploitation of women? Clearly. Against national oppression? Obviously. Lenin showed by his actions all through his life that he was prepared to fight against exploitation wherever it was found. What is the difference between him and Luxemburg? None at all on this point, unless it might be in the manner of phrasing and the priority given to economic (class) exploitation in Lenin's writings. Lenin thought that the class question was of overshadowing importance. But he was broad-minded enough to admit that under certain circumstances the national question might assume prior emphasis. Thus, the national question takes its proper place in the hierarchy of social values, and a rounded socialist ethic becomes possible.[13]

We find then that for Marxists to use phrases like the "right of self-determination" invites misunderstanding. Luxemburg's "freedom from national oppression" is superior on all counts.

In her basic theoretical articles, Luxemburg especially stressed the economic aspects of nationalism and understated the importance of the political aspects.[14] Her theory of nationalism thus lacks generality, and Lenin was right in criticizing her on this ground; further, the political aspects are of the greatest importance in the wars for national liberation which have dominated the scene since World War II. She also underestimated the importance, for the revolutionary struggle, of the allies of the proletariat, including both the minor nationalities and the peasants. However, we cannot accept a point that is sometimes made, namely that she overlooked the effect of national oppression on the working class. We interpret her eloquent denunciation of national oppression as such, and her insistence that resistance to such oppression has more emotional content than mere economic exploitation could evoke, as indicating a realization on her part that national movements affect the working classes profoundly. We cite here in proof a passage from a work heretofore not translated from the Polish, a preface to a compendium on the national question which she edited in 1905:

> To the credit of mankind, history has universally established that even the most inhumane *material* oppression is not able to provoke such wrathful, fanatical rebellion and rage as the suppression of intellectual life in general, or as religious or national oppression.[15]

The debate on self-determination continued up to and during World War I. When Luxemburg was in and out of prison in Germany, her point of view was argued in Bolshevik circles by Piatakov ("Kievsky") and Bukharin.

The First World War

In the "Junius" pamphlet, written anonymously from her prison cell in 1916, Rosa Luxemburg again discussed the question of self-determination. The phrasing is more moderate, but the point of view has not changed. "Socialism," she then said, "recognizes for every people the right of independence and the freedom of independent control of its own destinies." But at the same time she argued that self-determination was impossible to attain under capitalism, and added: "Today the nation is but a cloak that covers imperialistic desires, a battle cry for imperialistic rivalries."[16] National wars, said "Junius," are no longer possible. Lenin pointed out in the friendliest spirit (he did not at first know who had written the pamphlet) that, on the contrary, national wars *of liberation* were quite possible in the imperialist epoch and indeed were the order of the day.[17] He also did not altogether accept Luxemburg's contention that self-determination was impossible under capitalism.[18]

Poles holding Luxemburg's point of view submitted theses on the national question to the Zimmerwald Conference; these were published in 1916. They opposed the independence of Poland. Lenin drafted theses in opposition, and wrote a special article to answer the Polish theses ("The Discussion on Self-Determination Summed Up").

Lenin's Contradictory Position

In this "answer," Lenin conceded Luxemburg's main point, namely that Poland would not be a viable state under existing conditions. He therefore advised the Polish Social Democrats not to press for Polish independence. At the same time, he tried to stick to his former advice to the Social Democrats of Germany, Austria, and Russia that they should recognize the *right* of Poland *to* secede. The result was a hybrid policy which cleared up nothing. According to Lenin:

> People who have not thought out the question find it "contradictory" that Social Democrats of oppressing nations should insist on "freedom to *secede*" and Social Democrats of oppressed nations on "freedom to *unite.*" But a little reflection shows that there is not and cannot be any *other* road to internationalization and to the fusion of nations, any other road from *the present position* to that goal.[19]

Professor Carr calls this a "somewhat nebulous" foundation for Bolshevik nationality policy, a restrained judgment indeed. Lenin's position had become very difficult to grasp.[20]

However, Lenin's platform on the national question had other planks, and it was for these quite as much as for the rather meaningless demand for "self-determination" that Lenin was fighting in his battles on the nationality question. The principles which he succeeded in impressing on his followers were primarily two: (1) equality of nations; and (2) the right of nationalities to a cultural existence of their own. There were also other aspects. It was Lenin who led the fight for the legal protection of national minorities against discrimination, for the right to schools and court proceedings in the vernacular, for writing down languages that had never been written down before, and for directing new investment precisely into backward areas with the avowed aim of bringing their standards up to those of the most advanced areas.

Lenin did not invent these principles, which were in general circulation at the time. They had been developed in struggle, on the initiative of the minority peoples themselves. It was to Lenin's lasting credit that he perceived that a general principle was involved, the right—which Marxists could not deny—for the working class to be free of *national as well as class* oppression. Lenin believed in this principle and acted on it; Luxemburg made it the cornerstone of her position.

Lenin's "Theses on the Right of Nations to Self-Determination" (March 1916) emphasized the "politically conditional nature and the class content of all demands of political democracy, including this demand." He specifically denied that the right of self-determination was in a separate category from the other democratic demands. He also emphasized a point that was to be of increasing importance: "The necessity of drawing a distinction between the concrete tasks of the Social Democrats [then including the Communists] in the oppressing nations and those in the oppressed nations." These qualifications differentiated his theory of self-determination from certain unqualified statements then current in liberal political theory.

Self-Determination in the Russian Revolution

The Seventh Conference of the Bolshevik Party was held in April 1917. A major discussion on the national question resulted in the adoption of the Lenin-Stalin proposals. The Conference called for "broad regional autonomy" but not national cultural autonomy, for protection of national minorities, and for annulling all privileges enjoyed by any nationality whatever.[21]

The year 1918 found the Bolshevik Revolution victorious but beset on all sides. The attitude that the border nationalities would take became of crucial importance to its survival. Luxemburg was at this time in prison in Germany. She was full of misgivings. In a pamphlet written in 1918 and published after her death the next year ("The Russian Revolution"), she found that the slogan of national self-determination was a liability, indeed the source of the revolution's severest headaches. It was of course true that the border republics had become separated from the central government in the early stages of the October Revolution, and that they were brought back only with some difficulty. But was their separation due to the slogan of self-determination? Rosa Luxemburg was in no position to prove that it was; she merely stated that she believed this to be the fact.

To illustrate the difficulty of applying the principle of self-determination, she noted that the bourgeoisie in the border republics (meaning, no doubt, the Mensheviks in Georgia) had preferred the violent rule of Germany to making common cause with the Bolsheviks.[22] But was this government really representative of the people, the workers? She emphasized that there was no machinery available to test the sentiment of the masses of the population, where this was different from that of their (unrepresentative) government.

This rather legalistic approach was inconsistent with two points in Luxemburg's other writings. In the first place, as a revolutionary socialist she never thought that the revolution could be made peacefully; the sentiment of the workers would be expressed on the barricades and not in the ballot box. The question of self-determination would be settled as a matter of force, not of right. In the second place, she fully endorsed Lenin's effort to bring back into the new socialist state as many as possible of the peoples who had been subject to the rule of the tsar of Russia.

With this parting shot, the debate between Luxemburg and Lenin may be said to have concluded. But the issues she had raised were debated for some time after 1918.

A group around Bukharin and Piatakov had campaigned against the idea of self-determination during the war. In

November 1915 they spelled out their position in a set of "Theses on Self-Determination and a Fifteen-Point Program" which they submitted to the Central Committee of the Party. They argued as follows:

> In the epoch of imperialism, the tendency is for large capitalist states to become larger. This tendency is in the nature of the case and cannot be fought piecemeal; the only solution is to abolish capitalism. The Bolsheviks should not advise the proletariat to spend its forces campaigning for national "self-determination" within the capitalist orbit; this would be utopian, and would create illusions. It is no different from calling for "arbitration" or "disarmament" as a means of combating militarism. The task of the workers is to mobilize the proletariat of both the oppressing nation and the oppressed, under the slogan of a civil, class war for socialism. In colonial countries we can support the uprising of the popular masses as an event which weakens the imperialist countries; in such areas we can work with the national bourgeoisie. The question has to be reached not by stressing abstract rights, which have no meaning in this connection, but by an analysis of the situation of the given nation at a particular time.[23]

In 1919, at the Eighth Party Congress of the Bolsheviks, Bukharin took the point of view that the interests of the international revolution were paramount, and in this matter he was strongly seconded by Piatakov, then in actual charge of the Ukraine, who urged centralized control of all proletarian movements by the newly established Communist International. Piatakov condemned the slogan of the right of nations to self-determination as reactionary. The slogan of the hour was self-determination for the *working class* of each nationality, but this did not satisfy Piatakov, who said that Soviet Russia must keep control of the Ukraine, even against the wishes of the Ukrainian proletariat.[24] He thus pushed

Luxemburg's point of view to its logical conclusion (Lenin called Piatakov a Great Russian chauvinist).

The slogan of "self-determination for the working class" seems at first blush to incorporate the bourgeois ideal of self-determination for a nation into the revolutionary theory of the Bolsheviks, which is based on the working class. Lenin had used the slogan himself in 1903. The Armenian Social Democrats had taken a position in favor of self-determination for Armenia. Lenin wrote then: "We on our part concern ourselves with the self-determination of the *proletariat* in each nationality rather than with the self-determination of peoples or nations."[25] He was to repeat the same idea in "The National Question in Our Program" (July 1903).[26] He objected to the emphasis on the right of self-determination because it obscured the class point of view.[27]

By 1919 Lenin had come to realize that "self-determination of the working class" was an unacceptable formulation. A close analysis will show that the slogan is not realistic. The working class that won independence for a national unit and set up a state would thereby have constituted a nation, actual or potential. If that state was free of class oppression, there would still remain the question of abolishing or guarding against other kinds of oppression. A social class may control a state, or (in Marxist theory at least) it may constitute a state, but it cannot exist independent of and outside of a state. The classless state, which has existed so far only as a theoretical concept, does not by its existence solve all problems of nationality. The Bolsheviks conducted a victorious revolution under the slogans of internationalism and the ending of class domination; but if they had not been guided, to the extent they were, by Lenin's principles of the freedom of nationalities, the "classless" state would hardly have survived. And Russian nationalism was not held in abeyance for long. "Self-determination for the working class," taken in context, meant "all power to the working class," to the Bolsheviks, and down with the bourgeois nationalists, the bourgeoisie. The utilization of a slogan from the field of nationalism in what was essentially a class struggle may have been legitimate as a revolutionary tactic, but it made no sense as a logical proposition; it was no contribution to the argument on self-determination.

The Congress actually did remove the phrase "self-determination" from the Bolshevik program. However, it left in the right of secession, so that Stalin was later able to describe the change as having made no difference.[28]

Those who took Lenin's theory of self-determination seriously and attempted to apply it to concrete situations were faced with insuperable difficulties. In the Ukraine, for example, people were unable to find out just how self-determination was supposed to be applied. This problem was discussed at the time (1919) by two writers who professed to be loyal Communists but who were also interested in the freedom of the Ukraine. They said: Show us how self-determination should be applied, and we will "openly and publicly renounce the independence of the Ukraine and become the sincerest supporters of unification."[29] We do not have any means of checking up on these authors, but the point is that the dilemma they cite could have occurred. So Lenin laid himself open to an attack that was not long in coming. His "self-determination" was later called a "tactical propaganda trick to deceive [the non-Russians] and to bring about the 'speedy extinction of their national feelings.' "[30]

The situation in the Ukraine was not as bad for the Bolsheviks as Piatakov made it sound. The masses of the workers and peasants were, by and large, *for* the Bolsheviks, even if there was no possibility of testing the point by a plebiscite. The witness whose testimony has usually been accepted on this point is V. Vinnichenko, who headed the (bourgeois) Central Rada General Secretariat and the Directorate, and who was among those forced out of power when the Rada collapsed. He freely admitted that by the time of the Brest negotiations the Rada, whose representatives were admitted to the conference, had ceased to command the support of the people. By that time, he said, the "vast majority of the Ukrainian population was against us."[31] And again: "If our own peasants and working class had not risen, the Russian Soviet government would have been unable to do anything against us. . . . We were driven out of the Ukraine not by the Russian government but by our own people."[32]

Lenin's Two-Pronged Policy

The "official" Bolshevik version of this phase of Russian history is that Lenin's policy of self-determination for the border republics was a major reason for the success of the revolution. This contention calls for some discussion.

Lenin's policy toward the border peoples was two-pronged. On the one hand, the central Bolshevik government went to great lengths to recognize the desire of these peoples for freedom if they desired it. One of the first acts of the new government was to grant independence to Finland, and this was confirmed in an elaborate ceremony in which Stalin represented the Bolshevik government. The Baltic republics were also recognized.

The Georgian Mensheviks called themselves Georgian nationalists. They had never demanded secession from the tsar's empire, and did not seek to secede from the Kerensky government. When the Bolsheviks seized power, the Menshevik leaders proclaimed the independence of Georgia and organized a federation of Transcaucasian governments. Within a month, the Georgian authorities had invited the Germans to come in, and 3,000 German troops landed.[33]

With the defeat of the Germans in 1918, the Transcaucasian federation broke down. The British replaced the Germans in Georgia, at the invitation of the Menshevik government. In Azerbaijan, however, a Soviet republic was set up. On May 7, 1920, the Bolshevik government signed a treaty with the Georgian Menshevik government. According to this treaty, Georgia was required to break all contacts with the Russian counter-revolution, to have all foreign military forces withdrawn from Georgia, to grant legality to Bolshevik organizations, and to recognize the Soviet Republic of Azerbaijan.[34]

Nationalist Armenia was given a kind of *de facto* recognition. Turkey was fighting the Greeks in Asia Minor, and the Bolsheviks wished to assist the Turks: "The Armenian delegates in Moscow in May 1920 were offered assistance if Armenia allowed transport of Russian troops over the Kars Railway to go to the rescue of the Turks."[35] The Armenian government rejected the Russian offer.

Later Armenia, Azerbaijan, and Georgia were all brought into the USSR on a basis of formal equality with the RSFSR.

The Far Eastern Republic, which had been set up in eastern Siberia, faded out after the Bolsheviks established military control over the area. As a French newspaper headline put it at the time, the Far Eastern Republic "committed suicide for the beautiful eyes of Moscow."

The other prong of Lenin's policy toward the border peoples was to mobilize in each territory the friends of the revolution, to have them set up a revolutionary government, and to insure the accession of this government to power, with the aid of Red Army troops if necessary (as it was). This policy is defended as not inconsistent with self-determination, since any other policy would have endangered the revolution without benefiting the masses.[36]

Eventually most of the former tsarist colonies were reincorporated into the USSR. But where the Western powers had established their military occupation, as in Finland and the Baltic republics, or where the Red Army was defeated, as in Poland, it was the self-determination of the bourgeoisie that won out.

The case of Finland is instructive in this connection. The

newly recognized government of Finland asked to have the Red Army units then stationed in Finland withdrawn. Lenin did not do this. The intention had been to stage an uprising of the Finnish Communists, who would be aided by the Red Army in setting up a new government sympathetic to reunion with the Russians. But an expeditionary force of Germans under von der Goltz arrived in Finland in time to upset this plan.

In Poland it was the Luxemburgists, known as the "internationalists," who would have set up a government if the Red Army had won the war with the Polish army. The failure of the Polish workers and peasants to support the Russians was of course a major disappointment to Lenin. With regard to the peasants, the nationality question furnished part of the explanation. In the Ukraine the peasants supported the Bolsheviks, but in Poland they did not. Carr points out that the landlords in the western Ukraine were mostly of Polish extraction, so that there was an element of national antagonism between them and the Ukrainian peasants: "The national problem became acute when it acquired a social and economic content."[37] But in Poland, both peasants and landlords were by and large Poles. Also, the Polish Communist Party's land policy did not have sufficient appeal to attract many peasants.

The issue was settled finally, in the way that Rosa Luxemburg had predicted, by force of arms, although the outcome was as unpalatable to her as to Lenin.[38] The idea that the theory of self-determination was responsible for the breakup of the Russian empire was just as badly overdrawn as the opposite proposition, that the adherence of the border republics to the Bolsheviks was due to the same theory. Concrete evidence is lacking that the theory of self-determination had much to do with the outcome one way or the other.

The other points in Lenin's nationality program—equality of nations, freedom for national cultures to develop—were of very great importance. These were not issues between Lenin and Luxemburg. But they almost became an issue between Lenin and Stalin.

With the victory of the Russian Revolution, Lenin perceived that national oppression had not been abolished "as it were automatically," and he rose passionately to the defense of the minority peoples. In the summer of 1922, when his health was failing, Lenin learned of a proposal made by Stalin to limit the rights of the several republics in a plan that went by the name of "autonomization." Stalin's "autonomization" project would have had the national republics accede to the Soviet Union on a basis that would have led to a considerable paring of their rights. Lenin insisted that all of the nationalities should be equal: "We consider ourselves, the Ukrainian SSR and others, equal, and enter with them, on an equal basis, into a new union, a new federation."[39] The debate between Lenin and Stalin ended, as such debates always did, with the victory of Lenin, whose ideas were made the basis of the draft that was adopted.

Later History of Self-Determination

What has been the practice of Lenin's disciples, inside and outside the Soviet Union, with regard to the according of self-determination?

The Soviet Union will not countenance secessionist movements in its constituent republics. A recent article states specifically: "While giving every encouragement to the development of all genuinely national values, the Communist Party does not tolerate manifestations of nationalism and chauvinism, or anything that fosters national discord and isolation."[40] Plain enough, it would seem.

But perhaps some other socialist nation, confronted with the same problem, takes a more lenient line? It seemed for a while that Yugoslavia, with its excellent record on the national question, might fail to crack down on secession movements even as developed as that in Croatia in 1972. But the central party and the central government, with Tito acting as spokesman, did eventually clamp down on secessionist talk. The Croatian party officials who had sponsored secession were asked to resign, and while they were not purged like the Ukrainian nationalists in the 1930s, it was made quite clear that nationalism would not be tolerated if it meant splitting the Yugoslav state. The socialist governments have continued to give lip-service to the general principle of self-determination of nations while deciding each question in practice in a way that accorded with their own national interests. This generalization is just as true of China and Cuba as of the older socialist nations. It was of course not to be expected that China would accede to the demand for self-determination for Tibet, but its opposition to self-determination for Bangladesh (East Bengal) is more difficult to explain.[41] Fidel Castro's defense of the Soviet occupation of Czechoslovakia in 1968 was hardly a principled stand.

A Communist Party which is not in the government may be swept up in a nationalist psychology to the point where it forgets about self-determination. Thus it is hard to understand the position of the Communist Party of India on the Kashmiris, the Mizos, the Nagas, and other minor nationalities.[42] On the other hand, the position of the party in the 1940s favoring the independence of Pakistan has been attacked as "totally opportunist."[43] The Communists of India have been slow in working out a consistent revolutionary strategy. Lenin does not offer specific guidance in cases like this; each one has to be considered on its merits.

The proposition advanced by Lowy and others,[44] that denial of the right to form an independent state constitutes national oppression, is now generally accepted as far as colonies are concerned, but there are still arguments about what constitutes a colony. When the Algerians became insistent in their demand for independence, the stock answer of the French establishment was that Algeria was a constituent part of the French nation. The response failed to carry conviction, but that did not prevent the prerevolutionary government in Portugal from using it with regard to Portugal's African colonies. Spokesmen for the U.S. government deny that Puerto Rico is a colony.

Article 17 of the Soviet Union's constitution specifies that the national republics have the right of self-determination (secession), but that of the People's Republic of China does not. This provision has been in the Yugoslav constitution at times. But no state, capitalist or socialist, has spelled out in its basic law the modalities for bringing about such separation; nor can any be expected to do so. As Abraham Lincoln remarked, no state makes provision for its own dissolution.

The degree of freedom allowed to national dissidents in campaigning for independence has varied greatly among countries, and within particular countries at different periods. It may still be possible, even under capitalism, and presumably therefore under socialism, for an amicable separation arrangement to be worked out—Lenin never ceased to refer to the separation of Norway from Sweden in 1905. It may also be true that in the "last stage" of communism national rivalries will disappear, as contemplated by Marx and Lenin. But for the moment, socialist states are just as conscious of their national interests as capitalist states, and not any more likely to permit separatist propaganda—perhaps even less so. So, the multinational socialist states that include disaffected national groups are oppressing them, in Lowy's view. This was also the point of view of a substantial section of the Croatian Communist Party in 1971, as we noted above.

Before accepting this proposition, we need answers to certain questions. We need to know whether the demand for separation genuinely represents the sentiment of the proletarians, and is not the idea of some clique. We need information on whether the grievances complained of are demonstrably traceable to nationality discrimination, or whether they arise from other causes, or from the conjuncture as a whole. (This was the weak spot in the Croatians' argument.) Lenin always insisted on an analysis of the whole situation, "and then, perhaps, we shall not regard the rebellion of the Southern States of America in 1863 [sic] as a 'national rebellion.' "[45]

If we ask who is to make such an assessment, the answer of course is that the separationists and the central governments make their respective assessments, and there is no impartial arbiter to reconcile the conflicting claims. But Marxists have a duty to make their own judgments on such matters, and the "opinion of mankind" is not always devoid of influence, as we have noted above.

The traditional Marxist remedy for national grievances is more democracy in the country in question. This was the remedy offered by the French revolutionaries to the dissident national minorities in 1789, a solution retrospectively approved by Engels. The same solution was advanced before World War I by Lenin, and very strongly by Stalin in his 1913 essay. The bloodbath that accompanied the formation of Pakistan in 1947 was blamed, with some justice, on the traditional suppression of free speech by the British in colonial India. The Soviet Union cannot claim to be following a Leninist nationality policy when it suppresses nationalist agitation in the national republics as consistently and ferociously as has been customary.

But it is also true that in a condition of economic crisis, such as that which gripped Yugoslavia in 1971, the inflammation of national hatreds might cause a repetition of the bloodbaths of the period of World War I, when Croats slaughtered Serbs and vice-versa. For the central government to continue to follow a hands-off policy in such a situation would have been to risk disaster. National hatreds, like race hatreds, are sometimes more easily aroused than curbed.

Rosa Luxemburg's solution to the Polish problem was for "Kingdom Poland" to be reorganized as an autonomous province within a democratized Russia. Recent history has shown the limitations to this type of solution.

Eritrea is located between Ethiopia and the Red Sea, and has a certain strategic importance because it controls the entrance to the sea. It came under Italian colonial rule in 1890; in World War II it passed into the hands of the British. After the war it was proposed that Eritrea be annexed by Ethiopia, but an independence movement objected to this. In 1952 the United Nations sponsored an arrangement whereby Eritrea was to be a federative state under the Ethiopian crown, with full local autonomy, for a ten-year period, after which it was to exercise its right of self-determination. From the time the Ethiopian army marched in, Eritrean autonomy was a mirage. In 1962 Eritrea was formally annexed by Ethiopia. The Eritrean national liberation movement began guerrilla warfare, which was still continuing when the rule of Haile Selassie was ended in 1974.[46]

Or take the case of the Kurds, who campaigned all through the 1960s for freedom from the arbitrary rule of Iraq. The more extreme Kurdish nationalists favored an independent Kurdistan, to include parts of neighboring Iran and Turkey. The fighting ended in a stalemate, and in 1970 the Kurds were granted autonomy within Iraq and laid down their arms. The Communist Party of Iraq favored this arrangement,[47] provided that all of Iraq was democratized. Five years later, as part of a general settlement of differences between Iraq and Iran, the latter agreed to withdraw support from the Kurds in Iraq. The Iraqi army promptly marched into "autonomous" Kurdistan, and the Kurd national leader Mustapha al-Barzani took refuge abroad.

No movement for national liberation should campaign for

autonomy within the larger unit. Autonomy is like religious toleration; it can be terminated at any time, as the French Protestants learned when Louis XIV revoked the Edict of Nantes in 1685.

It is not enough to dump this whole issue in the lap of the United Nations, for this body is not constituted to deal with the problem. At most it can pass a resolution, and it does not do even that with any consistency. The United Nations is not set up to enforce any standard of behavior on the large states, which are the worst offenders against the principle of self-determination. But even if it had the power, it would not know how to proceed. The principles that would be applicable have not been developed. The General Assembly's "Declaration on Strengthening Internal Security," adopted in 1970 on Soviet initiative, envisages an end to repression and to the use of force against nations fighting for liberation from colonial rule, and urges aid for their legitimate struggle.[48] Much more important than this, however, was the furnishing of arms to Guinea-Bissau during its struggle with the Portuguese, and to the other Portuguese colonies since. (The Soviet Union, to its credit, did furnish arms to the liberation movements in Guinea-Bissau and Angola.)

"Right of Self-Determination" Receives Only Lip-Service

Soviet international lawyers have never accepted the idea that national self-determination is a principle that is valid regardless of the interests of the socialist revolution—nor, we should say, the interests of the Soviet Union.[49] Since other nations cannot be expected to accept the principle of self-determination in cases where it contravenes principles—or interests—that *they* consider important, the operation of the general principle of self-determination would appear to be limited to cases not considered vital by any party, and this is indeed what we observe.

Amilcar Cabral, the late leader of the national liberation movement in Guinea-Bissau, raised the question of whether the slogan of self-determination was not after all one invented by the imperialists as a means of covering their retreat. He pointed out that it was precisely the imperialist powers that had introduced national liberation as an objective:

> I would even go so far as to ask whether, given the advance of socialism in the world, the national liberation movement is not an imperialist initiative. Is the judicial institution which serves as a reference for the right of all peoples who are trying to liberate themselves a product of the peoples who are trying to liberate themselves? Was it created by the socialist countries who are our historical associates? It is signed by the imperialist countries, it is the imperialist countries who have recognized the right of all peoples to national independence, so I ask myself whether we may not be considering as an initiative of our people what is in fact an initiative of the enemy? Even Portugal, which is using napalm bombs against our people in Guiné, signed the declaration of the right of all peoples to independence. . . . The objective of the imperialist countries was to prevent the enlargement of the socialist camp, to liberate the reactionary forces in our countries which were being stifled by colonialism and to enable these forces to ally themselves with the international bourgeoisie. The fundamental objective was to create a bourgeoisie where one did not exist, in order specifically to strengthen the imperialist and the capitalist camp.[50]

A good example of the way the shibboleth of "self-determination" is used to gloss over differences without really settling anything is furnished by the recent experience of Portugal. When the Armed Forces Movement took power in 1974, the question of the future of the colonies was of key importance, but full agreement had not been reached within the government itself on the form that their liberation should take. If we are to believe an American who was on the spot, the first statements said that the colonies would have self-determination, this being intended as a kind of compromise. Later, the pro-independence element gained the upper hand and "self-determination" was forgotten.[51]

It is still true, as it was before World War I, that a consistent Marxist puts the interests of the international socialist revolution ahead of the interests of any one country. So any head of state, be it socialist or neutral, any spokesperson for a state, socialist or other, cannot be a consistent Marxist. He or she is obligated in the nature of the case to consider the interests of his or her country ahead of any other interests. This is just as true now as it was when Molotov signed the pact with von Ribbentrop in 1939.

Yet the truth of this proposition is challenged on every side. Is it not true (people say) that the interests of the international socialist revolution are best served by having strong socialist states, to help the weaker ones toward socialism? Would the long-run interests of socialism be served if China (or, the Soviet Union, or Vietnam) were to become a prey to capitalist imperialism?

A moment's thought will dispel any illusions on this head. All the successful socialist revolutions from 1917 to 1960 were made not only without the active assistance of the Soviet Union, but actually against its advice.[52] Powerful socialist states may lead weaker ones toward socialism or away from it.

Those who look to the socialist chiefs of state for guidance on particular problems as they come up may find themselves failing to condemn Yahya Khan in his attempt to liquidate the intelligentsia of East Pakistan (Bangladesh). Or they may justify the invasion of a peaceful smaller state. The truth is that neither Mao, nor Tito, nor Castro, nor any spokesperson for any of the socialist countries, can afford to take positions that conflict with the national diplomatic policies.[53]

Marxism is not a philosophy of power, of the strong and mighty; it is a philosophy of the poor, the downtrodden, the proletarians and the outcasts. Marxism is a philosophy of equality, of communism. And this philosophy can be advocated by anyone, at any time; only not when his or her point of view is warped and predetermined by considerations of national power.

The device of the plebiscite, in which high hopes were once placed, is still occasionally used, as in setting the boundaries of the Cameroons in 1961. One assumes that the areas in question in that case were not well enough endowed with natural resources to be of special concern to any major economic interest. There cannot have been much oil in the Cameroons. The use of the plebiscite requires the cooperation of both disputing parties, together with their willingness to accept the results; and where such agreement cannot be secured, as in Kashmir, no plebiscite can be held.

The ascendance of the doctrine of the right of self-determination at the time of World War I, and especially its implementation with regard to certain East European states (succession states), is seen by the historian Cobban as a happy accident—happy, that is, for the Polish, Czech, and other nationalists. The moral doctrine happened to coincide to a degree with the perceived interest of the Great Powers who made the Versailles treaty. The moral doctrine is even more widespread now than it was then, but the adoption of machinery to implement it has lagged.

As used today, the "right of self-determination" means that the political unit concerned—and we have to assume that it has been defined—may choose any status within its purview as far as the people according that right are concerned. Thus when the Federal Republic of Germany (West Germany) signs a treaty with the German Democratic Republic (East Germany), in which each accords the other the "right of self-determination," that means that each recognizes the existence of the other and is prepared to do business with it. When North Vietnam, the DRV, recognized that South Vietnam had the right of self-determination, it was saying that South Vietnam was independent as far as it, North Vietnam, was concerned. Of course, later events caused this declaration to be reconsidered.

Rosa Luxemburg was after all correct in one of her main points about self-determination. When the term is not defined with exactitude, adoption of the slogan may not be a solution of the problem but a means of avoiding it. The world is still waiting for Marxists to live up to the implications of this discovery.

Notes

1. Julius K. Nyerere, *Freedom and Socialism / Uhuru na Ujamaa: A Selection from Writings and Speeches 1965–1967* (Dar Es Salaam: Oxford University Press, 1968), pp. 26-32. Quoted in Lionel Cliffe and John S. Saul, *Socialism in Tanzania: An Interdisciplinary Reader, Vol. 1: Politics* (Dar es Salaam: Oxford University Press, 1972), p. 72. Here Cliffe and Saul develop this idea further. Nyerere is no Marxist, but his remarks apply if anything more forcefully to Marxian socialism than to the Nyerere variety.
2. This was noted by S. F. Bloom in *The World of Nations* (New York: 1941), p. 33. See also Horace B. Davis, *Nationalism and Socialism* (New York: 1967), p. 14.
3. *Le Courrier International* (London), March 16, 1867; emphasis not in original.
4. Communication from Bert Andreas, November 4, 1971.
5. The *schlachta,* nobility who for many years were the bearers of Polish nationalism, was, in fact, a quite stratified class and in-

cluded, besides landowners, a large number of pauperized "noblemen."

6. See "Marxism and the National Question," in Josef Stalin, *Marxism and the National Question: Selected Writings and Speeches* (New York: 1942), pp. 7-68.
7. The Maldive Islands, which were admitted to the United Nations in 1965, had at the time a population under 100,000, and some even smaller units have since been admitted.
8. V. I. Lenin, *Collected Works* (Moscow: 1961, 1964), XXI, 410.
9. In the "Junius" pamphlet, Luxemburg did speak of the "right of independence." But this was a qualified statement.
10. Michael Lowy, "Rosa Luxemburg et la question nationale," *Partisans* (Paris), May-August 1971, pp. 66-67. Actually, as we have seen, Luxemburg did recognize that nationalism has its constructive aspects.
11. V. I. Lenin, *Selected Works* (Moscow: 1961), III, 510-11.
12. Ibid., p. 512.
13. Lenin, *Collected Works,* VI, 434-63.
14. Lowy, "Rosa Luxemburg et la question nationale," pp. 65-66.
15. In J. Hentze, ed., *Rosa Luxemburg: Internationalismus und Klassenkampf* (Luchterhand: 1971), p. 217.
16. Rosa Luxemburg [Junius], *The Crisis in German Social Democracy* (New York: 1969), pp. 94-95, 98.
17. "The Junius Pamphlet," in *Collected Works,* XXII, 305-91.
18. See Lenin's "Theses" of 1916, in ibid., pp. 144-45.
19. Ibid., XIX, 297; emphasis in original.
20. E. H. Carr, *The Bolshevik Revolution, 1917-1923* (London: 1950), Vol. 1.
21. *History of the CPSU (B): Short Course* (Moscow: 1939), pp. 190-91.
22. Rosa Luxemburg, *The Russian Revolution* (New York: 1919), p. 27.
23. For the "Theses" and programs of the Bukharin-Piatakov group, see O. H. Gankin and H. H. Fisher, *The Bolsheviks and the World War: The Origin of the Third International* (Stanford: 1940), pp. 219ff.
24. R. V. Daniels, *The Conscience of the Revolution: Communist Opposition in Soviet Russia* (Cambridge: 1960), p. 97.
25. "On the Manifesto of the Armenian Social-Democrats," in *Iskra,* February 1, 1903; emphasis in the original. See Lenin, *Collected Works,* VI, 329.

26. See ibid., p. 454.
27. Ibid., p. 460.
28. Stalin, *Marxism and the National Question*, p. 140.
29. S. Mazlakh and V. Shakrai, *On the Current Situation in the Ukraine* (1919; Ann Arbor: 1970), p. 173.
30. R. Smal-Stocki, *The Captive Nations: Nationalism of the Non-Russian Nations in the Soviet Union* (New York: 1960), p. 43.
31. Carr, *The Bolshevik Revolution*, p. 298, quoting V. Vinnichenko, *Vidrozheniya Natsii* (Vienna: 1920), Vol. 2, p. 216.
32. Salov, *International Affairs* (Moscow), August 1972, p. 90, quoting V. E. Malanchuk, "Malicious Inventions of the Bourgeois 'Ukrainologists,' " in *Voprosy Istorii KPSS* (1971), p. 40.
33. L. Fischer, *The Soviets in World Affairs* (London: 1930), Vol. 1, p. 85.
34. *Bol'shaia Sovetskaia Entsiklopediia*, Vol. 7 (1970), p. 368; Carr, *The Bolshevik Revolution*, p. 350.
35. *The Encyclopaedia Britannica* (1955 ed.), Vol. 2, p. 380.
36. M. Rodinson, preface to Hélène Carrère d'Encausse, *Réforme et révolution chez les Musulmans de l'Empire russe* (Paris: 1966), p. 13.
37. Carr, *The Bolshevik Revolution*, p. 307.
38. The Luxemburgists favored the former Russian Poland (the "Congress Kingdom") becoming part of the Soviet Union. This point of view was advanced also after World War II, but did not prevail.
39. Lenin, *Collected Works*, XLII, 421-22; letter of September 26, 1922. See also Lenin, "The Question of Nationalities or 'Autonomisation,' " in *Collected Works*, XXXVI, 605-10.
40. Salov, in *International Affairs*, p. 93.
41. The Soviet Union eagerly recognized Bangladesh, "guided by the principles of self-determination of peoples" (see the *New York Times*, January 25, 1972). But this incident did not at all signify that the Soviets recognize the principle of self-determination or that the Chinese do not. What stand either country will take depends on the political conjuncture.
42. See N. Bhattacharya, "India's Colonial Legacy," *Guardian* (New York), December 25, 1974, p. 14.
43. Jairus Banaji, "Nationalism and Socialism," *Economic and Political Weekly* (Bombay), September 1974, p. 1539.
44. See Lowy in G. Haupt et al., *Les Marxistes et la Question Nationale, 1848-1914* (Paris: 1974), p. 378.

45. Letter to N. D. Kiknadze, October 1916, in *Collected Works,* XIX, 266.
46. An interesting point to investigate would be whether Ethiopian chauvinism, intent on preserving its rule over Eritrea, deflected the progressive impact of the movement that ended Haile Selassie's reign.
47. *Marxism Today* (London), September 1970, pp. 278-80.
48. J. Chikwe, "Africa: Unity and Differentiation," *World Marxist Review,* January 1972, p. 90.
49. Rudolf Schlesinger cites on this point M. Rappaport, "The Essence of Present International Law," *Sovietskoye Gosadarstvo i Pravo* (1940), p. 142; see Schlesinger, *Soviet Legal Theory: Its Background and Development* (London: 1951), p. 288.
50. "Analysis of the Social Structure," in A. Cabral, *Revolution in Guinea* (New York: 1969), p. 58.
51. J. Kramer, "Letter from Lisbon," *The New Yorker,* September 23, 1974.
52. Of course, the Soviet Union has assisted small socialist states when it was to its own advantage diplomatically to do so. As for Vietnam, who will doubt that it was against the interests of both China and the USSR to have the United States establish a military foothold on the mainland of Asia?
53. This point is well made with regard to Castro by M. Halpern, *The Rise and Decline of Fidel Castro* (Berkeley: 1972), p. 271.
54. Alfred Cobban, *The National State and National Self-Determination* (London: 1969), Vol. I, p. iv.

The National Question

The Polish Question at the International Congress in London[1]

Thirty-two years ago, when what was later to become the International met for the first time in London, it opened its proceedings with a protest against the subjugation of Poland, which just then was engaged, for the third time, in a fruitless struggle for independence. In a few weeks the International Workers' Congress will meet, also in London, and will be presented with a resolution in support of Polish independence. The similarity of circumstances quite naturally suggests a comparison of these two events in the life of the international proletariat.

The proletariat has come a long way in its development over these past thirty-two years. Progress is evident in every regard, and many aspects of the working-class struggle look quite different from the way they did thirty-two years ago. But the essential element in this entire development lies in the following: *from a sect of ideologues, socialists have grown into a major unified party capable of handling its own affairs.* Then, they barely existed in isolated little groups outside the mainstream of political life in every country; today, they represent the dominant factor in the life of society. This is particularly true in the major civilized countries; but in every country they are an element to be taken seriously and to be reckoned with at every step by government and ruling class alike. Then, it was a question of merely spreading the new message; today, the paramount question is how the struggle of the vast popular masses, now thoroughly imbued with the gospel of socialism, can best be led toward its goal.

The International Workers' Congress has undergone corresponding changes. In its beginning, the International was more of a council that met to formulate the basic principles of the new movement; today, it is primarily, even exclusively, a body for practical deliberations by the conscious proletariat on the urgent questions of its day to day struggle. All tasks and objectives are here subjected to rigorous evaluation as to their practicability; those, however, that appear to exceed the forces of the proletariat are laid aside, regardless of how attractive or appealing they may sound. This is the essential difference between the conference this year in St. Martin's Hall and the one that took place thirty-two years ago, and it is from this perspective that the resolution laid before the Congress must be examined.

The resolution on the restoration of Poland to be presented at the London congress reads as follows.[2]

> Whereas, the subjugation of one nation by another can serve only the interests of capitalists and despots, while for working people in both oppressed and oppressor nation it is equally pernicious; and whereas, in particular, the Russian tsardom, which owes its internal strength and its external significance to the subjugation and partition of Poland, constitutes a permanent threat to the development of the international workers' movement, the Congress hereby resolves: that the independence of Poland represents an imperative political demand both for the Polish proletariat and for the international labor movement as a whole.

The demand for the political independence of Poland is supported by two arguments: first, the general perniciousness of annexations from the point of view of the interests of the proletariat; and second, the special significance of the subjugation of Poland for the continued existence of the Russian tsardom, and thus, by implication, the significance of Polish independence for its downfall.

Let us take the second point first.

The Russian tsardom derives neither its inner strength nor its external significance from the subjugation of Poland. This assertion in the resolution is false from A to Z. The Russian tsardom derives its inner strength from the social relations within Russia itself. The historical basis of Russian absolutism is a natural economy resting on the archaic communal-property relations of the peasantry. The remains of this backward social structure—and there are many such remains still to be found in Russia today—along with the total configuration of other social factors, constitute the basis of the Russian tsardom. The nobility is kept under the tsar's thumb by an endless flow of handouts paid for by taxing the peasantry. Foreign policy is conducted to benefit the bourgeoisie with the opening of new markets as its main objective, while customs policy puts the Russian consumer at the mercy of the manufacturers. Finally, even the domestic activity of the tsardom is in the service of capital: the organization of industrial expositions, the construction of the Siberian railroad, and other projects of a similar nature are all carried out with a view to advancing the interests of capitalism. In general, under the tsardom the bourgeoisie plays an inordinately important role in shaping domestic and foreign policy, a role which its numerical inconsequence would never permit it to play without the tsar. This, then, is the combination of factors which gives the tsardom its strength internally. So it continues to vegetate, because the obsolete social forms have not yet completely disappeared, and the embryonic class relations of a modern society have not yet fully developed and crystallized.

Again: the strength of the tsardom abroad derives not from the partition of Poland, but from the particular features of the Russian Empire. Its vast human masses provide an unlimited source of financial and military resources, available almost on command, which elevates Russia to the level of a first-rate European power. Its vastness and geographic position give Russia a very special interest in the Eastern question, in which it vies with the other nations that are also involved in that part of the world. At the same time, Russia borders on the British possessions in Asia, which is leading it toward an inevitable confrontation with England. In Europe, too, Russia is deeply involved in the most vital concerns of the European powers. Especially in the nineteenth century, the revolutionary class struggles just now emerging have put the tsardom in the role of guardian of reaction in Europe, which fact also contributes to its stature abroad.

But above all, in speaking of Russia's foreign position, especially over the last few decades, it is not the partition of Poland but solely and exclusively the *annexation of Alsace-Lorraine* that lends it its power: by dividing Europe into two hostile camps, by creating a permanent threat of war, and by driving France further and further into the arms of Russia.

From false premises come false conclusions: as if the existence of an independent Poland could deprive Russia of its powers at home or abroad. The restoration of Poland could bring about the downfall of Russian absolutism only if it simultaneously abolished the social basis of the tsardom within Russia itself, i.e., the remains of the old peasant economy and the importance of the tsardom for both the nobility and the bourgeoisie. But of course this is arrant nonsense: it makes no difference—with or without Poland these relations remain unchanged. The hope of breaking the hold of Russian omnipotence through the restoration of Poland is an anachronism stemming from that bygone time when there seemed to be no hope that forces within Russia itself would ever be capable of achieving the destruction of the tsardom. The Russia of that time, a land of natural economy, seemed, as did all such countries, to be mired in total social stagnation. But since the sixties it has set a course toward the development of a modern economy, and in so doing has sown the seeds for a solution to the problem of Russian absolutism. The tsardom finds itself forced to support a capitalist economy, but in so doing it is sawing off the limb on which it sits.

Through its financial policies it is destroying whatever remains of the old agricultural-communal relationships, and is thus eliminating any basis for conservative modes of thought among the peasantry. What is more, in its plundering of the peasantry, the tsardom is undermining its own material foundations and destroying the resources with which it purchased the loyalty of the nobility. Finally, the tsardom has apparently made it its special task to ruin the major class of consumers at the bourgeoisie's expense, thus leaving with its pockets empty the very class to whose pecuniary interests it sacrificed the interests of the nation as a whole. Once a useful agent of the bourgeois economy, the ponderous bureaucracy has become its fetters. The result is the accelerated growth of the industrial proletariat, the one social force with which the tsardom cannot ally itself and to which it cannot give ground without jeopardizing its own existence.

These, then, are the social contradictions whose solution involves the downfall of absolutism. The tsardom is driving forward to that fatal moment like a rolling stone on a steep hill. The hill is the development of capitalism, and at its foot the iron fists of the working class are waiting. Only the political struggle of the proletariat throughout the entire Russian empire can accelerate this process. The independence of Poland has comparatively little to do with the fall of the tsardom, just as the partition of Poland had little to do with its continued existence.

Let us take now the first point of the resolution. "The subjugation of one nation by another," we read, "can serve only the interests of capitalists and despots, while for working people in both oppressed and oppressor nation it is equally pernicious . . ." On the basis of this proposition the independence of Poland is supposed to become an imperative demand of the proletariat. Here we have one of those great truths, so great, in fact, as to be one of the greatest of commonplaces, and as such it can lead to no practical conclusions whatsoever. If, from the assertion that the subjugation of one nation by another is in the interests of capitalists and despots, it is therefore concluded that all annexations are unjust or can be eliminated within the capitalist system, then this we hold to be absurd, for it makes no allowance for the basic principles of the existing order.

It is interesting to note that this point in the resolution is almost identical with the argument in support of the notorious Dutch resolution:[3] "Since the subjugation and control of one nation by another can lie only in the interests of the ruling classes . . . ," the proletariat is supposed to bring about the end of the war with the aid of the striking military. Both resolutions are based on the naive belief that it is enough to recognize any circumstance benefiting despots to the detriment of working people in order to do away with it immediately. The similarity goes further. The evil that must be rooted out is, in principle, the same in both resolutions: the Dutch resolution proposes to prevent future annexations by ending the war, while the Polish resolution intends to undo past wars by abolishing annexations. In both cases, the proletariat is supposed to eliminate war and annexations under capitalism without eliminating capitalism itself, though both, in fact, are part of the very essence of capitalism.

Granted that the truism just cited does not give any basis for the general abolition of annexations, it provides even less of a reason for abolishing the existing Polish annexation. In this case especially, without a critical assessment of the concrete historical conditions, nothing of value can be contributed to the problem. But on this point, on the question of how—and if—the proletariat can liberate Poland, the resolution maintains a deep silence. The Dutch resolution is more sophisticated in this respect: it at least proposes a specific means—a secret accord with the military—which allows us to see the utopian aspect of the resolution. The Polish resolution is more modest and contents itself with a "demand," although it is not any less utopian on that account than the other.

How is the Polish proletariat to build a classless state? In the face of the three governments ruling Poland; in the face of the bourgeoisie of the Polish congress pandering to the throne in Petersburg and recoiling from any thought of a restored Poland as a crime and a plot against its own pocketbook; in the face of the large Galician landholdings in the person of the governing Badani,[4] who watches over the unity of the Austrian monarchy (that is: guarantees the partition of Poland); and finally, in the face of the Prussian-Polish Junkers who provide the military budget and more supplies of bayonets to safeguard the Polish annexation—in the face of all these factors, what can the Polish proletariat do? Any rebellion would be bloodily suppressed. But if no rebellion is attempted, nothing at all can be done, since armed rebellion is the only way that Polish independence can be achieved. Certainly none of these states can be expected to relinquish voluntarily its provinces, which they have now ruled for a long hundred years. But under existing conditions, any rebellion of the proletariat would be crushed—there could be no other result. Perhaps then, the international proletariat would help? It, however, is in less of a position to act than the Polish proletariat; at most it can declare its sympathy. But suppose the entire campaign in support of the restoration of Poland limits itself to peaceful demonstrations? Well, then, in that case, of course, the partition states can continue to rule over Poland in all tranquility. So if the international proletariat makes the restoration of Poland its political demand—

as the resolution requires—it will have done no more than utter a pious wish. If one "demands" something, one must do something to achieve that demand. If one can do nothing, the empty "demand" may well make the air tremble, but it will certainly not shake the states ruling over Poland.

The adoption of the social-patriotic resolution by the International Congress could, however, have further-reaching implications than might be obvious at first glance. First and foremost, it would go in the face of the decisions of the previous Congress, especially those on the Dutch resolution about the military strike. In the light of their essentially parallel arguments and identical content, the adoption of the social-patriotic resolution would let the Dutch one in, once again, through the back door. How the Polish delegates, who voted against the Nieuwenhuis resolution, have now managed to propose what is essentially an identical resolution on that question, we shall not discuss for the moment. In any case, it would be worse if the entire Congress were to fall into such a contradiction with itself.

Secondly, this resolution, if adopted, would have an import for the Polish movement that the delegates to the upcoming Congress have surely not even dared to imagine. For the past three years—as I discussed at length in my essay in *Neue Zeit*, numbers 32 and 33[5]—the attempt has been made to impose on Polish Socialists a program for the restoration of Poland; the intention is to separate them from their German, Austrian, and Russian comrades by uniting them in a Polish party organized along nationalist lines. Given the utopianism of this program and the contradiction between it and any effective political struggle, the promoters of this tendency have not yet been able to provide any argument for the planned nationalist turn strong enough to withstand criticism. And so they have, up to now, been rather circumspect about any open disclosure of this tendency. While the Polish parties in the Prussian and Austrian sectors have not yet included the point concerning the restoration of Poland in their program, the advance guard of the nationalist tendency, the London group calling itself Zwiazek Zagraniczny Socjalistow Polskich,[6] has been working hard to arouse sympathy in the Western European parties, especially through the paper *Bulletin Officiel* and in countless articles: "Socialist Poland," "The Poland of the Workers," "Democratic Poland," "The Independent Republic of Poland," etc. These and similar slogans have been praised in Polish, German, and French by turns. The way is being prepared for the adoption of a Polish class state into the program. The crowning touch to this entire process is to be the London congress, and through the adoption of the resolution the nationalist position is to be smuggled in under the international banner. The international proletariat is presumably supposed to run up the red flag, with its own hand, on the nationalist edifice, and so consecrate it as a temple of internationalism. Moreover, the sanction by the representatives of the international proletariat is meant to provide an effective cover for social patriotism's total lack of any scientific basis and raise it to the level of a dogma, where it will be immune to criticism of any sort. Finally, this sanction is meant to encourage the Polish parties to adopt, once and for all, the nationalist program and organize themselves along national lines.

The adoption of the social-patriotic resolution would establish an important precedent for the socialist movement in other countries. What is good for one is purchased cheaply by the other. If the national liberation of Poland is elevated to a political goal of the international proletariat, why not also the liberation of Czechoslovakia, Ireland, and Alsace-Lorraine? All these objectives are equally utopian, and are no less justified than the liberation of Poland. The liberation of Alsace-Lorraine, in particular, would be far more important for the international proletariat, and far more likely at that; behind Alsace-Lorraine stand four million French bayonets, and in questions of bourgeois annexations, bayonets carry more weight than moralistic demonstrations. And if the Poles in the three partitioned sectors organize themselves along nationalist lines for the liberation of Poland, why should the other nationalities in Austria not also do the same, why should the Alsatians not organize themselves with the French? In a word, the door would be opened wide to national struggles and nationalist organizations. Rather than a working class organized in accordance with political realities, there would be an espousal of organization along national lines, which often goes astray from the start. Instead of political programs, nationalist programs would be drawn up. Instead of a coherent political struggle of the proletariat in every country, its disintegration through a series of fruitless national struggles would be virtually assured.

Here lies the greatest significance of the social-patriotic resolution, if adopted. We stated at the beginning that the greatest forward step that the proletariat has made since the days of the International is its development from a number of small sectarian groups into a major party capable of handling its own affairs. But to what does the proletariat owe this progress? Solely to its ability to understand the primacy of the political struggle in its activity. The old International gave way to parties organized in each country in conformity with the political conditions peculiar to that country, without, on that account, having regard for the nationality of the workers. Only political struggle in line with this principle makes the working class strong and powerful. But the social-patriotic resolution pursues a course in diametric opposition to this principle. Its adoption by the Congress would repudiate thirty-two years of the proletariat's accumulated experience and theoretical education.

The social-patriotic resolution was formulated quite cleverly: behind the protest against the tsardom lay the protest against annexation—after all, the demand for Poland's independence is raised against Austria and Prussia as well as against Russia: it sanctions nationalist tendencies with international interests; it tries to obtain backing for a practical program on the basis of a general moral demonstration. But the weakness of its argument is even greater than the artfulness of its formulation: a few commonplaces about the perniciousness of annexations and some nonsense about Poland's importance for the tsardom—this and no more—is all that this resolution is capable of offering.

Notes

1. This article appeared simultaneously in the Italian publication, *Critica Sociale,* no. 14, July 1896, and in *Sprawa Robotnicza,* no. 25, July 1896, where it was published in translation from the Italian. The present translation is from Jürgen Hentze, *Rosa Luxemburg: Internationalismus und Klassenkampf* (Luchterhand: 1971), pp. 142-52.
2. The text of the resolution is reproduced here in the form presented by Rosa Luxemburg in her essay, "Der Sozialpatriotismus in Polen," in *Neue Zeit.* Cf. *Collected Works,* I, I, 39ff.
3. This is a reference to a Dutch draft resolution at the International Socialist Congress in Zurich in 1893. It was rejected in favor of a German resolution on the same theme. Cf. "Protokoll des Internationalen Sozialistischen Arbeiterkongresses in der Tonhalle Zurich vom 6 bis 12 August 1893," Zurich, 1894, p. 25.
4. The reference is to a member of the Polish nobility in Austrian Poland, who was Austrian Prime Minister from 1895 to 1897.
5. "Neue Strömungen in der polnischen sozialistischen Bewegung in Deutschland und Österreich" ("New Tendencies in the Polish Socialist Movement in Germany and Austria"), in *Collected Works,* I, I.
6. Foreign Union of Polish Socialists, a special committee associated with the PPS.

Foreword to the Anthology
The Polish Question and the Socialist Movement[1]

Habent sua fata libelli! as the saying goes, and a fitting epigraph indeed to the present volume, a collection of articles on the Polish question that have appeared, written by various authors, in different journals, in different years, and in different languages. The book, in fact, contains a sampling of the intellectual history of Polish Socialism, and provides us with a conspectus of a truly unique phenomenon, namely, the lengthy debate that took place in the international press around the political program of Polish Socialists, in particular around the International Socialist Congress in London in 1896.

It was no mere coincidence that the internal affairs of Polish Socialists were brought into the European forum and placed before the tribunal of international socialism. Indeed, the exchange of opinion over the tactics of the labor parties in the various countries has become more and more the custom of late in the Socialist International. The history of Jaurèsism[2] or the general strike of the Belgian Labor Party in April 1902[3]–certainly illustrate the point; each provoked a lively discussion in the German, Dutch, and Russian press—and elsewhere as well.

In particular, the opportunist tendency, which reared its head throughout the entire international movement a few years ago, taking everywhere almost identical forms and provoking almost identical counterblasts from the revolutionary flank, gave rise to a curious confraternity among like-minded groups in different countries. Thus its net effect was actually to tighten international bonds, despite its inherent tendency to foster national and local parochialism and fragment the socialist movement. But Polish Socialism occupies—or at any rate once occupied—a unique position in its relation to international socialism, a position which can be traced directly to the Polish national question.

That the Polish insurrections should have aroused the warmest sympathies among European democrats need hardly cause surprise. But it was political interests—not merely the bonds of sympathy—that tied the Polish question to the cause of democracy in the West. From the time that Russian tsardom entered internal European politics, acting, through the Holy Alliance, as the gendarme of international reaction, democrats in France, and especially in Germany, have had to regard it as an actively hostile force which had to be effectively neutralized if a European revolution was to succeed. Yet within Russia itself, within the Russian society, no revolutionary signs were yet visible. The first manifestations along these lines—the Decembrist movement at the beginning of the nineteenth century,[4] and the attempted assassination by Karakozov[5] in the middle of the century—as well as other events occurring later, seemed to have erupted only to illuminate the black night of tsardom's unbending barbarism with a momentary ray of hope. It is quite understandable, then, that in the eyes of the West, the armed Polish insurrections appeared to be the only revolutionary force at hand; but even beyond that, they served the function of keeping the forces of Russian absolutism occupied, and thus safeguarding the cause of democratic revolution in the West.

Thus the viewpoint of German democracy toward Russia and Poland evolved quite naturally, and Karl Marx, in the *Neue Rheinische Zeitung,* was its radical and most consistent representative. The idea of a declaration of war against Russia, together with a call to insurrection in Poland, constituted the core of Marx's foreign policy during the March revolution. Marx, who belonged to the most radical left wing of the revolutionary democracy of the time, swung boldly from defensive to offensive tactics in this question as well: rather than postponing a clash with tsardom until such time as it should decide to intervene in Germany, he chose to challenge absolutism from the outset by carrying the torch of war and revolution into Russia itself.

What prospects this tactic actually had for success, or the extent to which it had any basis in reality, need not occupy us here. For the present, our only concern is to establish that in these circumstances, and in them alone, lies the basis for the traditional views on the Polish question that international socialism was later to inherit. Not socialist theory or tactics, but the burning political exigencies of German democracy at the time—the practical interests of the bourgeois revolution in Western Europe—determined the viewpoint that Marx, and later Engels, adopted with respect to Russia and Poland.[6] Even at first glance this standpoint reveals its glaring lack of inner relation to the social theory of Marxism. By failing to analyze Poland and Russia as class societies bearing economic and political contradictions in their bosoms, by viewing them not from the point of view of historical development but as if they were in a fixed, absolute condition as homogeneous, undifferentiated units, this view ran counter to the very essence of Marxism.

To Western democracy at that time Poland was the land of insurgents and Russia the land of reaction—nothing more. Neither the social circumstances, the economic basis, nor the political content of the Polish insurrections had any real existence for either German Socialists or bourgeois democrats, or at least they were accorded very little importance: so little, in fact, that as late as 1875, in his reply to Tkacev,[7] in the journal *Volkstaat,* Engels begins his enumeration of the factors undermining Russian absolutism thus: "First come *the Poles.*"[8]

But in point of fact, when Engels wrote these words "the Poles," i.e., that undifferentiated nation whose sole concern was presumably the struggle for independence, had long ceased to exist—if indeed they had ever existed. For at just this time Poland was experiencing the greatest orgies of "organic labor," the frantic dance of capitalism and capitalist enrichment over the graves of the Polish nationalist movements and the Polish nobility, by then a thing of the past. Shortly thereafter, history was to provide graphic proof that Poland had ceased to be the land of "the Poles" and had become a fully modern bourgeois society, rent by class contradictions and class struggle: only two or three years after Engels wrote these words, the Socialist movement was to make its first entry onto the stage of Polish history.

For a long time, these traditional views on Poland lay dormant in international socialism. After the last insurrection, the trumpet blasts of national struggle died away. Polish capitalists no longer drew the attention of all of Europe by the clatter of their arms. The bourgeois cry, "*enrichissez-vous,*" requires universal peace and tranquility; like the violet, it prefers to hide itself away among the shadows, and shies from nothing so much as from the envious eyes of its neighbors. And Polish Socialists, for their part, far from striving to link their politics with the traditions of rebellion at the outset, did, in fact, just the opposite: from the start they took up a fully conscious and determined stand *against* these traditions in Polish society, and what is more, abstained from any reliance on them even within the ranks of international socialism itself. Indeed, the first serious Socialist organization in Poland—the "Proletariat" Party—made its opposition to the nationalist movements and its sharp criticism of them the *keystone* of its class position.[9] The founders and theoretical leaders of the Proletariat Party were by no means unfamiliar with Marx's and Engels' opinions on the Polish question, yet they were not in the least confused by them; on the contrary, they regarded them merely as the outworn vestige of old views that had been based on an ignorance of the social content of the nationalist movements within Poland and of the social changes that had taken place within the country since the last insurrection. When the group, *Rovnosc,*[10] i.e., Ludwik Warynski, Stanislav Mendelson, Szymon Dickstein, and their comrades called an international meeting in Geneva in November 1880, on the fiftieth anniversary of the November insurrection to make clear once and for all their emphatically antinationalist position, among the various letters and telegrams they received was also one from Marx and Engels which tersely summed up the historical relationship between the slogan of Polish independence and the revolution in the West:

> The cry "Let Poland live!" which then resounded throughout Western Europe was not only an expression of sympathy and support for the patriotic fighters who had been crushed by brute force—this cry greeted the people all of whose revolts, in themselves so disastrous, always held back the advance of counter-revolution: the people, whose best sons never ceased to carry out armed resistance and always fought under the flag of the people's revolutions. On the other hand the partition of Poland consolidated the Holy Alliance, that mask for the hegemony of the Tsars over all European countries. Thus the cry "Let Poland live!" in and of itself meant: "Death to the Holy Alliance, death to the military despotisms of Russia, Prussia, Austria, death to the Mongolian supremacy over contemporary society."

The letter ends with the words:

> The Poles therefore played outside the borders of their country a great role in the battle for the freeing of the

> proletariat: they were its best international fighters. Today, since this battle is developing among the Polish people themselves, the propaganda and press of the revolutionary movement may support it, may join with the efforts of our Russian brothers; that will be one more reason for reviving the old cry: "Let Poland live!"[11]

In his wide-ranging address to the meeting, Ludwik Warynski said the following in reply to this letter:

> The Triple Alliance had its adversary in the International, which had called all working people to struggle under a common banner, the banner of international revolution. But not feeling itself in possession of enough forces to meet the reaction head-on, the International did not trouble itself to subsume the Polish question under a general program for the liberation of the proletariat. It was thought that the Polish revolutionary patriots were the only organized force in the Russian empire that could check the tsar's efforts to intervene in Europe in support of reaction. For a long time, our part in the international movement was reduced to this. *Even the authors of* "The Communist Manifesto" *linked their immortal rallying cry: "Proletarians of all countries unite," with another that was attractive even to the bourgeoisie and the privileged classes in general: the cry "Long live Poland!" This regard and sympathy for Poland, the Poland of the exploiters and the exploited, demonstrates that previous political expediencies have still today retained their force in the eyes of its defenders.* But the relevance of these earlier interests is gradually diminishing, and *we may hope that they will soon be forgotten.*

Warynski was wrong. The Polish traditions were, indeed, forgotten for a time in the international socialist movement; but they did not disappear—even though the historical conditions which had originally given rise to them had changed radically. Even ideology bears the stamp of conservatism, and the ideology of the working-class movement—even granting the thoroughly revolutionary spirit of its world view—is no exception to this rule. In its positions and attitudes on particular questions it lags considerably behind actual developments, to which it must from time to time readjust through a process of radical revision. But the Social Democracy is a party of political struggle, not of philosophical inquiry for the attainment of abstract truths. Hence, it takes up the revision of its old, out-of-date views only when the tangible interests of the working-class movement make such a revision necessary. Traditional views thus often lie for a long time uncontested in the treasure chest of Social Democracy, though the circumstances to which they were attuned may have long since disappeared from the scene. It is only when new developments cause the emergence of new vital needs for the movement which stand in flagrant contradiction with these musty old traditions, and collide with them, that political opinion drags them into the light for a thorough critical review.

That is what happened with Socialists' traditional views on the Polish question. Though they had been preserved in spirit, practical politics provided them no chance for public airing. There were no Polish national movements that might have given them a new breath of life, and the Polish Socialists had, as we have seen, avoided the embarrassment of these old ideas by simply ignoring them and pursuing a strongly anti-nationalist policy without asking anybody's permission.

But the entry of the social-patriotic tendency, represented by the Polish Socialist Party, onto the scene in 1893 changed all that.[12] True, there had been previous attempts to link the Polish Socialist movement with a programmatic demand for the restoration of Poland—for example, by the group, *Lud Polski,* in 1881, or the group, *Pobudka,*[13] in 1889, both under the aegis of B. Limanowski.[14] But both of these two ephemeral groups felt themselves so deeply isolated from the mainstream of international socialism that they made not the slightest effort to *link up* their views with the Marxist traditions—especially as their program was quite explicitly based not on the theory of modern socialism, but on a peculiar brand of sentimental and metaphysical phraseology.

The Polish Socialist Party was the first to attempt to revive and renovate the dormant legacy of Marx's 1848 position, and indeed it was quite ambitious in the undertaking. An entire system was created and set into motion to reclaim, so to speak, the old Polish traditions drifting about among socialists in Western Europe. The present volume contains several examples, in particular the article by Herr Häcker from Cracow.[15] This system relied—as one of our comrades aptly put it—on the collecting of "vouchers for the restoration of Poland" from all the luminaries of Western European socialism, vouchers that were obtained by convincing the French, English, Italian, German, etc. Socialists—the letter by Antonio Labriola is a good case in point—that "the whole of Polish socialism wants" the restoration of Poland, and then soliciting from them in advance a show of sympathy for this undertaking. Confronted in this manner by a *fait accompli*, and having no reason to rack their brains unbidden over the rationality or irrationality of the program of some foreign party, with whose language and terms of combat they were unfamiliar, the Western socialists of course granted the solicited voucher, wrote the requested letters or essays without too much reflection, and said a few words here and there at an occasional meeting—which of course was precisely why they had been invited.

Thus, the diligently accumulated endorsements by prominent figures of the international working-class movement became ritualized into an endlessly repeated litany for social patriotism in the literature of this tendency during the years

1895 to 1896—in the special May edition for 1896, in essays in *Przedswit,*[16] in *Gazeta Robotnicza,* etc., Marx, Engels, Liebknecht, Bebel, Kautsky, Bernstein, Guesde, Labriola, Hyndman, Eleanor Marx-Aveling, Moteler, Lessner, and so on, were incessantly cited as enthusiastic supporters of the restoration of Poland; at the same time, no opportunity was missed to rekindle the old traditions in the Western European press.

This unprecedented phenomenon was not the work of chance, nor was it merely the product of bad taste on the part of the custodians of social patriotism. When this tendency first surfaced in the Polish labor movement in 1893 and 1894 it met with an extremely hostile reception. Given the radical antinationalism with which *Rovnose* and *Przedswit* had shaped political opinion in Polish Socialist circles for fifteen years, in the spirit of the old Proletariat Party, this abrupt about-face entailed by the programmatic demand for the restoration of Poland was greeted with the greatest hostility.

From the antinationalist perspective long inculcated by the Proletariat Party, the espousal of patriotism, with its indulgent nostalgia for the old watchwords of the rebellions of the Polish nobility, could be viewed as nothing less than a betrayal of the socialist banner and of the class struggle. To overcome this hostile atmosphere and these firmly rooted traditions of the Proletariat Party, an artful argument, based on the class standpoint of the socialist movement, had to be found to justify these new nationalistic demands. But King Solomon himself could not have provided such an argument; for, as the saying goes, "*où il n'y a rien, le roi perd ses droits*": social patriotism simply *could not* be justified. The notorious bit of sophistry that was hit upon to make this "workers' " program more palatable, namely, that the constitution of an independent Poland would surely be more "democratic" than any Russian constitution which might follow after the fall of the tsardom, obviously satisfied only the modest intellectual needs of third- and fourth-rate sympathizers. Accordingly, the simplest way out of these difficulties was through a direct appeal to the traditions of international socialism, by calling upon the names of Marx and Engels and other prominent socialists who succeeded them. A long list of big names in the high court of socialism was made to serve in default of any sound argument in support of the social-patriotic program. In this way, the restoration of Poland lost its stigma as the betrayal of socialism—after all, the most accomplished theoreticians and practitioners of the European movement had come out in support of this slogan—and the Polish Socialist Party's program had obtained the direct sanction of Marxism—hadn't "Marx himself" attested to its correctness? From this point on, all doubts, misgivings, or aversions in Polish socialist circles with regard to this about-face toward social patriotism were set to rest by reciting over again the litany: Marx, Engels, Liebknecht, Bebel, Eleanor Aveling, Labriola, etc., or perhaps even the other way around: Labriola, Bebel, Liebknecht, Engels, Marx, and so on.

A moment's reflection is enough to convince one that such a solution to the problem rested upon an utterly primitive, double deception. Socialists abroad were misled into believing that the entire Polish labor movement regarded the restoration of Poland as their programmatic demand, a demand no longer even subject to question, and on this basis expressed their support of it. And Polish Socialists were, in their turn, beguiled by all these proclamations of sympathy from socialists abroad into assuming, also falsely, that the entire international socialist movement urgently required that they stand actively behind the restoration of Poland. Thus, in both quarters, this policy of social patriotism maintained itself only by stifling any critical appraisal, and rested solely on the force of authority—in Europe, on the authority of the entire Polish labor movement, and in Poland itself, on the prestigious names of Marx, Engels, etc.

As we have seen, the authority of Marx himself on this question, even while he was still alive, had no great influence on socialists of the caliber of Ludwik Warynski; it caused them to waver not at all in their views. But for the petit-bourgeois, patriotically minded intelligentsia, from whom the social-patriotic tendency had originally drawn its recruits—*because* of and not in spite of the nationalist aspects of its program—for them the personal authority of Marx, Engels, Bebel, Liebknecht, etc., was sufficient to purge their minds of any and all doubts. After the long years of a veritable antinationalist crusade on the part of socialists of the Warynski stamp, it was an especially agreeable discovery to find that perhaps one had been a nationalist all along, and even so—indeed, *almost on that account*—the purest of socialists.

Now that the traditional views of the Socialist International on the Polish question had finally obtruded into the realm of practical concerns of the labor movement, it became a matter of crucial importance for Polish and international socialism to subject them to a critical analysis. Specifically, it was necessary to do away with the illusions and obsolete views on Poland from which social patriotism had created an imposing obstacle to a socialist class standpoint in the labor movement in Poland—a critical analysis had to be applied to the traditions which had been transformed by the adherents of social patriotism into a veritable *article of faith* for Polish Socialists. At the heart of the matter was a revision of the obsolete views of Marx on the Polish question, in order to open the way to the *principles of Marxist theory* for the Polish labor movement.

On the other hand, there was a very immediate aim behind this revival and renovation of the Polish nationalist traditions among socialists in Germany and elsewhere. In fact, these traditions had been specifically cultivated for several years by a newsletter entitled *Bulletin Officiel du Parti Socialiste Polonais.* It was hoped that by imposing the programmatic demand for Poland's restoration not only on the socialists in the kingdom, but on those in Galicia and the Prussian sector as well, it would be possible to bring the three sectors of the Polish labor movement—which were struggling under totally different circumstances—together on a nationalist basis, and thus in opposition to the most vital political interests of the Polish proletariat. Of course, the other thrust of this tendency was obviously to isolate the Polish Socialist movement politically from the class-wide German and Austrian Social Democracy movement, and hence to split the ranks of the German and Austrian proletariat, at that time homogeneous, along nationalist lines.

The high point, the crowning touch to the two-year efforts of the social patriots was to have been the International Socialist Congress in London in August 1896, where the Polish Socialists were to put forward a resolution that would have given sanction to their campaign to get the restoration of Poland recognized as an absolute necessity for the international labor movement. In this way, the nationalist tendency in the Polish labor movement meant to obtain the sanction of the highest Socialist body, with all the material consequences that entailed. Such a sanction would have effectively quashed any subsequent protest that might have arisen from within the ranks of Polish Socialists.

Under these circumstances, the proposal put forward by the Polish Socialist Party at the London congress naturally gave rise to an extensive debate on the Polish question. This debate, which was in part of a theoretical nature, but also extended into the realm of tactics and practical politics, was initiated in *Neue Zeit,* and later taken up by *Vorwärts,* the central organ of the German Social Democracy and other German party newspapers (*Leipziger Volkszeitung, Sach-*

sische Arbeiterzeitung), and even found its way into the Italian press. The reader will find the entire lively discussion of 1896 and the years following in the present volume.[17] As we—contrary to the social-patriotic tendency—consider it a governing maxim of Social Democracy to encourage rather than stifle critical thinking in socialist ranks, we offer the reader all the stated opinions unaltered, all the pros and cons uttered on the issue at that time, without making the least attempt to impose ready-made answers or final conclusions. We have reproduced all of this abundant material so that the reader himself may have the opportunity to evaluate the discussion independently and form his own opinion and judgment on this problem, so fundamental to the Polish labor movement.

Politically, the immediate objectives of the debate launched in *Neue Zeit* were certainly achieved. It stirred up quite a few minds, and induced Western European socialists to devote some thought to the political meaning and concrete implications of the Social Patriotic Party, so that the latter's proposal at the London congress was tabled, and in its place a resolution unanimously adopted that once again, in general terms, affirmed the sympathy of socialists for all oppressed nationalities and gave recognition to their right to self-determination. Of course there had never been any doubts about the sympathy and compassion of socialists for oppressed nations! Indeed, such sentiments follow naturally from the socialist world view. And no less clear and self-evident was—and is—to socialists, the *right* of every nation to independence; that too flowed directly from the most elementary principles of socialism. But the social patriots who submitted the resolution were not interested in a mere blanket declaration of *sympathy* for *all* nationalities; rather, they wanted the restoration of Poland acclaimed as a specific political desideratum of the labor movement. The *right* of a nation to independence was neither here nor there; the crucial concern was to have the campaign of Polish Socialists to establish this right in Poland recognized as *correct* and *necessary.* But in effect the London congress ruled precisely to the contrary. Not only did it set the Polish situation squarely on a level with the situation of all other oppressed peoples; it at the same time called for the workers of *all* such nations to enter the ranks of international socialism as the only remedy for national oppression, rather than dabbling off and on with the restoration of independent capitalist states in their several countries; only in this way could they hasten the introduction of a socialist system that, by abolishing class oppression, would do away with all forms of oppression, including national, once and for all.

This immediate result of our critical attack shows clearly the extent to which the traditional views on the Polish question—on which the very existence of the patriotic tendency in the international movement depended—had, for the most part, already outlived their time, and moreover, how diametrically opposed they were to the real interests of the labor movement. This was brought out especially clearly by the fact that the question of Poland's restoration was posed by the proletariat on the level of practical politics in such a way that it inevitably provoked a whole new series of international questions which opened up perspectives that previously, the time of the *Neue Rheinische Zeitung* and the 1848 Revolution, had not even existed. Thus, the question was immediately posed: If the international proletariat were to recognize the national restoration of the Polish state as a goal of socialist politics, why then should it not recognize the separation of Alsace-Lorraine from Germany and its restitution to France also as a goal of Social Democracy? or support Italian nationalism in its efforts to regain Trieste and the Trentino? Even the question of the separatist ambitions in the Bohemian territories was raised.

Furthermore, recognition of the tendency calling for

Polish Socialist organizations to separate themselves from the existing socialist parties in the countries involved in the Partition, and, conversely, for the proletariat in the three Polish territories to merge into one workers' party, gave rise to a whole series of organizational questions. In Germany, not only Poles, but a large number of Danes, Alsatian French, and Lithuanians in East Prussia, live side by side with the German population. The practical consequences of the principle the social-patriotic tendency had adopted for the benefit of the Polish proletariat would have been the splitting up of the united German Social Democracy into particular parties defined along nationalist lines. The same consequences would certainly have followed for many other countries as well, since almost none of the larger modern states has a homogeneous population.

For these reasons, a sanctioning of the social-patriotic tendency would have necessitated a thoroughgoing revision of the existing positions of the international Social Democracy and a regression—in program, tactics, and organizational principles—from a solid foundation in class politics to a policy based on nationalism.

It sufficed, then, to draw attention to the concrete implications and questions inherent in the social-patriotic tendency for the entire affair to be raised from the level of a specifically *Polish* question to one of truly international import, and thus to draw German, Italian, and Russian comrades as well into the discussion.

Especially the last named. The resolution of the Polish Socialist Party at the London congress, and indeed the whole tendency which would have been sanctioned by its adoption, was of major political importance for the labor movement in Russia itself.

Polish readers who are reasonably well acquainted with the publications of the Polish Socialist Party know that ever since 1893, the year when it first appeared in the public arena, the

Polish social-patriotic tendency has attempted to justify its existence before the *Polish* public principally, and in fact almost solely, on the basis of the social stagnation in Russia and the hopeless prospects of the Russian labor movement.* By rekindling and cultivating the traditional policy on Poland in the West, social patriotism tried to preserve as well these traditional views on Russia within the ranks of international socialism. By systematically portraying the Polish labor movement as the only serious revolutionary element in tsardom, it succumbed to the delusion that the same views on the social situation in Russia that were prevalent at the time of the 1848 Revolution in the Russia of Nicholas I, the Russia of serfdom, had entrenched themselves among German, French, and other socialists. Thus, when the Russian labor movement emerged at the end of the eighties, it found itself faced with a highly unreceptive atmosphere in international socialist circles. And just at the time when the eruption of a mammoth strike of forty thousand workers in the spring of 1896 in Petersburg heralded the beginnings of a mass movement of the Russian proletariat, at precisely this time, international socialism was to declare officially, on the strength of a social-patriotic resolution, that it placed its hope for the fall

* This finds its most pointed formulation in the lead article of issue number 11 of *Przedswit*, 1894; the following extract is characteristic:

> There are some among us who support our program, or imagine that they do, yet make the following reservation: in all our efforts to achieve an independent Polish republic we must not forget that if a powerful rebellion occurs in Russia promising success of the constitutional movement, we too should join forces with this movement and do our part to obtain a constitution. Others go even further, saying: to be sure, independence is imperative for the Polish workers, and sooner or later they must obtain it, but to do so they must first possess constitutional freedoms; only when we are able to organize the masses of workers will we struggle for the ultimate objective of our political efforts—a democratic republic. As we have already stated, such persons are in error if they think we are in their camp; and if they still agree with our

of tsardom not in the political class struggle of this proletariat but in the national struggle of the Poles—in effect, a public proclamation that it placed no stock whatsoever in the Russian workers or their revolutionary struggle.

Thus, the criticism at the London congress of the social patriots' resolution, and hence, by extension, of the entire traditional standpoint on the Polish question, developed almost immediately into a criticism of the traditional views on Russia; instead of outdated images of the patriarchal Russia of Nicholas I, Western socialists were once again confronted with the picture of a modern capitalist Russia, the Russia of a struggling proletariat, demonstrating categorically that the Russian labor movement had come of age, and had earned the recognition of the international movement as a reality, and a crucial one, that had to be reckoned with.

What had originally begun as an internal affair among Polish Socialists provoked a debate that ended in a thoroughgoing revision of prevailing opinions in Western European socialism in three areas: the international situation, the situation in Russia, and the situation in Poland.

One hears a great deal of talk about Marxist "dogmatism." But the revision of the views on the Polish question provides

demand for independence they do so only because they have not taken the trouble to draw all the consequences from this step. *How can one make room for the possibility of a struggle for a constitution in the program when one does not believe in the existence of the forces that could achieve such a constitution? And yet this disbelief is still rampant among us, even since the present political program was formulated. Further, how can our supporters of a "possible" constitution reconcile their efforts with their belief in the reactionary nature of Russian society and the impotence of the socialist elements in Russia,* when the combination of these factors forces them to assume from the outset that in Russia our constitutional freedoms are either quite negligible or totally nonexistent. *In the meantime, none of our arguments enjoys such popularity among our comrades as does the argument of the reactionary nature of Russia.*

a forceful demonstration of how utterly superficial such objections are. True, Polish social patriotism did try hard for some time to transform a particular view of Marx's on a current issue into a genuine dogma, timeless, unchangeable, unaffected by historical contingencies, and subject to neither doubt nor criticism—after all, "Marx himself" once said it. However, such an abuse of Marx's name to sanction a tendency that in its entire spirit was in jarring contradiction to the teachings and theory of Marxism could only be defended as a temporary delusion suited primarily to the intellectual demoralization of the nationalist Polish intelligentsia.

Indeed, the essence of "Marxism" lies not in this or that opinion on current questions, but in two basic principles: the dialectical materialist method of historical analysis—with the theory of class struggle as one of its corollaries—and Marx's basic analysis of the principles of capitalist development. The latter theory, which explains the nature and origin of value, surplus value, money, and capital, of the concentration of capital and capitalist crises, is, strictly speaking, simply the application—albeit a brilliant one—of dialectics and historical materialism to the period of bourgeois economy. Thus, the vital core, the *quintessence*, of the entire Marxist doctrine is the dialectical materialist method of social inquiry, a method for which no phenomena, or principles, are fixed and unchanging, for which there is no dogma, for which Mephistopheles' comment, "reason turns to madness, kindness to torment,"[18] stands as a motto over the affairs of human society; and for which every historical "truth" is subject to a perpetual and remorseless criticism by actual historical developments.

Nor did the Polish Social Democracy ever see as its task the seeking of sanctions for earlier nationalist slogans in Marx's obsolete views on Poland: instead, the *method* and underlying principles of the Marxist doctrine had to be applied to the conditions of Polish society. But here it found a theoretical *tabula rasa* in the archives of Polish Socialism. The original founders of Polish Socialism, Warynski and his comrades, who brought scientific socialism to our country, encountered the remains of the nationalist ideology of the Polish nobility, including the theory of "organic labor," at that time the dominant social ideology. As representatives of the interests of the new class, the proletariat, they had above all to settle accounts with the ideological legacy of the ruling classes, and they proceeded right to the task by branding the theories and earlier movements of Polish nationalism as the expression of the selfish class and caste interests of the nobility, and the theory of organic labor as the expression of the no less material, narrow, class interests of our industrial bourgeoisie. Thus, the Polish Socialists, at the end of the seventies and beginning of the eighties, prepared the way for the theory of class contradiction by struggling against the nationalism of the nobility no less than against the bourgeois notion of "organic labor," which, as theory, proclaimed the harmony of interests of all social strata. That was the way Marx's general analysis of capitalist society and its concrete implications—class struggle of the proletariat and socialist program—were brought to Poland. This, too, was a meritorious historical contribution of Ludwik Warynski, Dickstein, and comrades.

However, by setting *socialist* revolution as the *immediate* task of the Polish proletariat to counter the political program of the ruling class, Polish Socialists left the labor movement without any political program at all, and placed socialism on a conspiratorial and utopian foundation. In so doing, they condemned the socialist movement to stagnate within the narrow confines of a sect, and within a short time, to disappear from the political scene.* One could use the above-

* Our views on the successive transformations in the political position of the Warynski group can be found especially in "Dem Andenken des *Proletariat*" ["In Memory of the Proletariat Group"].

cited argument to hold one's own against the nationalist social patriots as long as they opposed socialism on open grounds, under the old, worn-out slogan of harmony of interests and national unity in the spirit of T. T. Jež-Milkowski,[19] or even when they attempted to ally themselves with socialism, if only in the primitive, incompetent, and naive manner of Mr. Limanowski's ventures with "national socialism." But confronted with the modern version of nationalism this argument was bound to miscarry, since the latter had disavowed the discredited theory of national unity and instead hid itself behind the theory of class struggle, appearing on the political stage with the program of the proletariat as its calling card.

Hence, Social Democracy found itself propelled by the precipitous growth of the Polish labor movement into mass dimensions at the beginning of the nineties, and after the collapse of the conspiratorial tendency within socialism was obliged to work out a solid *political program* for the class struggle of the proletariat. This could only be achieved—in accordance with Marxist theory—by investigating the current trends of Polish society, an investigation which sought the key to the understanding of phenomena of a political, intellectual, and moral nature in relations of production, and the class relations which grew out of them. It was no longer a question of *describing* the development of capitalism in Poland, to what extent it produced capital concentration, proletarianization, exploitation, in a word, social anarchy and class struggle. Rather, what was necessary was an *analysis* of this development, and of the extent to which it gave rise to specific political tendencies within society. That is, there was no longer any need to show that the patterns of capitalist development *typical* to all countries were now appearing in Poland as well; what was needed was to explain the *specific* features which capitalist development had brought to the social life of *Poland* as a result of our country's particular historical and political conditions. In a word, the mere application of the stock, general conclusions of the Marxian analysis of bourgeois society to the case of Poland was not sufficient; it was necessary to undertake an original analysis of bourgeois Poland and in so doing bring socialism back down from its abstract clouds and empty schematism to the soil of Poland. This analysis, the economic aspects of which we attempted to sketch out in *The Industrial Development of Poland* [Leipzig: Duncker and Humbolt, 1898], was presented in summary form together with all the essential conclusions in an official report of the Social Democracy at the International Socialist Congress in Zurich in 1893.[20]

The result was twofold, with both aspects—one positive, the other negative—logically related: first, it provided a theoretical confirmation of a conclusion which the labor movement had already reached empirically in its mass development, namely, that the immediate political task of the Polish proletariat in the Kingdom of Poland was to join in common struggle with the Russian proletariat to bring about the downfall of absolutism, and institute democracy into political life. Second, it made clear that the struggle for the restoration of Poland was hopelessly utopian in the face of the development of capitalism in Poland, that, on the contrary, this very development had led to the above political program with the inevitability of the iron laws of history.

In this way, Polish Social Democracy was forced to find an independent explanation, as it were, for the social development of modern Poland by applying the principles of scientific socialism to Polish circumstances, in the same way that the Russian Social Democracy was forced to establish a positive program for the Russian proletariat by analyzing the specific social relations existing in Russia itself, and simultaneously mark out the path it was to take by its annihilating criticism of Narodnik theory.[21] Thus, after having traveled along completely different paths, in the positive results of their theories the Polish and Russian Social Democracies found themselves on common grounds—a common political program. There was just one difference: whereas Friedrich Engels had, in 1875, already shown a brilliant insight into the principal mistakes of the Russian Narodniks in his answer to Tkacev in *Volkstaat,* where he traced out the main lines of capitalist development from the disintegration of the village commune, in the case of Poland, neither Marx nor Engels had bothered to the very end to revise their old position of 1848; in fact, toward the last, they even mechanically applied this standpoint to the Polish Socialist movement, as we saw in their letter to the November Commemorative meeting in Geneva in 1880, and as was more recently made evident in Engels' preface to the Polish edition of "The Communist Manifesto" in 1892.[22]

No sooner had Social Democracy come forward for the first time, in 1893, with its criticism of social patriotism based on Marxian social theory,[23] than it became plain that social patriotism was capable of mustering no more than sophomoric arguments for its own defense and justification. This intellectual poverty naturally still maintained a particular brilliance about it since it had to appear in the international arena as well as before the humble Polish public. The partisans of nationalism proved themselves totally incapable of even *understanding* this Marxian analysis, let alone providing some plausible refutation of it. For example, when it was pointed out what direction capitalist development was taking in Poland, namely, that the material interests of the ruling class were creating increasingly stronger ties between our country and Russia—the social patriots tried to "brand" this whole objective, extraordinarily complex historical process—a process extending from the purely economic foundations through key political interests and issues to the most subtle aspects of ideology—as the subjective striving of Social Democrats toward "organic integration," or as a subjective concern for whether Polish manufacturers would still have anywhere to sell their "percale" once Poland was restored. The rejoinders of the supporters of social nationalism were on the same level: indignation that socialists should even acknowledge such a contemptible subject as capitalist development; or such magnanimous assurances as we find, for example, in the October 1894 issue of *Przedswit,* that Socialist delegates to parliament in restored Poland would make it their special concern to ponder over how one might find employment for the workers who would lose their jobs as a consequence of the collapse of Polish industry brought about by the loss of Russian markets.*

In the face of a real *embarras de richesses,* of this and similar such naivetés, uttered in all seriousness, it is hard to decide whether the prize should not go after all to the argument of a certain Mr. Zborowicz, who, like a true Moses, gave social patriotism its ten commandments: these anticipated every conceivable stupidity of this tendency as early as 1892 in the pamphlet, *Beitrag zur Program der Polnischen Sozialen Demokraten* [Contribution to the Program of the Polish Social Democrats, Berlin: Morawski]. The author, who in his quest for "markets" for "our" industry, naively reveals the enthusiasm that he and his followers derive from an objective

* The future historian studying the "national humor" in modern Poland will find invaluable treasures in the social-patriotic publications. We offer the following pearl in its entirety: "Let Messrs. Scheibler & Co. lose millions in profits they are presently getting from the sale of their percale to various Kalmuks or to Chiwa; we shall hardly grieve about that, and even if a certain number of workers should have to lose their jobs on account of diminished market outlets for the products of Polish factories, we will not renounce independence on that account. It will be the responsibility of the future Socialist faction in parliament to provide for these unfortunates through appropriate parliamentary proposals and to agitate for a shortening of the working day, the right to work, etc."

analysis of Social Democracy, develops the question in the following way, worthy of a Machiavelli: ". . . if political independence means we lose southern Russian markets, Russia will lose the Lithuanian market, presently dominated by Moscow industries, for the same reason. It will then be open to our industry; and add to that the Galician market which is presently inundated with Viennese products. It seems to me *the compensation is worth the loss.*"

This mindless and banal reduction of the whole of social relations in bourgeois Poland to the question of market outlets, this attempt to explain the dynamics of the objective historical process in terms of the subjective wishes, apprehensions, and concerns of socialists, showed that in the minds of social patriots the theory of historical materialism and the whole of Marx's teachings had suffered the same caricaturing as in the minds of the bourgeois critics who periodically "demolish" Marxist doctrine by distorting it and perverting it into some horrible monstrosity. That such arguments, from a tendency that was trying to pass itself off as socialist, could even find their way into the Polish press and into similar articles in the German press—this fact in itself was appalling testimony to the intellectual level of the Polish intelligentsia. This was the harvest of long years during which the minds of our "radical" intelligentsia were educated in the banal and mindless eclectic mishmash of a Limanowski, that insipid socialist slumgullion that flaunts the name of "The Social Theories of the 18th and 19th Centuries,"[24] or in that vulgar, obstreperous "revolutionary" version of socialism that the foreign publishers of the former *Proletariat* had been dishing up in *Walka* and *Przedswit*[25] since the middle of the eighties. The sad fact had at last come out: the Polish intelligentsia had, at best, been educated to *believe* in the socialist faith but not to *think* in the spirit of scientific socialism. Just as it becomes immediately apparent in the debates between Marxists and their French and German bourgeois opponents that each side considered the other barbarians, that it was not differences of opinion on particular issues but their entire modes of thought, their *Weltanschauung,* that separated them, in exactly the same manner the feud with social patriotism resembled a dialogue at the Tower of Babel. Even the replies of the social patriots bore, from the beginning, that characteristic tremolo of exasperation and whining lament that usually accompanies the ripostes of the bourgeois adversaries of Marxism.

The Polish social patriots have this in common with all petit bourgeois utopians: both consider that the discovery of historical facts which controvert their utopian dreams is an act of personal baseness on the part of the discoverer. Not for all the world can they be brought to understand that if there is any baseness involved, it is at most the "baseness" of the objective process of history, but hardly the baseness of those that draw our attention to the particular trends of this process, and that this "base" process is by no means brought to a halt merely by closing one's eyes to it. It is likewise beyond their grasp that any talk of the "baseness" of history necessarily misses the mark. The dialectic of history has this advantage, that as it undermines and abolishes traditional forms of satisfying social needs, it at the same time creates new forms. "Interests," on the other hand, for whose preservation social evolution provides no material guarantees whatsoever, are usually, if one looks closely, for the most part obsolete, bankrupt, or even no more than merely imagined.

When the German and French democrats announced their position on the Polish question in 1848 they were guided on the one hand by consideration for the existing national movement of the Polish *schlachta;* on the other hand, however, they were merely being consistent with the interests of their own democratic politics. They had no connections with the Polish Socialist movement, nor indeed could they have had, since at that time no such movement existed. Today, however, there is one question that takes precedence over all others for us Polish Socialists in adopting a position on any social phenomenon: what are the implications of that position for the class interests of the Polish proletariat? Any analysis of objective social developments in Poland requires the conclusion that a campaign for the restoration of Poland at this juncture is a petit bourgeois utopian fantasy, and, as such, is capable only of interfering with the class struggle of the proletariat and diverting it from its path. For this reason, the Polish Social Democracy today rejects the nationalist standpoint out of consideration for the interests of the Polish Socialist movement, and in so doing adopts an attitude diametrically opposed to that formerly held by Western democrats. Thus, the same historical change which turned the restoration of Poland into a utopian dream and put it in opposition to the interests of socialism in Poland, brought along with it a *new* solution for meeting international democratic interests on this point. After it had become apparent that the idea of making an independent Poland into a buffer and protective barrier for the West against the reactionary Russian tsardom was unrealizable, the development of capitalism, which had buried this idea in the first place, created in its place the revolutionary class movement of the united proletariat in Russia and Poland and in it a far more stalwart ally for the West, an ally that would not merely mechanically protect Europe from absolutism but would itself undermine and crush it.

Nor does this solution stand counter to the national interests of the Polish proletariat. Its real interests in this respect—liberty, the free development of the national cultural heritage, bourgeois equality, and the abolition of all national oppression—find their only effective, nay, only possible expression in the universal class strivings of the proletariat for the broadest democratization of the partition countries, to which national autonomy is a self-evident corollary. Beyond this, however, to think that appropriation of the state apparatus in an independent class society under existing conditions is in the interests of the working class is no more than a utopian delusion, rooted in the prejudices of the petite bourgeoisie, and, as such, is alien to the real interests of the proletariat as it is to the thought of scientific socialism in general.

Social patriotism's total lack of any argument capable of understanding criticism found its most blatant demonstration in the remarkable fact that a foreign theoretician, no less than Karl Kautsky, was needed to defend its position in the discussion being carried on in the foreign press.[26] In preparing this defense, Kautsky found himself faced with the necessity of having to develop entirely from his own resources a wholly original theory in support of the restoration of Poland, inasmuch as among the actual advocates of this program not a trace of a well-grounded argument could be discerned. The reader will see what difficulties confronted this illustrious representative of Marxism in grappling with the problem. Lacking any knowledge whatsoever of social life in Poland, he was forced to deduce the interests of the different Polish social classes from the nature of things—by mere abstract reasoning. In this way, as often happens with abstract reasoning, he arrived at the quite remarkable conclusion that the restoration of Poland was, in fact, an urgent necessity not only for the Polish proletariat, or even for any one particular class, but for all the social classes without exception—the bourgeoisie, the *schlachta,* the peasants, the petite bourgeoisie, the intelligentsia, and the proletariat. Thus, although the reputedly pure "workers' program" of social patriotism had achieved in this altogether too congenial conclusion of Kautsky's a net gain in terms of its actual basis and prospects for success, it had also lost whatever class character it may previously have had; whereupon it regressed to an earlier, more primitive phase, when it represented the harmony of interests of all social strata, to the national-unity theme of the blessed memory of Zygmunt Fortunat Milkowski.[27]

The fact that Kautsky's article received no direct rebuttal was mainly due to the circumstance that its appearance coincided almost exactly with the opening of the London congress, and it was quite impossible for a reply to be published in such a short space. After the Congress, the discussion of the restoration of Poland no longer possessed the same timeliness and practical import, since, as we have mentioned, the Congress did not adopt the social-patriotic resolution which Kautsky's essay was meant to support.

Kautsky admitted that the only factual basis for his general argument—the theory of the economic interests of the bourgeoisie and landed aristocracy—had been taken on faith from an article by a Mr. S. G. in *Neue Zeit.*[28] Behind these modest initials a *Przedswit* journalist had attempted to place the program for the restoration of Poland on "materialist" foundations, using as a basis a string of statistical fabrications, concocted historical facts, and quotations from various authors he happened to have at his finger tips. From these questionable sources, he shows that Polish capitalism, oppressed by tsardom, must give rise to a national-separatist tendency among the Polish bourgeoisie. As a writer of European stature, Kautsky, of course, could not suspect that such a weed, of the same species as the one that Lassalle had once already pulled up by the roots from German soil in his immortal excoriation of Julian Schmidt,[29] still flourished in the wretched fields of Polish journalism: as the saying goes, *"la vermine pullule chez les mendicants."* So he fell prey to the fraud perpetrated by this "national" purveyor of facts. For this reason, it was just and proper that this Polish faker bore the brunt of our criticism, and not the misled German theoretician. As a matter of fact, *The Industrial Development of Poland* contains a quite substantial, if not complete, survey of the principal statistical falsifications of our Mr. S. G., who, at *Przedswit,* is presently engaged in drawing up plans of war and gunrunning for the national cause, and has not yet offered one word in rebuttal. Finally, as regards those arguments in Kautsky's article that are of a purely political and tactical nature, the reader should have no trouble in determining for himself from Kautsky's articles in the present volume that he has brought his views on the Polish question more closely in line with the Social Democratic position under the influence of facts which reaffirm this position anew every day.

This kind of revision of the traditional views on the national question was begun in Poland in 1896, and has continued down to the present time. In that same year, the Polish Socialist movement in Germany began to dissociate itself from the German movement, a process which has ended—after a long series of unspeakably painful incidents—in 1901 with the Polish Socialist Party in the Prussian sector finding itself completely cut off from German Social Democracy.[30] Much of what we had argued—at that time on an a priori basis—in the first article in *Neue Zeit,* in spring 1896, to be the logical consequence of the nationalist tendency, was later to be verified with the utmost precision. The political contradiction which the social-patriotic tendency had inevitably to produce between Polish and international socialism—as we pointed out from the very beginning—became a tangible fact in the history of the labor movement in Germany. These experiences could not help but have an impact on the views of German Social Democracy, and they indeed found official expression in the famous declaration of August Bebel and the party's executive committee: he found it impossible, he said, to reconcile, or even to link up, the program for the restoration of Poland with the class struggle of the Polish proletariat.

In Russia, events took a similar course. The contradiction between the social-patriotic tendency and the Russian labor movement was bound eventually to find expression in practical terms, as the Russian Social Democracy began to grow into a cohesive party. The resultant revision that the Russian Social Democracy had to undertake with respect to the tendency represented by the PPS was set forth in several articles in *Iskra,* also to be found in this volume.[31] Finally, Franz Mehring, who at that time was engaged in editing the literary remains of Marx, Engels, and Lassalle, and examining their previously expressed views in the light of later developments, undertook a criticism of Marx's statements on the Polish question from a purely theoretical perspective.[32] The review of the position taken in the *Neue Rheinische Zeitung,* through application of the principles and methods of Marxism, led to a full acceptance of the views of Polish Social Democracy, so that we can now speak of a decisive and conscious shift on the Polish question all down the line, throughout the ranks of international socialism.* Kautsky came out against the separatist tendencies of certain sections of the Armenian Socialists in a comprehensive article in the *Leipziger Volkszeitung* of May 1, 1905.

* One can even say that this turn affects not only the Polish question, but nationalist tendencies of any sort within the labor movement, which today provoke pronounced hostility, and, where called for, sharp rejection.

The political independence of the *Bohemian territories* was discussed as early as the end of 1898 in *Neue Zeit* where Karl Kautsky argued with exceptional trenchancy against this proposition (at that time defended by a certain F. Stampfer), on the basis of the principles and tactics of the Austrian Social Democracy. See this article of Kautsky's in *Die Neue Zeit,* 1898–1899, Vol. I, nos. 10 and 16.

The efforts of Italian separatists in Trieste and the Trentino, and parallel nationalist tendencies in Italy, led to a special party conference of the Italian and Austrian Socialists in May 1905 in Trieste, where any solidarity or support of this nationalist movement was expressly rejected by *both* parties, thanks largely to the presence of the Austrian, Victor Adler, and the Italian, Bissolati.

Finally, the past week has provided us with a thoroughly characteristic phenomenon that was not without a touch of comedy: a violent confrontation between the Galician party and the separatist tendency of the *Jewish* Socialists within the Polish organization. Following faithfully in the Prussian and Russian territories, the position of the PPS, whose separatism is publicly supported by the leaders of the Galician party, and even using some of the arguments of the PPS, the Jewish Social Democrats isolate themselves from the party of the Galician proletariat as a whole, and thereby give the supporters of social patriotism the opportunity to see the other side of the coin: the fragmentation of the proletariat as the logical result of their tendency. To overcome this tendency, which was threatening its existence, the Galician party took refuge in the authority of the pan-Austrian Social Democracy from which they received a flat condemnation of the separatists, i.e., the Jewish ones.

But the most emphatic proof of the theory offered by Polish Social Democracy in 1893, and which it began to defend in the international movement in 1896, is furnished by the events of the past few months and years. Indeed, as this book is going to press [1905], our country and Russia find themselves in the throes of a deep social crisis. The period from 1896, when the first of these articles appeared, up to the present, comprised an entire epoch in the development of both countries, and today the Hegelian revolutionary "transformation of quantity to quality"[33] is taking place for all to see; the quantitative changes that have accumulated unnoticed are now being transformed into a new quality. We are witnessing the culmination of capitalism's slow erosion of absolutism from within, a process on which Social Democracy had based its programmatic perspective. And in this process, the two aspects of capitalist growth—to which we have called attention from the first—are finding their raw political expression. The economic merging of Poland with

Russia into an economic unit that abolishes the material basis for national separatist tendencies in our society has found reflection in the remarkable circumstance that the Polish nationalist movement, as an effective political force calling for the restoration of Poland, has disappeared without a trace. The war summons all to life and action, and has brought to the surface all revolutionary and oppositional elements in Russian society; even such an essentially trivial phenomenon as Russian liberalism has found itself carried away in quite open revolutionary raptures. The war, the last appeal, which once and for all put to the test of history all aspirations toward independence, wherever even a spark still existed, unveiled before an astonished world a picture of ghostly silence in bourgeois Poland. Indeed, the only significant ways in which the nationalist movement registered the impact of the new revolutionary developments were the renunciation of the program of national independence by one wing of the nationalists, the National Democrats' *formal* renunciation in an official declaration of policy in 1903,[34] and in the *actual* suppression of this program by the Polish Socialist Party, which completely abandoned its slogan of armed insurrection for the liberation of Poland from Russia at the first outbreak of revolution in tsardom. This party's "Political Declaration" at the end of January of this year, which makes the demand for a "legislative sejm in Warsaw," shows the utter bankruptcy of social patriotism in the face of the revolutionary crisis in Russia. In spite of all, it retains its reactionary, nationalistic core intact, as revealed in the fact that the slogan, a "legislative sejm in Warsaw," is linked with no program for democratic freedoms for the Russian empire as a whole. The Social Democratic program, by contrast, demands a republic for all of Russia with national autonomy for Poland as an organic part of any general democratic freedoms. By its *silence,* and by its aloof *disregard* of freedom for all of the tsarist empire, social patriotism reveals its nationalist character and shows after all that it has retained its utopianism *fully* intact. Indeed, this utopianism becomes all the more absurd, in that the idea of a legislative sejm in Warsaw, suspended in mid-air, so to speak, and not tied down to earth by even a general notion of democracy for Russia, is even more utopian than the restoration of Poland; the latter, at least, was only a reactionary regression to the blunted, historically obsolete idea of an autonomous constitution for the Kingdom of Poland within the absolutist Russian state, as granted by the grace of the Congress of Vienna.

However, by disavowing the slogan of armed resistance to wrench Poland loose from Russia, and by reverting to the slogan of an autonomous Poland, which takes no account of the question of freedom in Russia, social patriotism openly admits that the course of events has quite simply reduced its political program to impotence. The only aspect remaining of nationalism today is its negative side—an aloofness from the revolutionary struggle for freedom in Russia—while its positive side, the demand for Polish autonomy, has turned out to be no more than an empty phrase. This much is clear: those who do not raise the call for Poland's separation from Russia now, when tsardom is seething with violent revolution, will never do so. In other words, when revolution broke out, the *only thing* that remained of nationalism was *reaction,* while its *outwardly* and *formally* revolutionary side, that which flaunted the slogan of armed insurrection for national independence, vanished at the first wave of the present revolutionary upsurge, never to be seen again.

The other aspect of this capitalist process manifested itself at the same time in the form of the unified revolutionary class action of the Polish and Russian proletariat against absolutism and vindicated to the world the conclusions with which the author of the present article ended her book, *The Industrial Development of Poland,* in 1897: "As the Russian government incorporates Poland economically into the empire and cultivates capitalism as an 'antidote' to its nationalist opposition, it breeds, by this very process, a new social class in Poland—the mighty industrial proletariat—a class, which by its very nature, must inevitably become the resolute opponent of the absolutist regime. Although the opposition of the proletariat cannot have a national character, this inability can only render its opposition all the more effective, since it must then counter the solidarity of the Russian and Polish bourgeoisie, so coveted by the government, with the only logical response: the political solidarity of the Polish and Russian proletariat. The result of the merging of Poland and Russia was a circumstance overlooked by the Russian government, the Polish bourgeoisie, and the Polish nationalists alike: *the unification of the Polish and Russian proletariat into a single body to preside over the coming bankruptcy of, first, Russian tsardom, and then the combined rule of Polish and Russian capital."* The first liquidation has already begun. The spirit of Marxism has triumphed in the revolution of the proletariat on the streets of Warsaw and Petersburg.

The whole course of social development, now reaching its culmination in the revolutionary upheavals in the tsarist empire, has struck a fatal blow to our nationalism—but not to the cause of Polish national identity. Where reactionary utopianism, mired in the past, sees only ruin, defeat, and destruction, the scrutinizing eye, trained to decipher the historical dialectic of revolution, cannot but perceive the opening of new vistas for the deliverance of Polish national culture.

The accusations of "dogmatism" against Social Democracy are no less frequent than complaints about its "doctrinairism": its alleged intellectual narrowness that is said to be bent on forcing the vast and infinitely varied world of social phenomena into a rigid schema that recognizes nothing but "material interests," and is deaf and blind to the higher forms of psychic phenomena—national sentiments, for example. Marxism can really have only one response to such critics: in Goethe's words, *"Ihr gleicht dem Geist, den Ihr begreift, nicht mir!"*[35]

The Social Democratic world view is reduced to a narrow, intellectually stifling doctrine by just those critics who complain of its doctrinairism. The contrary is true: Marxism is, by its very nature, the most fecund, the most universal product of thought, a theory that makes the mind soar, vast as the world is wide, and as rich in color and tones as nature, urging to action, and pulsating with the vitality of youth. This theory, and no other, provides the key to the riddles of past history, and opens the way to our understanding of society as it continues to unfold; lifting us, "with one wing sustained in the past, the other grazing the future," it impels us forward in the present to creative, truly revolutionary deeds.

But our being aware of the actual trends of historical development by no means absolves us from involvement in our own social history, or allows us to fold our arms fatalistically across our breasts and like an Indian fakir wait to see what the future will bring. "Men make their own history, but they do so not as free individuals," says Marx.[36] One could, with full justification, state the converse: men do not make history as free individuals, *but they make their own history.* Far from blunting or sapping our revolutionary fervor, a sensitivity to the objective movement of history tempers the will and pushes us to action by showing us ways to drive the wheel of social progress effectively forward and by sparing us from impotently and fruitlessly knocking our heads against the wall, which sooner or later inevitably brings disappointment, despair, and quietism; through this knowledge we are protected as well from mistaking, as revolutionary activity, aspirations that have long since been transformed by the forces of social evolution into their reactionary opposites.

As the reader will perceive from the modest selection contained in this book, Marxism alone is in a position to provide an exhaustive explanation for the remarkable, puzzle-ridden history of our society over the last half-century, even to the most subtle nuances of its intellectual physiognomy, its ideology. Only a blustering simpleton would not find it puzzling that a society suffering such outrageous subjugation, whose most elementary national rights have been so systematically trampled under foot, whose intellectual and cultural life has been so brutally stunted—that such a society would not only give up its armed struggle for independence for fifty years, but would also abandon all efforts, however slight, to obtain a European, democratic way of life, and renounce all active opposition to its savage tyrants. Only people who "make" revolution and "rebellions" in small schoolboy cliques can toss off such historical problems and be done with them merely by branding certain classes as "conciliators" and blaming conciliation on a "handful" of their representatives; they, of course, do not understand that given the factual material circumstances of our social development, this "handful" of conciliators turns out to be the entire Polish bourgeoisie with its present historical mission, and hardly that other handful of individuals who discourse on "guns" and rebellions of petit bourgeois utopians. Only the Marxist scholar can best comprehend the deepest inner motives of Polish bourgeois society, its shameful past and its shameful present; he is in the best position to see in what directions our country's history and the class struggle are driving. Only a penetrating study into the causes of the decline of the rebellious Polish nobility and of the disgraceful history of bourgeois-capitalist Poland, a study unclouded by romantic utopianism, made it possible to foresee the revolutionary regeneration of working-class Poland presently occurring before our eyes. Now, as in the past, it is an understanding of national and class development that enables us to grasp that the only real revolutionary deed at this juncture is bringing *consciousness* into this spontaneous historical process, thereby foreshortening its course and speeding it onward toward its goal.

Doubtless the cause of nationalism in Poland bears a special historical relationship to the class struggle of the proletariat; but not at all in the sense imagined by the social patriots. For them the modern proletarian movement was a scapegoat from which one could exact payment for all the back debts, long since swept away by history, of the aristocracy and petite bourgeoisie, or which could be ordered to make good all the obligations of the bankrupt classes. The relationship was, in fact, quite otherwise. In the framework, in the spirit of the Polish proletarian class struggle, the cause of nationalism itself takes on quite a different appearance than it has in the aspirations of the *schlachta* and the petite bourgeoisie.

The cause of nationalism in Poland is not alien to the working class—nor can it be. The working class cannot be indifferent to the most intolerably barbaric oppression, directed as it is against the intellectual and cultural heritage of society. To the credit of mankind, history has universally established that even the most inhumane *material* oppression is not able to provoke such wrathful, fanatical rebellion and rage as the suppression of intellectual life in general, or as religious or national oppression. But only classes which are revolutionary by virtue of their *material* social situation are capable of heroic revolt and martyrdom in defense of these intellectual riches.

To tolerate national oppression, to toady to it servilely—that is the special talent of the *schlachta* and bourgeoisie, i.e., the possessing classes whose interests today are reactionary to the core, classes that are the perfect embodiment of that vulgar "gut materialism" into which the materialist philosophy of Marx and Feuerbach is usually transformed in the empty skulls of our humdrum journalists. As a class possessing no material stake in present society, our proletariat, whose historical mission is to overthrow the entire existing system—in short, the revolutionary class—must experience national oppression as an open wound, as a shame and disgrace, and indeed it does, although this does not alter the fact that this particular injustice is only a drop in the ocean of the entire social privation, political abuse, and intellectual disinheritance that the wage laborer suffers at the hands of present-day society.

But this, as we said, by no means implies that the proletariat is capable of taking upon itself the historical task of the *schlachta,* as the anachronistic minds of petit bourgeois nationalism would have it; this task, to restore Poland to its existence as a class state, is an objective which the *schlachta* itself abandoned, and the bourgeoisie has rendered impossible through its own development. But our proletariat can and must fight for the defense of national identity as a cultural legacy, that has its own right to exist and flourish. And today our national identity cannot be defended by national separatism; it can only be secured through the struggle to overthrow despotism and solidly implant the advantages of culture and bourgeois life throughout the entire country, as has long since been done in Western Europe.

Consequently, it is precisely the untarnished class movement of the Polish proletariat, which grew to maturity, along with capitalism, on the grave of the movements for national autonomy, that constitutes the best and *only* guarantee of attaining, along with bourgeois equality and autonomy, freedom in political life and in our national culture. Thus, from even a purely national perspective, everything that contributes to promoting, expanding, and expediting the working-class movement must be viewed as a contribution to *national patriotism* in the best and truest sense of the word. But anything that checks or impedes this development, anything that might delay it or cause it to depart from its principles, must be regarded as injurious and hostile to the national cause. From this perspective, the efforts to cultivate the old traditions of nationalism and to divert the Polish working class from the path of class struggle to the utopian folly of Polish restoration, as social patriotism did for twelve long years, represents the politics of a profound *anti-nationalism,* despite its outwardly nationalist trappings. Social Democracy, sailing under the banner of international socialism, bears in its keeping the Polish national cultural heritage—that is the present consequence of the dialectics of history. To understand and foresee this process, and act in consonance with it—that is what the Marxist method enables us to do.

Notes

1. The book to which this essay was the Foreword was published in Polish in Cracow in 1905. In addition to the Foreword, it contained several other articles by Rosa Luxemburg, and reprints of articles by Karl Kautsky, Franz Mehring, and "Parvus" (A. Helphand). The articles by Rosa Luxemburg have all been translated into German, and this translation is based on the German version.
2. Jean Jaurès was a leading French exponent of revisionism, and as such subject to ceaseless attack by Rosa Luxemburg.
3. In April 1902, the Belgian workers staged a general strike in order to secure the vote. They were unsuccessful.
4. In December 1825, young officers (Decembrists) in the Tsar's army sought to introduce Western ideas of reform into autocratic Russia. The uprising was quickly put down.
5. In 1866, Karakozov made an unsuccessful attempt on the life of Tsar Alexander II.
6. Rosa Luxemburg's point of view on this matter has recently been sustained by Hans-Ulrich Wehler—see his *Sozialdemokratie und Nationalstaat* (Würzburg: 1962), pp. 17ff.
7. Tkacev (1844-1885) was a Nihilist who developed a Blanquist theory of revolution, especially in the journal *Nabat* (*Tocsin*), which he edited and published in Switzerland.

8. This quote by Engels is given in German in Rosa Luxemburg's original, which, it will be recalled, was written in Polish. The quote is from Engels, "Soziales aus Russland" ("Social Perspectives from Russia"), Marx-Engels *Werke* (Berlin: 1962), XVIII, 585.
9. The first Marxist group to become active in Poland was founded in 1882 by Ludwik Warynski and others, with the name "Proletariat." It was obliged to work underground, but still succeeded in organizing several big strikes in 1883. It was in close touch with the Russian organization, *Narodnaya Volya* (People's Will), and, like it, adopted terrorist tactics in the late 1880s. Rosa Luxemburg did not approve of terrorism, then or later, but still traced her spiritual ancestry to Warynski, including his rejection of Polish independence.
10. "Equality." The periodical and group by this name were the immediate precursors of the Proletariat group.
11. Marx-Engels, op. cit., XIX, 239-41.
12. The Polish Socialist Party (PPS) was founded in London toward the end of 1892, and thereafter worked closely with the sister parties in Germany and Austrian Poland for the independence of Poland. Associated with the PPS was a special committee in London, the Ziriazelc Zagraniczny Socjalistow Palskich.
13. Pobudka means "alarm," "reveille."
14. Limanowski was also the chairman at the founding conference of the PPS.
15. S. Häcker, "Der Sozialismus in Polen: Eine Entgegnung" ("Socialism in Poland: A Reply") [i.e., to Rosa Luxemburg], in *Die Neue Zeit, 1895–1896*, vol. II.
16. "Dawn." At this time the journal was the organ of the internationalist Proletariat group. Later it became a voice for the PPS.
17. That is, the volume *The Polish Question and the Socialist Movement*, to which this essay was the Foreword. Cf. footnote 1.
18. Given in German in the original Polish text: "Vernunft wird Unsinn, Wohltat–Plage."
19. Zygmunt Milkowski (pseudonym Jež), 1824-1915. Writer and politician, spokesman for the "organic labor" movement, which took the point of view that the main job for Poland was to industrialize, with independence as a secondary consideration. He preached the philosophy of harmony of interests, i.e., against class war.
20. See Volume I of R. L.'s *Collected Works* for both of these items.
21. The Narodnik, or Populist movement in Russia, was active in the last part of the nineteenth century. Its "socialism" was not Marxist.

22. Marx–Engels, op. cit., XXII, 282ff.
23. The *Sprawa Robotnicza* (The Workers' Cause) was founded in Paris in July 1893 with the collaboration of Leo Jogiches, Rosa Luxemburg (under the name "R. Kruszynska"), and Adolf Warszawski, and later, Julian Marchlewski. The following month this group founded the political party, Socjaldemokracja Krolesta Polskiego (SDKP), which, in 1899, through the incorporation of a Lithuanian group, became the SDKPiL.
24. *Historia ruchu spolecznego v drugiej polowie XVIII stulecia* (Lemberg: 1888); and *Historia ruchu spolecznego w XIX stulecia* (Lemberg: 1890).
25. "Class Struggle."
26. Karl Kautsky, "Finis Poloniae?," in *Die Neue Zeit, 1895–1896*, Vol. II.
27. Cf. footnote 19.
28. "Die industrielle Politik Russlands in dessen polnischen Provinzen" ("Russia's Industrial Policy in its Polish Provinces") in *Die Neue Zeit, 1893–1894*, Vol. II.
29. Ferdinand Lassalle, "Herr Julian Schmidt der Literaturhistoriker" ("Julian Schmidt the Historian of Literature"), 1862.
30. The increasing difficulties between the Prussian branch of the PPS and the German Social Democratic Party, ending in the expulsion of the former group, must have been a painful experience for Rosa Luxemburg. She was delegated to work for the Social Democratic Party among the Poles in East Prussia; she was the Polish expert of the German party. She had even joined the PPS, although continuing to criticize its excessive nationalism.
31. Lenin, "The National Question in Our Program," in *Collected Works*, Vol. VI. In his attitude toward the PPS, Lenin's position appears to be largely identical with Rosa Luxemburg's.
32. Mehring, ed., *Aus dem literarischen Nachlass von Karl Marx, Friedrich Engels und Ferdinand Lassalle*, Vol. III (Stuttgart: 1902).
33. This phrase is given in German in the original.
34. The National Democrats were an outgrowth of a party founded in 1887. They included segments of the bourgeoisie and the big landowners. Their leading figure was R. Dmowski.
35. "You are not equal [to me]. You are only equal to what you think I am." From Goethe's *Faust*, trans. Bryan Fairley (Toronto: 1970), Scene 1, p. 10.
36. Karl Marx, "The 18th Brumaire of Louis Bonaparte," op. cit., VIII, 115.

The National Question and Autonomy[1]

1. The Right of Nations to Self-Determination

Among other problems, the 1905 Revolution in Russia has brought into focus the nationality question. Until now, this problem has been urgent only in Austria-Hungary. At present, however, it has become crucial also in Russia, because the revolutionary development made all classes and all political parties acutely aware of the need to solve the nationality question as a matter of practical politics. All the newly formed or forming parties in Russia, be they radical, liberal, or reactionary, have been forced to include in their programs some sort of a position on the nationality question, which is closely connected with the entire complex of the state's internal and external policies. For a workers' party, nationality is a question both of program and of class organization. The position a workers' party assumes on the nationality question, as on every other question, must differ in method and basic approach from the positions of even the most radical bourgeois parties, and from the positions of the pseudo-socialistic, petit bourgeois parties. Social Democracy, whose political program is based on the scientific method of historical materialism and the class struggle, cannot make an exception with respect to the nationality question. Moreover, it is only by approaching the problem from the standpoint of scientific socialism that the politics of Social Democracy will offer a solution which is *essentially uniform,* even though the program must take into account the wide variety of forms of the nationality question arising from the social, historical, and ethnic diversity of the Russian empire.

In the program of the Social Democratic Labor Party (RSDLP) of Russia, such a formula, containing a general solution of the nationality question in all its particular manifestations, is provided by the ninth point; this says that the party demands a democratic republic whose constitution would insure, among other things, *"that all nationalities forming the state have the right to self-determination."*

This program includes two more extremely important propositions on the same matter. These are the seventh point, which demands the abolition of classes and the full legal equality of all citizens without distinction of sex, *religion, race,* or *nationality,* and the eighth point, which says that the several ethnic groups of the state should have the right to schools conducted in their respective national languages at state expense, and the right to use their languages at assemblies and on an equal level with the state language in all state and public functions. Closely connected to the nationality question is the third point of the program, which formulates the demand for wide self-government on the local and provincial level in areas which are characterized by special living conditions and by the special composition of their populations. Obviously, however, the authors of the program felt that the equality of all citizens before the law, linguistic rights, and local self-government were not enough to solve the nationality problem, since they found it necessary to add a special paragraph granting each nationality the "right to self-determination."

What is especially striking about this formula is the fact that it doesn't represent anything specifically connected with socialism nor with the politics of the working class. "The right of nations to self-determination" is at first glance a paraphrase of the old slogan of bourgeois nationalism put forth in all countries at all times: "the right of nations to freedom and independence." In Poland, the "innate right of nations" to freedom has been the classic formula of nationalists from the Democratic Society to Limanowski's *Pobudka,* and from the national socialist *Pobudka* to the antisocialist "National League" before it renounced its program of independence.[2] Similarly, a resolution on the "equal rights of all nations" to freedom was the only tangible result of the famous pan-Slav congress held in Prague, which was broken up in 1848 by the pan-Slavic bayonets of Windischgraetz. On the other hand, its generality and wide scope, despite the principle of "the right of nations to self-determination"—which obviously can be applied not only to the peoples living in Russia but also to the nationalities living in Germany and Austria, Switzerland and Sweden, America—strangely enough is not to be found in any of the programs of today's socialist parties. This principle is not even included in the program of Austrian Social Democracy, which exists in a state with an extremely mixed population, where the nationality question is of crucial importance.

The Austrian party would solve the nationality question not by a metaphysical formula which leaves the determination of the nationality question up to each of the nationalities according to their whims, but only by means of a well-defined plan. Austrian Social Democracy demands the elimination of the existing state structure of Austria, which is a collection of "kingdoms and princely states" patched together during the Middle Ages by the dynastic politics of the Hapsburgs, and includes various nationalities mixed together territorially in a hodgepodge manner. The party rather demands that these kingdoms and states should be divided into territories on the basis of nationality, and that these national territories be joined into a state union. But because the nationalities are to some extent jumbled together through almost the entire area of Austria, the program of Social

Democracy makes provision for a special law to protect the smaller minorities in the newly created national territories.

Everyone is free to have a different opinion on this plan. Karl Kautsky, one of the most knowledgeable experts on Austrian conditions and one of the spiritual fathers of Austrian Social Democracy, shows in his latest pamphlet, *Nationality and Internationalism,* that such a plan, even if it could be put into effect, would by no means completely eliminate the conflicts and difficulties among the nationalities. Nonetheless, it does represent an attempt to provide a practical solution of these difficulties by the party of the proletariat, and because of the importance of the nationality question in Austria, we shall quote it in full.

The nationality program of the Austrian party, adopted at the Brünn Congress in 1899, says:

> Because national conflicts in Austria are obstructing all political progress and the cultural development of the nationalities, because these conflicts result primarily from the backwardness of our public institutions and because the prolongation of these conflicts is one of the methods by which the ruling classes insure their domination and prevent measures in the true interests of the people, the congress declares that:
>
> The final settlement of the nationality and language question in Austria in the spirit of equality and reason is primarily a cultural demand, and therefore is one of the vital interests of the proletariat.
>
> This is possible only under a truly democratic regime based on universal, equal, and direct elections, a regime in which all feudal privileges in the state and the principalities will have been abrogated. Only under such a regime will the working classes, the elements which really support the state and society, be able to express their demands.
>
> The nurturing and development of the national peculiarities of all peoples in Austria are possible only

on the basis of equal rights and the removal of oppression. Therefore, state–bureaucratic centralism and the feudal privileges of the principalities must be opposed.

Only under such conditions will it be possible to create harmony among the nationalities in Austria in place of the quarreling that takes place now, namely, through the recognition of the following guiding principles:

1. Austria is to be transformed into a democratic federation of nationalities (*Nationalitätenbundesstaat*).

2. The historic Crown lands are to be replaced by nationally homogeneous self-ruling bodies, whose legislation and administration shall be in the hands of national chambers, elected on the basis of universal, equal, and direct franchise.

3. All self-governing regions of one and the same nation are to form together a nationally distinct union, which shall take care of this union's affairs autonomously.*

4. A special law should be adopted by the parliament to safeguard the rights of national minorities.

5. We do not recognize any national privilege; therefore we reject the demand for a state language. Whether a common language is needed, a federal parliament can decide.

The party congress, as the organ of international social democracy in Austria, expresses its conviction that on the basis of these guiding principles, understanding among peoples is possible.

It solemnly declares that it recognizes the right of each nationality to national existence and national development.

Peoples can advance their culture only in close solidarity with one another, not in petty quarrels; particularly the working class of all nations must, in the

*** That is, linguistic and cultural, according to the explanation given in the draft by the party's leadership.**

> interest of the individual nationalities and in the general interest, maintain international cooperation and fraternity in its struggle and must conduct its political and economic struggle in closely united ranks.
>
> In the ranks of international socialism, the Russian Workers' Party is the only one whose program includes the demand that "nationalities be granted the right to self-determination."

Apart from Russian Social Democracy, we find this formula only in the program of the Russian Social Revolutionaries, where it goes hand in hand with the principle of state federalism. The relevant section of the political declaration of the Social Revolutionary Party states that "the wide application of the principle of federalism in the relations between individual nationalities is possible," and stresses the "recognition of their unlimited right to self-determination."

It is true that the above formula exists in another connection with international socialism: namely, it is a paraphrase of one section of the resolution on the nationality problem adopted in 1896 by the International Socialist Congress in London. However, the circumstances which led to the adoption of that resolution, and the way in which the resolution was formulated, show clearly that if the ninth paragraph in the program of the Russian party is taken as an application of the London Resolution, it is based on a misunderstanding.

The London resolution was not at all the result of the intention or need to make a statement at an international congress on the nationality question in general, nor was it presented or adopted by the Congress as a formula for the *practical resolution of that question* by the workers' parties of the various countries. Indeed, just the opposite was true. The London Resolution was adopted on the basis of a motion presented to the Congress by the social-patriotic faction of the Polish movement, or the Polish Socialist Party (PPS), a motion which demanded that the reconstruction of an independent Poland be recognized as one of the most urgent demands of international socialism.* Influenced by the criticism raised at the Congress by Polish Social Democracy and the discussion concerning this in the socialist press, as well as by the first mass demonstration of the workers' movement in Russia—the memorable strike of forty thousand textile workers in Petersburg in May 1896—the International Congress did not consider the Polish motion, which was directed in its arguments and in its entire character against the Russian revolutionary movement. Instead, it adopted the London Resolution already mentioned, which signified a rejection of the motion for the reconstruction of Poland.

The Congress—the resolution states—declares itself in favor of

> the complete right of all nations to self-determination, and expresses its sympathy for the workers of every country now suffering under the yoke of military, national, or other despotism; the Congress calls on the workers of all these countries to join the ranks of the class-conscious workers of the whole world in order to fight together with them for the defeat of international capitalism and for the achievement of the aims of international Social Democracy.

* The above motion read: "Whereas, the subjugation of one nation by another can serve only the interests of capitalists and despots, while for working people in both oppressed and oppressor nation it is equally pernicious; and whereas, in particular, the Russian tsardom, which owes its internal strength and its external significance to the subjugation and partition of Poland, constitutes a permanent threat to the development of the international workers' movement, the Congress hereby resolves: that the independence of Poland represents an imperative political demand both for the Polish proletariat and for the international labor movement as a whole."

As we can see, in its content, the London Resolution replaces the exclusive consideration of the Polish question by the generalization of the question of all suppressed nationalities, transferring the question from a national basis onto an international one, and instead of a definite, completely concrete demand of practical politics, which the motion of the PPS demanded—the reconstruction of independent Poland—the resolution expresses a general socialist principle: sympathy for the proletariat of all suppressed nationalities and the recognition of their *right* to self-determination. There can be no doubt that this principle was not formulated by the Congress in order to give the international workers' movement a practical solution to the nationality problem. On the contrary, a practical guideline for socialist politics is contained not in the first part of the London Resolution quoted above, but in the second part, which "calls upon the workers of all countries suffering national oppression to enter the ranks of international Social Democracy and to work for the realization of its principles and goals." It is an unambiguous way of emphasizing that the principle formulated in the first part—the right of nations to self-determination—can be put into effect only in one way: viz., by first realizing the principles of international socialism and by attaining its ultimate goals.

Indeed, none of the socialist parties took the London Resolution to be a practical solution of the nationality question, and they did not include it in their programs. Even Austrian Social Democracy, for which the solution of the nationality problem was a question involving its very existence, did not do this; instead, in 1899, it created for itself independently the practical "nationality program" quoted above. What is most characteristic, even the PPS did not do this, because, despite its efforts to spread the tale that the London Resolution was a formula in "the spirit" of socialism, it was obvious that this Resolution meant rather a rejection of its motion for the reconstruction of Poland, or at the very least, a dilution of it into a general formula without any practical character.* In point of fact, the political programs of the modern workers' parties do not aim at stating abstract principles of a social ideal, but only at the formulation of those practical social and political reforms which the class-conscious proletariat needs and demands in the framework of bourgeois society to facilitate the class struggle and their ultimate victory. The elements of a political program are formulated with definite aims in mind: to provide a direct, practical, and feasible solution to the crucial problems of political and social life, which are in the area of the class struggle of the proletariat; to serve as a guideline for everyday politics and its needs; to initiate the political action of the workers' party and to lead it in the right direction; and finally, to separate the revolutionary politics of the proletariat from the politics of the bourgeois and petit bourgeois parties.

The formula, "the right of nations to self-determination," of course doesn't have such a character at all. It gives no practical guidelines for the day to day politics of the proletariat, nor any practical solution of nationality problems. For example, this formula does not indicate to the Russian proletariat in what way it should demand a solution of the Polish national problem, the Finnish question, the Caucasian question, the Jewish, etc. It offers instead only an unlimited authorization to all interested "nations" to settle their national problems in any way they like. The only practical conclusion for the day to day politics of the working class which can be drawn from the above formula is the guideline that it is the duty of that class to struggle against all mani-

* Only the German branch of the Polish Socialist Party thought it relevant to include the London Resolution in its program during its struggles with German Social Democracy. After it joined the German party again, the PPS adopted the Erfurt program as its own without reservations.[3]

festations of national oppression. If we recognize the right of each nation to self-determination, it is obviously a logical conclusion that we must condemn every attempt to place one nation over another, or for one nation to force upon another any form of national existence. However, the duty of the class party of the proletariat to protest and resist national oppression arises not from any special "right of nations," just as, for example, its striving for the social and political equality of sexes does not at all result from any special "rights of women" which the movement of bourgeois emancipationists refers to. This duty arises solely from the general opposition to the class regime and to every form of social inequality and social domination, in a word, from the basic position of socialism. But leaving this point aside, the only guideline given for practical politics is of a purely negative character. The duty to resist all forms of national oppression does not include any explanation of what conditions and political forms the class-conscious proletariat in Russia at the present time should recommend as a solution for the nationality problems of Poland, Latvia, the Jews, etc., or what program it should present to match the various programs of the bourgeois, nationalist, and pseudosocialist parties in the present class struggle. In a word, the formula, "the right of nations to self-determination," is essentially not a political and problematic guideline in the nationality question, but only a means of *avoiding that question.*

II

The general and cliché-like character of the ninth point in the program of the Social Democratic Labor Party of Russia shows that this way of solving the question is foreign to the position of Marxian socialism. A "right of nations" which is valid for all countries and all times is nothing more than a metaphysical cliché of the type of "rights of man" and "rights of the citizen." Dialectic materialism, which is the basis of scientific socialism, has broken once and for all with this type of "eternal" formula. For the historical dialectic has shown that there are no "eternal" truths and that there are no "rights." . . . In the words of Engels, "What is good in the here and now, is an evil somewhere else, and vice versa"—or, what is right and reasonable under some circumstances becomes nonsense and absurdity under others. Historical materialism has taught us that the real content of these "eternal" truths, rights, and formulae is determined only by the *material* social conditions of the environment in a given historical epoch.

On this basis, scientific socialism has revised the entire store of democratic clichés and ideological metaphysics inherited from the bourgeoisie. Present-day Social Democracy long since stopped regarding such phrases as "democracy," "national freedom," "equality," and other such beautiful things as eternal truths and laws transcending particular nations and times. On the contrary, Marxism regards and treats them only as expressions of certain definite historical conditions, as categories which, in terms of their material content and therefore their political value, are subject to constant change, which is the *only* "eternal" truth.

When Napoleon or any other despot of his ilk uses a plebiscite, the extreme form of political democracy, for the goals of Caesarism, taking advantage of the political ignorance and economic subjection of the masses, we do not hesitate for a moment to come out wholeheartedly against that "democracy," and are not put off for a moment by the majesty or the omnipotence of the people, which, for the metaphysicians of bourgeois democracy, is something like a sacrosanct idol.

When a German like Tassendorf or a tsarist gendarme, or a "truly Polish" National Democrat defends the "personal freedom" of strikebreakers, protecting them against the moral and material pressure of organized labor, we don't hesitate a minute to support the latter, granting them the fullest moral and historical right to *force* the unenlightened rivals into solidarity, although from the point of view of formal liberalism, those "willing to work" have on their side the right of "a free individual" to do what reason, or unreason, tells them.

When, finally, liberals of the Manchester School demand that the wage worker be left completely to his fate in the struggle with capital in the name of "the equality of citizens," we unmask that metaphysical cliché which conceals the most glaring economic inequality, and we demand, point-blank, the legal protection of the class of wage workers, thereby clearly breaking with formal "equality before the law."

The nationality question cannot be an exception among all the political, social, and moral questions examined in this way by modern socialism. It cannot be settled by the use of some vague cliché, even such a fine-sounding formula as "the right of all nations to self-determination." For such a formula expresses either absolutely nothing, so that it is an empty, noncommittal phrase, or else it expresses the unconditional duty of socialists to support all national aspirations, in which case it is simply false.

On the basis of the general assumptions of historical materialism, the position of socialists with respect to nationality problems depends primarily on the concrete circumstances of each case, which differ significantly among countries, and also change in the course of time in each country. Even a superficial knowledge of the facts enables one to see that the question of the nationality struggles under the Ottoman Porte in the Balkans has a completely different aspect, a different economic and historical basis, a different degree of international importance, and different prospects for the future, from the question of the struggle of the Irish against the domination of England. Similarly, the complications in the relations among the nationalities which make up Austria are completely different from the conditions which influence the Polish question. Moreover, the nationality question in each country changes its character with time, and this means that new and different evaluations must be made about it. Even our three national movements beginning from the time of the Kościuszko Insurrection could be seen as a triple, stereotyped repetition of the same historical play (that is, "the struggle of a subjugated nationality for independence") only in the eyes of either a metaphysician of the upper-class Catholic ideology such as Szujski, who believed that Poland had a historical mission to be the "Christ of nations," or in the eyes of an ignoramus of the present-day social-patriotic "school." Whoever cuts deeper with the scalpel of the researcher—more precisely, of the historical-materialist researcher—will see beneath the surface of our three national uprisings three completely different sociopolitical movements, which took on an identical form of struggle with the invader in each case only because of external circumstances. To measure the Kościuszko Insurrection and the November and January insurrections by one and the same yardstick—by the sacred laws of the "subjugated nation"—actually reveals a lack of all judgment and the complete absence of any historical and political discrimination.[4]

A glaring example of how the change of historical conditions influences the evaluation and the position of socialists with respect to the nationality question is the so-called Eastern question. During the Crimean war in 1855, the sympathies of all democratic and socialist Europe were on the side of the Turks and against the South Slavs who were seeking their liberty. The "right" of all nations to freedom did not prevent Marx, Engels, and Liebknecht from speaking against the Balkan Slavs and from resolutely supporting the integrity of the Turks. For they judged the national movements of the Slavic peoples in the Turkish empire not from the standpoint of the "eternal" sentimental formulae of liberalism, but from the standpoint of the material conditions which determined the *content* of these national movements, according to their views of the time. Marx and Engels saw in the freedom movement of the socially backward South Slavs only the machinations of Russian tsardom trying to irritate the Turks, and thus, without any second thoughts, they subordinated the question of the national freedom of the Slavs to the interests of European democracy, insisting on the integrity of Turkey as a bulwark of defense against Russian reaction. This political position was maintained in German Social Democracy as late as the second half of the 1890s, when the gray-haired Wilhelm Liebknecht, on the occasion of the struggle of the Ormian Turks, still spoke in that spirit. But by this time the position of German and international Social Democracy on the Eastern question had changed. Social Democracy began to support openly the aspirations of the suppressed nationalities in Turkey to a separate cultural existence, and abandoned all concern for the artificial preservation of Turkey as a whole. And at this time it was guided not by a feeling of duty toward the Ormians or the Macedonians as subjugated nationalities, but by the analysis of the material base of conditions in the East in the second half of the last century. By this analysis, the Social Democrats became convinced that the political disintegration of Turkey would result from its economic-political development in the second half of the nineteenth century, and that the temporary preservation of Turkey would serve the interests of the reactionary diplomacy of Russian absolutism. Here, as in all other questions, Social Democracy was not contrary to the current of objective development, but with it, and, profiting from its conclusions, it defended the interests of European civilization by supporting the national movements within Turkey. It also supported all attempts to renew and reform Turkey from within, however weak the social basis for such a movement may have been.

A second example of the same thing is provided by the diametrically opposite attitudes of Marx and Engels during the revolution of 1848 with respect to the national aspirations of the Czechs and the Poles. There is no doubt that from the point of view of the "right of nations to self-determination" the Czechs deserved the support of the European socialists and democrats no less than the Poles. Marx, however, did not pay any attention to that abstract formula, and hurled thunderbolts at the heads of the Czechs and their aspirations for freedom, aspirations which he regarded as a harmful complication of the revolutionary situation, all the more deserving of severe condemnation, since, to Marx, the Czechs were a dying nationality, doomed to disappear soon. The creators of "The Communist Manifesto" put forth these views at the same time that they were defending the nationalist movement of the Poles with all their strength, calling upon all revolutionary and progressive forces to help our patriots.

The sober realism, alien to all sentimentalism, with which Marx examined the national problems during the revolution itself, is shown by the way he treated the Polish and Czech questions:

"The Revolution of 1848," wrote Marx in his articles[5] on the revolution which appeared in February 1852 in the American paper, *Daily Tribune,*

> calling forth at once the claim of all oppressed nations to an independent existence, and to the right to settle their own affairs for themselves, it was quite natural that the Poles should at once demand the restoration of their country within the frontiers of the old Polish Republic before 1772. It is true, this frontier, even at that time, had become obsolete, if taken as the delimitation of German and Polish nationality; it had become more so every year since by the progress of Germanization; but then, the Germans had proclaimed such an

enthusiasm for the restoration of Poland, that they must expect to be asked, as a first proof of the reality of their sympathies, to give up *their* share of the plunder. On the other hand, should whole tracts of land, inhabited chiefly by Germans, should large towns, entirely German, be given up to a people that as yet had never given any proofs of its capability of progressing beyond a state of feudalism based upon agricultural serfdom? The question was intricate enough. The only possible solution was in a war with Russia. The question of delimitation between the different revolutionized nations would have been made a secondary one to that of first establishing a safe frontier against the common enemy. The Poles, by receiving extended territories in the east, would have become more tractable and reasonable in the west; and Riga and Milan would have been deemed, after all, quite as important to them as Danzig and Elbing. *Thus the advanced party in Germany, deeming a war with Russia necessary to keep up the Continental movement, and considering that the national re-establishment even of a part of Poland would inevitably lead to such a war, supported the Poles;* while the reigning, middle-class party clearly foresaw its downfall from any national war against Russia, which would have called more active and energetic men to the helm, and, therefore, with a feigned enthusiasm for the extension of German nationality, they declared Prussian Poland, the chief seat of Polish revolutionary agitation, to be part and parcel of the German Empire that was to be.

Marx treated the Czech question with no less political realism:

The question of nationality gave rise to another struggle in Bohemia. This country, inhabited by two millions of Germans, and three millions of Slavonians of the Czechian tongue, had great historical recollections, almost all connected with the former supremacy of the Czechs. But then the force of this branch of the Slavonic family had been broken ever since the wars of the Hussites in the fifteenth century. The province speaking the Czechian tongue was divided, one part forming the kingdom of Bohemia, another the principality of Moravia, a third the Carpathian hill country of the Slovaks, being part of Hungary. The Moravians and Slovaks had long since lost every vestige of national feeling and vitality, although mostly preserving their language. Bohemia was surrounded by thoroughly German countries on three sides out of four. The German element had made great progress on her own territory; even in the capital, in Prague, the two nationalities were pretty equally matched; and everywhere capital, trade, industry, and mental culture were in the hands of the Germans. The chief champion of the Czechian nationality, Professor Palacky, is himself nothing but a learned German run mad, who even now cannot speak the Czechian language correctly and without foreign accent. But as it often happens, dying Czechian nationality, dying according to every fact known in history for the last four hundred years, made in 1848 a last effort to regain its former vitality—an effort whose failure, independently of all revolutionary considerations, was to prove that Bohemia could only exist, henceforth, as a portion of Germany, although part of her inhabitants might yet, for some centuries, continue to speak a non-German language.*

We quote the above passages in order to stress the *methods* which Marx and Engels used with respect to the nationality question, methods not dealing in abstract formulae, but only in the real issues of each individual case. That method did not, though, keep them from making a faulty evaluation of

* *Revolution und Konterrevolution in Deutschland,* pp. 57-62.

the situation, or from taking a wrong position in certain cases. The present state of affairs shows how deeply Marx was in error in predicting, sixty years ago, the disappearance of the Czech nationality, whose vitality the Austrians today find so troublesome. Conversely, he overestimated the international importance of Polish nationalism; this was doomed to decay by the internal development of Poland, a decay which had already set in at that time. But these historical errors do not detract an ounce from the value of Marx's method, for there are in general no *methods* of research which are, a priori, protected against a wrong application in individual cases. Marx never claimed to be infallible, and nothing, in the last resort, is so contrary to the spirit of his science as "infallible" historical judgments. It was possible for Marx to be mistaken in his position with respect to certain national movements, and the author of the present work tried to show in 1896 and 1897 that Marx's views on the Polish question, as on the Eastern question, were outdated and mistaken. But it is this former position of Marx and Engels on the question of Turkey and the South Slavs, as well as on the national movement of the Czechs and Poles, that shows emphatically how far the founders of scientific socialism were from solving all nationality questions in one manner only, on the basis of one slogan adopted a priori. It also shows how little they were concerned with the "metaphysical" rights of nations when it was a matter of the tangible material problems of European development.

Finally, an even more striking example of how the creators of modern socialist politics treated the national question is their evaluation of the freedom movement of the Swiss in the fourteenth century. This is part of history, therefore free from the influence of all the expectations and passions of day to day politics. The uprising of the Swiss cantons against the bloody oppression of the Hapsburg despotism (which, in the form of the historical myth of William Tell, is the object of absolute worship by the liberal-bourgeois romantic idealist) was appraised by Friedrich Engels in 1847 in the following way:

> The struggle of the early Swiss against Austria, the famous oath at Rytli, the heroic shot of Tell, the immortal victory at Morgarten—all this represented the struggle of restless shepherds against the thrust of historical development, a struggle of hidebound, conservative, local interests against the interests of the entire nation, a struggle of primitivism against enlightenment, barbarism against civilization. They won their victory over the civilization of that period, but as punishment they were cut off from the whole later progress of civilization.[6]

To this evaluation Kautsky adds the following commentary:

> A question mark could be added to the above concerning the civilizing mission which the Hapsburgs were carrying out in Switzerland in the fourteenth century. On the other hand it is correct that the preservation of the independence of the cantons was an event which was conservative to the nth degree, and in no way revolutionary, and that thenceforth the freedom of those cantons served as a means of preserving an element of blackest reaction in the center of Europe. It was those forest cantons which defeated Zwingli and his army in 1531 at the battle of Kappel, and thereby put a stop to the spread of Protestantism in Switzerland. They provided armies to all the despots of Europe, and it was the Swiss of the forest cantons who were the staunchest supporters of Louis XVI against the revolution. For this the republic raised a magnificent monument to them in Lucerne.*

* *Die Neue Zeit, 1904–1905*, Vol. II, p. 146.

From the point of view of the "right of nations to self-determination," the Swiss uprising obviously deserves the sympathy of socialists on all scores. There is no doubt that the aspirations of the Swiss to free themselves from the Hapsburg yoke were an essential expression of the will of the "people" or a huge majority of them. The national movement of the Swiss had a purely defensive character, and was not informed by the desire to oppress other nationalities. It was intended only to throw off the oppression of a foreign and purely dynastic invader. Finally, this national movement formally bore all the external characteristics of democratism, and even revolutionism, since the people were rebelling against absolute rule under the slogan of a popular republic.

In complete contrast to this movement is the national uprising in Hungary in 1848. It is easy to see what would have been the historical outcome of the victory of the Hungarians because the social and national conditions of that country insured the absolute domination of the Magyar minority over the mixed majority of the other, subjugated nationalities. A comparison of these two struggles for national independence—the Hungarian in 1848 and the Swiss five centuries earlier—is all the more significant since both were directed against the same enemy: the absolutism of the Austrian Hapsburgs. The method and the viewpoint on national politics of Marx and Engels are brought into high relief by this comparison. Despite all the external evidences of revolutionism in the Swiss movement, and despite the indisputable two-edged character of the Magyar movement, obvious in the flunkeyism with which the Hungarian revolutionaries helped the Vienna government to suppress the Italian revolution, the creators of scientific socialism sharply criticized the Swiss uprising as a reactionary event, while they supported fervently the Hungarian uprising in 1848. In both cases they were guided not by the formula of "the right of nations to self-determination," which obviously was much more applicable to the Swiss than to the Magyars, but only by a realistic analysis of the movements from a historical and political standpoint. The uprising of the fragmented peasant cantons, with their regionalism against the centralist power of the Hapsburgs, was, in the eyes of Engels, a sign of historical reaction, just as the absolutism of the princely power, moving toward centralism, was *at that time* an element of historical progress. From a similar standpoint, we note in passing, Lassalle regarded the peasant wars, and the parallel rebellion of the minor knights of the nobility in Germany in the sixteenth century against the rising princely power, as signs of reaction. On the other hand, in 1848, Hapsburg absolutism was already a reactionary relic of the Middle Ages, and the national uprising of the Hungarians—a natural ally of the internal German revolution—directed against the Hapsburgs naturally had to be regarded as an element of historical progress.

III

What is more, in taking such a stand Marx and Engels were not at all indulging in party or class egoism, and were not sacrificing entire nations to the needs and perspectives of Western European democracy, as it might have appeared.

It is true that it sounds much more generous, and is more flattering to the overactive imagination of the young "intellectual," when the socialists announce a general and universal introduction of freedom for all existing suppressed nations. But the tendency to grant all peoples, countries, groups, and all human creatures the right to freedom, equality, and other such joys by one sweeping stroke of the pen, is characteristic only of the youthful period of the socialist movement, and most of all of the phraseological bravado of anarchism.

The socialism of the modern working class, that is, scientific socialism, takes no delight in the radical and wonderful-sounding solutions of social and national questions, but examines primarily the real issues involved in these problems.

The solutions of the problems of Social Democracy are not in general characterized by "magnanimity," and in this respect they are always outdone by socialist parties which are not hampered by scientific "doctrines," and which therefore always have their pockets full of the most beautiful gifts for everyone. Thus, for example, in Russia, the Social Revolutionary Party leaves Social Democracy far behind in the agricultural question; it has for the peasants a recipe for the immediate partial introduction of socialism in the village, without the need of a boring period of waiting for the conditions of such a transformation in the sphere of industrial development. In comparison with such parties, Social Democracy is and always will be a poor party, just as Marx in his time was poor in comparison with the expansive and magnanimous Bakunin, just as Marx and Engels were both poor in comparison with the representatives of "real" or rather "philosophical" socialism. But the secret of the magnanimity of all socialists with an anarchist coloration and of the poverty of Social Democracy, is that anarchistic revolutionism measures "strength by intentions, not intentions according to strength"; that is, it measures its aspirations only by what its speculative reason, fumbling with an empty utopia, regards as "good" and "necessary" for the salvation of humanity. Social Democracy, on the other hand, stands firmly on historical ground in its aspirations, and therefore reckons with historical possibilities. Marxian socialism differs from all the other brands of socialism because, among other things, it has no pretensions to keeping patches in its pocket to mend all the holes made by historical development.

Actually, even if as socialists we recognized the immediate right of all nations to independence, the fates of nations would not change an iota because of this. The "right" of a nation to freedom as well as the "right" of the worker to economic independence are, under existing social conditions, only worth as much as the "right" of each man to eat off gold plates, which, as Nicolaus Chernyshevski wrote, he would be ready to sell at any moment for a ruble. In the 1840s the "right to work" was a favorite postulate of the Utopian Socialists in France, and appeared as an immediate and radical way of solving the social question. However, in the Revolution of 1848 that "right" ended, after a very short attempt to put it into effect, in a terrible fiasco, which could not have been avoided even if the famous "national workshops" had been organized differently. An analysis of the real conditions of the contemporary economy, as given by Marx in his *Capital,* must lead to the conviction that even if present-day governments were forced to declare a universal "right to work," it would remain only a fine-sounding phrase, and not one member of the rank and file of the reserve army of labor waiting on the sidewalk would be able to make a bowl of soup for his hungry children from that right.

Today, Social Democracy understands that the "right to work" will stop being an empty sound only when the capitalist regime is abolished, for in that regime the chronic unemployment of a certain part of the industrial proletariat is a necessary condition of production. Thus, Social Democracy does not demand a declaration of that imaginary "right" on the basis of the existing system, but rather strives for the abolition of the system itself by the class struggle, regarding labor organizations, unemployment insurance, etc., only as temporary means of help.

In the same way, hopes of solving all nationality questions within the capitalist framework by insuring to all nations, races, and ethnic groups the possibility of "self-determination" is a complete utopia. And it is a utopia from the point of view that the objective system of political and class forces condemns many a demand in the political program of Social Democracy to be unfeasible in practice. For example, important voices in the ranks of the international workers' movement have expressed the conviction that a demand for the universal introduction of the eight-hour day by legal enactment has no chance of being realized in bourgeois society because of the growing social reaction of the ruling classes, the general stagnation of social reforms, the rise of powerful organizations of businessmen, etc. Nonetheless, no one would dare call the demand for the eight-hour day a utopia, because it is in complete accordance with the progressive development of bourgeois society.

However, to resume: the actual possibility of "self-determination" for all ethnic groups or otherwise defined nationalities is a utopia precisely because of the trend of historical development of contemporary societies. Without examining those distant times at the dawn of history when the nationalities of modern states were constantly moving about geographically, when they were joining, merging, fragmenting, and trampling one another, the fact is that all the ancient states without exception are, as a result of that long history of political and ethnic upheavals, extremely mixed with respect to nationalities. Today, in each state, ethnic relics bear witness to the upheavals and intermixtures which characterized the march of historical development in the past. Even in his time, Marx maintained that these national survivals had no other function but to serve as bastions of the counter-revolution, until they should be completely swept from the face of the earth by the great hurricane of revolution or world war. "There is no country in Europe," he wrote in the *Neue Rheinische Zeitung,*

> which doesn't have in some corner one or more of these ruins of nations, the remains of an ancient people displaced and conquered by a nation which later became a standard-bearer of historical development. These remains of nationalities, mercilessly trampled on by history—as Hegel says—these national left-overs will all

> become and will remain until their final extermination or denationalization fanatic partisans of the counter-revolution, since their entire existence is in general a protest against the great historical revolution. For example, in Scotland the Gaels were the mainstays of the Stuarts from 1640 to 1745; in France, it was the Bretons who were the mainstays of the Bourbons from 1792 to 1800; while in Spain, the Basques were the supporters of Don Carlos. In Austria, to take another example, the pan-Slavic South Slavs are nothing more than the national left-overs of a highly confused thousand-year-long development.*

In another article, treating the pan-Slavs' strivings for the independence of all Slavic nations, Marx writes,

> The Germans and Hungarians, during the times when great monarchies were a historical necessity in Europe, forged all those petty, crippled, powerless little nations into one big state, thereby allowing them to participate in the development of history which, if left to themselves, they would have completely missed. Today, because of the huge progress of industry, trade, and communications, political centralization has become an even more pressing need than it was in the fifteenth and sixteenth centuries. What is not yet centralized is being centralized.**

We abandoned Marx's views on the South Slavs a long time ago; but the general fact is that historical development, especially the modern development of capitalism, does not tend to return to each nationality its independent existence, but moves rather in the opposite direction, and this is as well known today as during the time of the *Neue Rheinische Zeit-*

* *Aus dem literarischen Nachlass von Karl Marx, Friedrich Engels und Ferdinand Lasalle,* Vol. III, p. 241.

** Ibid., p. 255.

ung. In his most recent paper, *Nationality and Internationalism,* Karl Kautsky makes the following sketch of the historical fates of nationalities:

> We have seen that language is the most important means of social intercourse. As that intercourse grows with economic development, so the circle of people using the same language must grow as well. From this arises the tendency of unified nations to expand, to swallow up other nations, which lose their language and adopt the language of the dominant nation or a mixture.

According to Kautsky, three great cultural communities of humanity developed simultaneously: the Christian, the Muslim, and the Buddhist.

> Each of these three cultural groupings includes the most variegated languages and nationalities. Within each one most of the culture is not national but international. But universal communication has further effects. It expands even more and everywhere establishes the domination of the same capitalist production. . . . Whenever a closely knit community of communication and culture exists for a fairly long time among a large number of nations, then one or a few nations gain ascendancy over the government, the military, the scientific and artistic heights. Their language becomes indispensable for every merchant and educated man in that international cultural community. Their culture—in economy, art, and literature—lends its character to the whole civilization. Such a role was played in the Mediterranean basin until the end of ancient times by Greek and Latin. In the Mohammedan world it is played by Arabic; in the Christian, including Jews and atheists, German, English, and French have become universal languages. . . . Perhaps economic and political development will add Russian to these three languages. But it is equally possible that one of them, English, will become

the only common language. . . . The joining of nations to the international cultural community will be reflected in the growth of universal languages among merchants and educated people. And this union was never as closely knit as it is now; never was a purely national culture less possible. Therefore it strikes us as very strange when people talk always of only a *national* culture and when a goal of socialism is considered to be the endowing of the masses with a *national* culture. . . . When socialist society provides the masses with an education, it also gives them the ability to speak several languages, the universal languages, and therefore to take part in the entire *international* civilization and not only in the separate culture of a certain linguistic community. When we have got to the point where the masses in our civilized states can master one or more of the universal languages besides their native language, this will be a basis for the gradual withdrawal and ultimately the complete disappearance of the languages of the smaller nations, and for the union of all civilized humanity into one language and one nationality, just as the peoples in the eastern basin of the Mediterranean were united in Hellenism after Alexander the Great, and the peoples of the western area later merged into the Roman nationality.

The variety of languages within our circle of civilization makes understanding among members of the various nations difficult and is an obstacle to their civilized progress. But only socialism will overcome that obstacle, and much work will be needed before it can succeed in educating entire masses of people to obtain visible results. And we must keep in mind already today that *our internationalism is not a special type of nationalism differing from bourgeois nationalism only in that it does not behave aggressively—that it leaves to each nation the same right which it demands for its own nation,**

* Emphasis here and in the following sentences is ours.

and thereby recognizes the complete sovereignty (*souveränität*) of each nation. *Such a view, which transfers the position of anarchism concerning individuals onto nations, does not correspond to the close cultural community existing between nations of contemporary civilization.**

These last, in fact, in regard to economy and civilization, form one single social body whose welfare depends on the harmony of the cooperation of the parts, possible only by the subordination of all the parts to the whole. *The Socialist International is not a conglomerate of autocratic nations, each doing what it likes, as long as it does not interfere with the equality of rights of the others; but rather an organism wherein the better it works, the easier it is for its parts to come to agreement and the more they work together according to a common plan.***

Such is the historical scheme as described by Kautsky. To be sure, he presents the matter from a different point of view than Marx does, emphasizing mainly the side of cultural, peaceful development, whereas Marx accents its political side, an external armed conquest. Both, however, characterize the fate of nationalities in the course of events, not as tending to separate themselves and become independent, but completely vice-versa. Kautsky formulates—as far as we know, for the first time in socialistic literature of recent times—the historical tendency to remove completely all national distinctions within the socialist system and to fuse all of civilized humanity into one nationality.

However—that theoretician believes—at the present time capitalist development gives rise to phenomena which seem to work in the opposite direction: the awakening and inten-

* K. Kautsky, *Nationalität und Internationalität*, pp. 12-17.
** Ibid., p. 23.

sification of national consciousness as well as the need for a national state which is the state form "best corresponding to modern conditions, the form in which it can most easily fulfill its tasks."*

That "best" national state is only an abstraction which can be easily described and defined theoretically, but which doesn't correspond to reality. Historical development toward a universal community of civilization will, like all social development, take place in the midst of a contradiction, but this contradiction, with respect to the consolidating growth of international civilization, lies in another area than where Kautsky seeks it, not in the tendency toward the idea of a "national state," but rather where Marx indicates it to be, in the deadly struggle among nations, in the tendency to create —alongside the great areas of civilization and despite them— great capitalist states.

The development of *world powers,* a characteristic feature of our times growing in importance along with the progress of capitalism, from the very outset condemns all small nations to political impotence. Apart from a few of the most powerful nations, the leaders in capitalist development, which possess the spiritual and material resources necessary to maintain their political and economic independence, "self-determination," the independent existence of smaller and petty nations, is an illusion, and will become even more so. The return of all, or even the majority of the nations which are today oppressed, to independence would only be possible if the existence of small states in the era of capitalism had any chances or hopes for the future. Besides, the big-power economy and politics—a condition of survival for the capitalist states—turn the politically independent, formally equal, small European states into mutes on the European stage and

* Ibid.

more often into scapegoats. Can one speak with any seriousness of the "self-determination" of peoples which are formally independent, such as Montenegrins, Bulgarians, Rumanians, the Serbs, the Greeks, and, as far as that goes, even the Swiss, whose very independence is the product of the political struggles and diplomatic game of the "Concert of Europe"? From this point of view, the idea of insuring all "nations" the possibility of self-determination is equivalent to reverting from Great-Capitalist development to the small medieval states, far earlier than the fifteenth and sixteenth centuries.

The other principal feature of modern development, which stamps such an idea as utopian, is capitalist *imperialism.* The example of England and Holland indicates that under certain conditions a capitalist country can even completely skip the transition phase of "national state" and create at once, in its manufacturing phase, a colony-holding state. The example of England and Holland, which, at the beginning of the seventeenth century, had begun to acquire colonies, was followed in the eighteenth and nineteenth centuries by all the great capitalist states. The fruit of that trend is the continuous destruction of the independence of more and more new countries and peoples, of entire continents.

The very development of international trade in the capitalist period brings with it the inevitable, though at times slow ruin of all the more primitive societies, destroys their historically existing means of "self-determination," and makes them dependent on the crushing wheel of capitalist development and world politics. Only complete formalist blindness could lead one to maintain that, for example, the Chinese nation (whether we regard the people of that state as one or several nations) is today really "determining itself." The destructive action of world trade is followed by outright partition or by the political dependence of colonial countries in various degrees and forms. And if Social Democracy struggles with all its strength against colonial policy in all its manifestations, trying to hinder its progress, then it will at the same time realize that this development, as well as the roots of colonial politics, lies at the very foundations of capitalist production, that colonialism will inevitably accompany the future progress of capitalism, and that only the innocuous bourgeois apostles of "peace" can believe in the possibility of today's states avoiding that path. The struggle to stay in the world market, to play international politics, and to have overseas territories is both a necessity and a condition of development for capitalist world powers. The form that best serves the interests of exploitation in the contemporary world is not the "national" state, as Kautsky thinks, but a state bent on conquest. When we compare the different states from the point of view of the degree to which they approach this ideal, we see that it is not the French state which best fits the model, at least not in its European part which is homogeneous with respect to nationality. Still less does the Spanish state fit the model; since it lost its colonies, it has shed its imperialist character and is purely "national" in composition. Rather do we look to the British and German states as models, for they are based on national oppression in Europe and the world at large—and to the United States of America, a state which keeps in its bosom like a gaping wound the oppression of the Negro people, and seeks to conquer the Asiatic peoples.

The following table illustrates the imperialist tendency of national conquest. The figures refer to the number of oppressed people in colonies belonging to each country.

The huge figures quoted, which include around five hundred million people, should be increased by the colossal addition of the countries which do not figure as colonies, but are actually completely dependent on European states, and then we should break these totals down into countless nationalities and ethnic groups to convey an idea of the ef-

	In Asia	In Africa	In America	In Australasia
Great Britain	361,445,000	40,028,000	7,557,300	5,811,000
France	18,073,000	31,500,000	428,819	89,000
Germany	120,041	11,447,000	–	448,000
Holland	37,734,000	–	142,000	–
Belgium	–	19,000,000	–	–
Denmark	–	–	42,422	–
Spain	–	291,000	–	–
Portugal	810,000	6,460,00	–	–
USA	7,635,426	–	953,243	13,000

fects to date of capitalist imperialism on the fates of nations and their ability to "determine themselves."

Of course, the history of the colonial expansion of capitalism displays to some extent the contradictory tendency of the legal, and then political gaining of independence of the colonial countries. The history of the breaking away of the United States from England at the end of the eighteenth century, of the countries of South America from Spain and Portugal in the twenties and thirties of the last century, as well as the winning of autonomy by the Australian states from England, are the most obvious illustrations of this tendency. However, a more careful examination of these events will point at once to the special conditions of their origins. Both South and North America, until the nineteenth century, were the victims of a still primitive system of colonial administration, based more on the plundering of the country and its natural resources for the benefit of the treasures of European states than on a rational exploitation for the benefit of capitalist production. In these cases, it was a matter of an entire country, which possessed all the conditions for the independent development of capitalism, making its own way by breaking the rotting fetters of political dependence. The force of that capitalist thrust was stronger in North America, which was dependent on England, while South America, until then predominantly agricultural, met a much weaker resistance from Spain and Portugal, which were economically backward. Obviously, such an exceptional wealth of natural resources is not the rule in all colonies. On the other hand, the contemporary system of colonization has created a dependence which is much less superficial than the previous one. But the winning of independence by the American colonies did not remove national dependence, it only transferred it to another nationality—only changed its role. Take first the United States: the element freeing itself from the scepter of England was not a foreign nation but only the same English emigrants who had settled in America on the ruins and corpses of the redskin natives—which is true also of the Australian colonies of England, in which the English constitute 90 percent of the population. The United States is today in the vanguard of those nations practicing imperialist conquest. In the same way, Brazil, Argentina, and the other former colonies whose leading element is immigrants—Portuguese and Spanish—won independence from the European states primarily in order to exercise control over the trade in Negroes and their use on the plantations, and to annex all the weaker colonies in the area. Most likely the same conditions prevail in India, where lately there has appeared a rather serious "national" movement against England. The very existence in India of a huge number of nationalities at different degrees of social and civilized development, as well as their mutual dependence, should warn against too hasty evaluation of the Indian movement under the simple heading of "the rights of the nation."

Apparent exceptions only confirm on closer analysis the conclusion that the modern development of capitalism cannot be reconciled with the true independence of all nationalities.

It is true the problem appears much simpler if, when discussing nationality, we exclude the question of colonial partitions. Such a technique is often applied, consciously or unconsciously, by the defenders of the "rights of nations"; it also corresponds to the position with respect to colonial politics taken, for example, by Eduard David in the German Social Democracy or van Kol in the Dutch. This point of view considers colonialism in general as the expression of the civilizing mission of European peoples, inevitable even in a socialist regime. This view can be briefly described as the "European" application of the philosophical principle of Fichte in the well known paraphrase of Ludwig Brone: "*Ich bin ich–was ausser mir ist Lebensmittel*" ["I am myself–what is outside of me is the means of life"]. If only the European peoples are regarded as nations proper, while colonial peoples are looked on as "supply depots," then we may use the term "nation-state" in Europe for countries like France, Denmark, or Italy, and the problem of nationality can be limited to intra-European dimensions. But in this case, "the right of nations to self-determination" becomes a theory of the ruling races and betrays clearly its origin in the ideologies of bourgeois liberalism together with its "European" cretinism. In the approach of socialists, such a right must, by the nature of things, have a universal character. The awareness of this necessity is enough to indicate that the hope of realizing this "right" on the basis of the existing setup is a utopia; it is in direct contradiction to the tendency of capitalist development on which Social Democracy has based its existence. A general attempt to divide all existing states into national units and to re-tailor them on the model of national states and statelets is a completely hopeless, and historically speaking, reactionary undertaking.*

* In the minds of legal formalists and professors, this development appears in the form of the "degeneration of the national idea."

The other stream of nationalist trends appears in the strivings of nations which have already gained political independence, to assert their superiority and ascendancy over other nations. These

IV

The formula of the "right of nations" is inadequate to justify the position of socialists on the nationality question, not only because it fails to take into account the wide range of historical conditions (place and time) existing in each given case and does not reckon with the general current of the development of global conditions, but also because it ignores completely the fundamental theory of modern socialism—the theory of social classes.

When we speak of the "right of nations to self-determination," we are using the concept of the "nation" as a homogeneous social and political entity. But actually, such a concept of the "nation" is one of those categories of bourgeois ideology which Marxist theory submitted to a radical revision, showing how that misty veil, like the concepts of the "freedom of citizens," "equality before the law," etc., conceals in every case a definite historical content.

In a class society, "the nation" as a homogeneous sociopolitical entity does not exist. Rather, there exist within each nation, classes with antagonistic interests and "rights." There literally is not one social area, from the coarsest material

strivings are expressed on the one hand in the glorification of their past historical virtues or the present features of their national character, the "soul," or finally as completely undefined hopes for a future cultural role, for some kind of a mission of destiny given to certain nations, strivings which are now christened with the name of nationalism. On the other hand, these political tendencies bring about the expansion of the territorial boundaries of a given nation, the strengthening of its global position by partitioning various other countries and by increasing its colonial possessions—that is, the politics of imperialism. These movements embody the further development of the national idea, but they represent a contradiction of the original contents of that idea, and in its fatal results, so degrading for civilization, it is impossible not to see the degeneration of that idea and its death. It is obvious that the century of nationalities has finished. We must await a new age, colored by new trends.—W. M. Ustinow, *Idyeya Natsyonalnovo Gosudarstva* (Kharkov: 1906).

relationships to the most subtle moral ones, in which the possessing class and the class-conscious proletariat hold the same attitude, and in which they appear as a consolidated "national" entity. In the sphere of economic relations, the bourgeois classes represent the interests of exploitation—the proletariat the interests of work. In the sphere of legal relations, the cornerstone of bourgeois society is private property; the interest of the proletariat demands the emancipation of the propertyless man from the domination of property. In the area of the judiciary, bourgeois society represents class "justice," the justice of the well-fed and the rulers; the proletariat defends the principle of taking into account social influences on the individual, of humaneness. In international relations, the bourgeoisie represent the politics of war and partition, and at the present stage, a system of trade war; the proletariat demands a politics of universal peace and free trade. In the sphere of the social sciences and philosophy, bourgeois schools of thought and the school representing the proletariat stand in diametric opposition to each other. The possessing classes have their world view; it is represented by idealism, metaphysics, mysticism, eclecticism; the modern proletariat has its theory—dialectic materialism. Even in the sphere of so-called "universal" conditions—in ethics, views on art, on behavior—the interests, world view, and ideals of the bourgeoisie and those of the enlightened proletariat represent two camps, separated from each other by an abyss. And whenever the formal strivings and the interests of the proletariat and those of the bourgeoisie (as a whole or in its most progressive part) seem identical—for example, in the field of democratic aspirations—there, under the identity of forms and slogans, is hidden the most complete divergence of contents and essential politics.

There can be no talk of a collective and uniform will, of the self-determination of the "nation" in a society formed in such a manner. If we find in the history of modern societies "national" movements, and struggles for "national interests," these are usually class movements of the ruling strata of the bourgeoisie, which can in any given case represent the interest of the other strata of the population only insofar as under the form of "national interests" it defends progressive forms of historical development, and insofar as the working class has not yet distinguished itself from the mass of the "nation" (led by the bourgeoisie) into an independent, enlightened political class.

In this sense, the French bourgeoisie had the right to come forth as the third estate in the Great Revolution in the name of the French people, and even the German bourgeoisie in 1848 could still regard themselves, to a certain degree, as the representatives of the German "nation"–although "The Communist Manifesto" and, in part, the *Neue Rheinische Zeitung* were already the indicators of a distinct class politics of the proletariat in Germany. In both cases this meant only that the revolutionary class concern of the bourgeoisie was, at that stage of social development, the concern of the class of people who still formed, with the bourgeoisie, a politically uniform mass in relation to reigning feudalism.

This circumstance shows that the "rights of nations" cannot be a yardstick for the position of the Socialist Party on the nationality question. The very existence of such a party is proof that the bourgeoisie has *stopped* being the representative of the entire mass of the people, that the class of the proletariat is no longer hidden in the skirts of the bourgeoisie, but has separated itself off as an independent class with its own social and political aspirations. Because the concepts of "nations," of "rights," and the "will of the people" as a uniform whole are, as we have said, remnants from the times of immature and unconscious antagonism between the proletariat and the bourgeoisie, the application of that idea by the class-conscious and independently organized proletariat would be a striking contradiction—not a contradiction against academic logic, but a *historical* contradiction.

With respect to the nationality question in contemporary society, a socialist party must take class antagonism into account. The Czech nationality question has one form for the young Czech petite bourgeoisie and another for the Czech proletariat. Nor can we seek a single solution of the Polish national question for Koscielski and his stable boy in Miroslawie, for the Warsaw and Lodz bourgeoisie and for class-conscious Polish workers all at the same time; while the Jewish question is formulated in one way in the minds of the Jewish bourgeoisie, and in another for the enlightened Jewish proletariat. For Social Democracy, the nationality question is, like all other social and political questions, primarily *a question of class interests.*

In the Germany of the 1840s there existed a kind of mystical-sentimental socialism, that of the "true socialists" Karl Grün and Moses Hess; this kind of socialism was represented later in Poland by Limanowski. After the 1840s there appeared in Poland a Spartan edition of the same—see the *Lud Polski* [Polish People] in the early 1870s and *Pobudka* [Reveille] at the end of that decade. This socialism strove for everything good and beautiful. And on that basis, Limanowski, later the leader of the PPS, tried to weld together Polish socialism and the task of reconstructing Poland, with the observation that socialism is an idea that is obviously beautiful, and patriotism is a no less beautiful idea, and so "Why shouldn't two such beautiful ideas be joined together?"

The only healthy thing in this sentimental socialism is that it is a utopian parody of the correct idea that a socialist regime has, as the final goal of the proletariat's aspirations, taken the pledge that by abolishing the domination of classes, for the first time in history it will guarantee the realization of the highest ideals of humanity.

And this is really the content and the essential meaning of the principle presented to the International Congress at London [in 1896] in the resolution quoted. "The right of nations to self-determination" stops being a cliché only in a social regime where the "right to work" has stopped being an empty phrase. A socialist regime, which eliminates not only the domination of one class over another, but also the very existence of social classes and their opposition, the very division of society into classes with different interests and desires, will bring about a society which is the sum total of individuals tied together by the harmony and solidarity of their interests, a uniform whole with a common, organized will and the ability to satisfy it. The socialist regime will realize directly the "nation" as a uniform will—insofar as the nations within that regime in general will constitute separate social organisms or, as Kautsky states, will join into one—and the material conditions for its free self-determination. In a word, society will win the ability to freely determine its national existence when it has the ability to determine its political being and the conditions of its creation. "Nations" will control their historical existence when human society controls its social processes.

Therefore, the analogy which is drawn by partisans of the "right of nations to self-determination" between that "right" and all democratic demands, like the right of free speech, free press, freedom of association and of assembly, is completely incongruous. These people point out that we support the freedom of association because we are the party of political freedom; but we still fight against hostile bourgeois parties. Similarly, they say, we have the democratic duty to support the self-determination of nations, but this fact does not commit us to support every individual tactic of those who fight for self-determination.

The above view completely overlooks the fact that these "rights," which have a certain superficial similarity, lie on completely different historical levels. The rights of association and assembly, free speech, the free press, etc., are the legal forms of existence of a mature bourgeois society. But "the right of nations to self-determination" is only a metaphysical formulation of an idea which in bourgeois society is completely nonexistent and can be realized only on the basis of a socialist regime.

However, as it is practiced today, socialism is not at all a collection of all these mystical "noble" and "beautiful" desires, but only a political expression of well-defined conditions, that is, the fight of the class of the modern proletariat against the domination of the bourgeoisie. Socialism means the striving of the proletariat to bring about the dictatorship of its class in order to get rid of the present form of production. This task is the main and guiding one for the Socialist Party as the party of the proletariat; it determines the position of that party with respect to all the several problems of social life.

Social Democracy is the class party of the proletariat. Its historical task is to express the class interests of the proletariat and also the revolutionary interests of the development of capitalist society toward realizing socialism. Thus, Social Democracy is called upon to realize not the right of nations to self-determination but only the right of the working class, which is exploited and oppressed, of the proletariat, to self-determination. From that position Social Democracy examines all social and political questions without exception, and from that standpoint it formulates its programmatic demands. Neither in the question of the political forms which we demand in the state, nor in the question of the state's internal or external policies, nor in the questions of law or education, of taxes or the military, does Social Democracy allow the "nation" to decide its fate according to its own vision of self-determination. All of these questions affect the class interests of the proletariat in a way that questions of national-political and national-cultural existence do not. But between those questions and the national-political and national-cultural questions, exist usually the closest ties of mutual dependence and causality. As a result, Social Democracy cannot here escape the necessity of formulating these demands individually, and demanding actively the forms of national-political and national-cultural existence which best correspond to the interests of the proletariat and its class struggle at a given time and place, as well as to the interests of the revolutionary development of society. Social Democracy cannot leave these questions to be solved by "nations."

This becomes perfectly obvious as soon as we bring the question down from the clouds of abstraction to the firm ground of concrete conditions.

The "nation" should have the "right" to self-determination. But who is that "nation" and who has the authority and the "right" to speak for the "nation" and express its will? How can we find out what the "nation" actually wants? Does there exist even one political party which would not claim that it alone, among all others, truly expresses the will of the "nation," whereas all other parties give only perverted and false expressions of the national will? All the bourgeois, liberal parties consider themselves the incarnation of the will of the people and claim the exclusive monopoly to represent the "nation." But conservative and reactionary parties refer no less to the will and interests of the nation, and within certain limits, have no less of a right to do so. The Great French Revolution was indubitably an expression of the will of the French nation, but Napoleon, who juggled away the work of the Revolution in his *coup* of the 18th Brumaire, based his entire state reform on the principle of "*la volonté générale*" [the general will].

In 1848, the will of the "nation" produced first the republic and the provisional government, then the National Assembly, and finally Louis Bonaparte, who cashiered the Republic, the provisional government, and the national assembly. During the [1905] Revolution in Russia, liberalism demanded in the name of the people a "cadet" ministry; absolutism, in the name of the same people, arranged the pogroms of the Jews, while the revolutionary peasants expressed their national will by sending the estates of the gentry up in smoke. In Poland, the party of the Black Hundreds, National Democracy, had a claim to be the will of the people, and in the name of "the self-determination of the nation" incited "national" workers to assassinate socialist workers.

Thus the same thing happens to the "true" will of the nation as to the true ring in Lessing's story of Nathan the Wise: it has been lost and it seems almost impossible to find it and to tell it from the false and counterfeit ones. On the surface, the principle of democracy provides a way of distinguishing the true will of the people—by determining the opinion of the majority.

The nation wants what the majority of the people want. But woe to the Social Democratic Party which would ever take that principle as its own yardstick: that would condemn to death Social Democracy itself as the revolutionary party. Social Democracy by its very nature is a party representing the *interests* of a huge majority of the nation. But it is also for the time being in bourgeois society, insofar as it is a matter of expressing the *conscious* will of the nation, the party of a minority which only seeks to become the majority. In its aspirations and its political program it seeks to reflect not the will of a majority of the nation, but on the contrary, the embodiment of the conscious will of the proletariat alone. And even within that class, Social Democracy is not and does not claim to be the embodiment of the will of the majority. It expresses only the will and the consciousness of the most advanced and most revolutionary section of the urban-industrial proletariat. It tries to expand that will and to clear a way for a majority of the workers by making them conscious of their own interests. "The will of the nation" or its majority is not therefore an idol for Social Democracy before which it humbly prostrates itself. On the contrary, the historical mission of Social Democracy is based above all on revolutionizing and forming the will of the "nation"; that is, its working-class majority. For the traditional forms of consciousness which the majority of the nation, and therefore the working classes, display in bourgeois society are the usual forms of bourgeois consciousness, hostile to the ideals and aspirations of socialism. Even in Germany, where Social Democracy is the most powerful political party, it is still today, with its three and a quarter million voters, a minority compared to the eight million voters for bourgeois parties and the thirty million who have the right to vote. The statistics on parliamentary electors give, admittedly, only a rough idea of the relation of forces in times of peace. The German nation then "determines itself" by electing a majority of conservatives, clerics, and freethinkers, and puts its political fate in their hands. And the same thing is happening, to an even greater degree, in all other countries.

V

Let us take a concrete example in an attempt to apply the principle that the "nation" should "determine itself."

With respect to Poland at the present stage of the revolution, one of the Russian Social Democrats belonging to the editorial committee of the now defunct paper, *Iskra*, in 1906 explained the concept of the indispensable Warsaw constituent assembly in the following way:

> If we start from the assumption that the political organization of Russia is the decisive factor determining the current oppression of the nationalities, then we must conclude that the proletariat of the oppressed nationalities and the annexed countries should be ex-

tremely active in the organization of an all-Russian constituent assembly.

This assembly could, if it wished, carry out its revolutionary mission, and break the fetters of force with which tsardom binds to itself the oppressed nationalities.

*And there is no other satisfactory, that is, revolutionary way of solving that question than by implementing the rights of the nationalities to determine their own fate.** The task of a united proletarian party of all nationalities in the assembly will be to bring about such a solution of the nationality question, and this task can be realized by the Party only insofar as it is based on the movement of the masses, on the pressure they put on the constituent assembly.

But in what concrete form should the admitted right to self-determination be realized?

Where the nationality question can be more or less identified with the existence of a legal state—as is the case in Poland—then the organ which can realize the nation's right to self-determination can and should be a *national constituent assembly whose special task is to determine the relation of a given "borderland country" to the state as a whole, to decide whether it should belong to the state or break away from it, to decide its internal setup and its future connection with the state as a whole.*

And therefore the constituent assembly of Poland should decide whether Poland will become part of a new Russia and what its constitution should be. *And the Polish proletariat should use all its strength to insure that its class makes its mark on the decision of that organ of national self-government.*

If we should ask the all-Russian assembly to hand the

* Emphasis in the entire citation is ours.

solution of the Polish national question* over to the Warsaw sejm, I do not believe that there is any need to put off calling that sejm until the Petersburg constituents should take up the nationality question.

On the contrary, I think that the slogan of a constituent assembly in Warsaw should be put forth now, at the same time as the slogan for an all-Russian constituent assembly. The government which finally calls a constituent assembly for all Russia should also call (or sanction the calling of) a special constituent sejm for Poland. *The job of the all-Russian assembly will be to sanction the work of the Warsaw sejm,* and in the light of the different social forces involved in the Petersburg constituent assembly, the more this is given on the basis of the real principles of democracy the more decisively and clearly will the Polish nation express its national will. It will do this most clearly in the elections to the sejm especially called to decide the future fate of Poland. On the basis of this sejm's decisions, the representatives of the Polish and Russian proletariat in the all-Russian assembly will be able to energetically defend the real recognition of the right to self-determination.

Thus, the simultaneous calling of all-Russian and all-Polish constituent assemblies: this should be our slogan.

The presentation by the proletariat of the demand for a constituent assembly for Poland should not be taken to mean that the Polish nation would be represented in the all-Russian assembly by any delegation of the Warsaw sejm.

I think that such representation in the all-Russian assembly would not correspond to the interests of revolutionary development. It would join the proletariat and bourgeois elements of the Polish sejm by bonds of mu-

* The above article appeared in *Robotnik*, the organ of the PPS, no. 75, February 7, 1906.–*Note of the editorial board of* Przeglad Sozialdemokratyczny.

> tual solidarity and responsibility, in contradiction to the real mutual relations of their interests.
>
> In the all-Russian assembly, the proletariat and bourgeoisie of Poland should not be represented by one delegation. But this would occur even if a delegation were sent from the sejm to an assembly which included representatives of all the parties of the sejm proportionally to their numbers. In this case, the direct and independent representation of the Polish proletariat in the assembly would disappear, and the very creation of real political parties in Poland would be made difficult. Then the elections to the Polish sejm, whose main task is to define the political relations between Poland and Russia, would not show the political and social faces of the leading parties, as elections to an all-Russian assembly could do; for the latter type of elections would advance, besides the local, partial, historically temporary and specifically national questions, *the general questions of politics and socialism, which really divide contemporary societies.* *

This article gives a moral sanction on the part of the opportunist wing of Russian Social Democracy to the slogan put forth by the PPS in the first period of the revolution: that is, to the Warsaw constituent assembly. However, it had no practical result. After the dissolution of the PPS, the so-called left wing of that party, having publicly rejected the program of rebuilding Poland, found itself forced to abandon its partial program of nationalism in the form of the slogan of a Warsaw constituent assembly. But the article remains a characteristic attempt to give practical effect to the principle of "the right of nations to self-determination."

* Here as everywhere I speak of a definite manner of solving the nationality question for Poland, not touching those changes which may prove themselves indispensable while resolving this question for other nations. –*Note of the author of the cited article.*

In the above argument, which we quoted in full in order to be able to examine it from all aspects, several points strike the reader. Above all, according to the author, on the one hand "a constituent assembly of Poland should decide whether Poland should enter the formation of a new Russia and what kind of constitution it should have." On the other, "the Polish proletariat should use its strength to insure that its class will make the greatest mark on the decisions of that organ of national self-government." Here the class will of the Polish proletariat is expressly opposed to the passive will of the Polish "nation." The class will of the proletariat can obviously leave "its mark" on the decisions of the Warsaw constituent assembly only if it is clearly and expressly formulated; in other words, the class party of the Polish proletariat, the Socialist Party, must have a well-defined program with respect to the national question, which it can introduce in the Warsaw constituent assembly—a program which corresponds not to the will of "the nation" but only to the will and interests of the Polish proletariat. Then, in the constituent assembly, in the national question, one will, or "the self-determination of the proletariat" will come out against the will or "the self-determination of the nation." For Polish Socialists, the "nation's right to self-determination" as an obligatory principle in fact disappears, and is replaced by a clearly defined political program on the national question.

The result is rather strange. The Russian Social Democratic Labor Party leaves the solution of the Polish question up to the Polish "nation." The Polish Socialists should not pick it up but try, as hard as they can, to solve this question according to the interests and will of the proletariat. However, the party of the Polish proletariat is organizationally tied to the all-state party, for instance, the Social Democracy of the Kingdom of Poland and Lithuania is a part of the Russian Social Democratic Labor Party. Thus, Social Democracy of all of Russia, united both in ideas and factually, has two different positions. As a whole, it stands for the "nations"; in its constituent parts, it stands for the separate proletariat of each nation. But these positions can be quite different and may even be completely opposed to each other. The sharpened class antagonism in all of Russia makes it a general rule that in the national-political question, as in questions of internal politics, the proletarian parties take completely different positions from the bourgeois and petit bourgeois parties of the separate nationalities. What position should the Labor Party of Russia then take in the case of such a collision?

Let us suppose for the sake of argument, that in the federal constituent assembly, two contradictory programs are put forth from Poland: the autonomous program of National Democracy and the autonomous program of Polish Social Democracy, which are quite at odds with respect to internal tendency as well as to political formulation. What will the position of Russian Social Democracy be with regard to them? Which of the programs will it recognize as an expression of the will and "self-determination" of the Polish "nation"? Polish Social Democracy never had any pretensions to be speaking in the name of the "nation." National Democracy comes forth as the expresser of the "national" will. Let us also assume for a moment that this party wins a majority at the elections to the constituent assembly by taking advantage of the ignorance of the petit bourgeois elements as well as certain sections of the proletariat. In this case, will the representatives of the all-Russian proletariat, complying with the requirements of the formula of their program, come out in favor of the proposals of National Democracy and go against their own comrades from Poland? Or will they associate themselves with the program of the Polish proletariat, leaving the "right of nations" to one side as a phrase which binds them to nothing? Or will the Polish Social Democrats be forced, in order to reconcile these contradictions in their program, to come out in the Warsaw constituent assembly, as well as in their own agitation in Poland, in favor of their own autonomous program, but in the federal constituent assembly, as members well aware of the discipline of the Social Democratic Party of Russia, for the program of National Democracy, that is, against their own program?

Let us take yet another example. Examining the question in a purely abstract form, since the author has put the problem on that basis, let us suppose, to illustrate the principle, that in the national assembly of the Jewish population of Russia—for why should the right to create separate constituent assemblies be limited to Poland, as the author wants? —the Zionist Party somehow wins a majority and demands that the all-Russian constituent assembly vote funds for the emigration of the entire Jewish community. On the other hand, the class representatives of the Jewish proletariat firmly resist the position of the Zionists as a harmful and reactionary utopia. What position will Russian Social Democracy take in this conflict?

It will have two choices. The "right of nations to self-determination" might be essentially identical with the determination of the national question by the proletariat in question—that is, with the nationality program of the concerned Social Democratic parties. In such a case, however, the formula of the "right of nations" in the program of the Russian party is only a mystifying paraphrase of the class position. Or, alternatively, the Russian proletariat as such could recognize and honor only the will of the national *majorities* of the nationalities under Russian subjugation, even though the proletariat of the respective "nations" should come out against this majority with their own class program. And in this case, it is a political dualism of a special type; it gives dramatic expression to the discord between the "national" and class positions; it points up the conflict between the position of the federal workers' party and that of the parties of the particular nationalities which make it up.

A special Polish constituent assembly is to be the organ of realizing the right of the nation to self-determination. But that right is, in reality, severely limited by the author, and in two directions. First, the competence of the Warsaw constituent assembly is reduced to the special question of the relation of Poland to Russia and to the constitution for Poland. Then, even within this domain, the decisions of the "Polish nation" are subordinated to the sanction of an all-Russian constituent assembly. The assembly, however—if this reservation is to have any meaning at all—can either grant or deny these sanctions. Under such conditions the unlimited "right of the nation to self-determination" becomes rather problematic. The national partisans of the slogan of a separate Warsaw constituent assembly would not at all agree to the reduction of their competence to the narrow area of relations between Poland and Russia. They wanted to give the assembly the power over all the internal and external relations of the social life of Poland. And from the standpoint of the "right of nations to self-determination," they would undoubtedly have right and logic on their side. For there seems to be no reason why "self-determination" should mean only the solution of the external fate of the nation and of its constitution, and not of all social and political matters. Besides, the separation of the relation of Poland to Russia and the constitution of Poland from the "general problems of politics and socialism" is a construction which is artificial to the highest degree. If the "constitution of Poland" is to determine—as it evidently must—the electoral law, the law of unions and meetings, the law of the press, etc., etc., for Poland, then it is not clear what political questions remain for the federal constituent assembly to solve with respect to Poland. From this point of view, only one of two points of view is possible: either the Warsaw constituent assembly is to be the essential organ for the self-determination of the Polish nation, and in this case it can be only an organ on the same level as the Petersburg constituent assembly; or, the constituent assembly of Warsaw plays only the role of a national sejm in a position of dependence on and subordination to the federal constituent assembly, and in this case, "the right of the nation to self-determination," dependent on the sanction of the Russian "nation," reminds one of the German concept: *"Die Republik mit dem Grossherzog an der Spitze"* ["The Republic with the Grand Duke at the Head"].

The author himself helps us to guess how, in his understanding, the "right of the nation," proclaimed in the introduction so charmingly in the form of a Warsaw constituent assembly, is finally canceled out by the competence and right of sanction of the Petersburg constituent assembly.

In this matter, the Menshevik journalist adopts the view that the Warsaw constituent assembly will be the organ of national interests, whereas the federal assembly will be the organ of the class and general social interests, the terrain of the class struggle between the proletariat and the bourgeoisie. Thus, the author shows so much mistrust of the Warsaw organ of the "national will" that he opposes the representation of that national sejm in the Petersburg constituent assembly, for which he demands direct elections from Poland to insure the best representation of the interests of the Polish proletariat. The defender of two constituent assemblies feels instinctively that even with universal and equal elections to the Warsaw assembly, its very individual nature would weaken the position of the Polish proletariat, while the combined entry of the Polish proletariat with the proletariat of the entire state in a general constituent assembly would strengthen the class position and its defense. Hence arises his vacillation between one and the other position and his desire to subordinate the organ of the "national" will to the organ of the class struggle. This is, then, again an equivocal political position, in which the collision between the "national" point of view and the class point of view takes the form of the opposition between the Warsaw and the Petersburg constituent assemblies. Only one question remains: since the representation in a federal constituent assembly is more useful for the defense of the Polish proletariat, then why cannot that body resolve the Polish national question, in order to insure the preponderance of the will and interests of the Polish proletariat? So many hesitations and contradictions show how desirable it would be for the "nation" and the working class to develop a common position.

Apart from this, we must add that the entire construction of the Warsaw constituent assembly as the organ of national "self-determination" is only a house of cards; the dependence or independence of nation-states is determined not by the vote of majorities in parliamentary representations, but only by socioeconomic development, by material class interests, and as regards the external political affairs, by armed struggle, war, or insurrection. The Warsaw assembly could only really determine the fate of Poland if Poland had first, by means of a successful uprising, won factual independence from Russia. In other words, the Polish people can realize its "right" to self-determination only when it has the actual ability, the necessary force for this, and then it will realize it not on the basis of its "rights" but on the basis of its power. The present revolution did not call forth an independence movement in Poland; it did not show the least tendency to separate Poland from Russia. On the contrary, it buried the remains of these tendencies by forcing the national party (National Democracy) to renounce the program of the reconstruction of Poland, while the other party (the PPS) was smashed to bits and also, midway in the struggle, was forced to renounce this program explicitly. Thus, the "right" of the Polish nation to self-determination remains—the right to eat off gold plates.

The demand for a Warsaw constituent assembly is therefore obviously deprived of all political or theoretical importance and represents only a momentary tentative improvisation of deteriorated Polish nationalism, like a soap bubble which bursts immediately after appearing. This demand is useful only as an illustration of the application of "the right of a nation to self-determination" in practice. This illustration is a new proof that by recognizing the "right of nations to self-determination" in the framework of the present regime, Social Democracy is offering the "nations" either the cheap blessing to do what they (the "nations") are in a position to do by virtue of their strength, or else an empty phrase with no force at all. On the other hand, this position brings Social Democracy into conflict with its true calling, the protection of the class interests of the proletariat and the revolutionary development of society, which the creators of scientific socialism used as the basis of their view on the nationality question.

The preservation of that metaphysical phrase in the program of the Social Democratic Party of Russia would be a betrayal of the strictly class position which the party has tried to observe in all points of its program. The ninth paragraph should be replaced by a concrete formula, however general, which would provide a solution of the nationality question in accordance with the interests of the proletariat of the particular nationalities. That does not in the least mean that the program of the Social Democratic organization of the respective nationalities should become, *eo ipso,* the program of the all-Russian party. A fundamental critical appraisal of each of these programs by the whole of the workers' party of the state is necessary, but this appraisal should be made from the point of view of the actual social conditions, from the point of view of a scientific analysis of the general tendencies of capitalist development, as well as the interests of the class struggle of the proletariat. This alone can indicate a uniform and consistent position of the party as a whole and in its constituent parts.

Notes

1. Rosa Luxemburg published a series of articles under the general title, "The Problem of Nationality and Autonomy," in her theoretical journal, *Przeglad Sozialdemokratyczny* (Cracow), in nos. 6-10, 12, and 14-15, 1908 and 1909. The paging was as follows: Article 1, pps. 482-515; 2, 597-612; 3, 613-631; 4, 687-710; 5, 795-818; 6 ("Special Problems of Poland"), pp. 136-63, 351-76. The first five articles (but not the sixth) are included in the present collection.
2. *Towarzystwo Demokratyczne Polskie* (Democratic Society/Polish), 1832–1862, was the biggest organization of Polish emigrants in France and in England, professing revolutionary and democratic views. After 1840, it was involved in preparing an insurrection in the three parts of partitioned Poland.

   Pobudka (Reveille), also called "La Diane," was a journal of the Polish National Socialist Party published in Paris, 1889–1893.

   Liga Narodwa (National League), founded 1893 as a successor of the "Polish League," was a secret political organization in Russian, German, and Austrian Poland. It promoted class solidarity and nationalism; it represented the interests of the propertied classes. In 1896, it founded the Party of National Democrats (Endecja), which was considered bourgeois, with strong nationalist tendencies.
3. The three partitions (1772, 1793, 1795) had left Poland divided among Russia, Prussia, and Austria (62 percent, 20 percent, and 18 percent of Polish territory respectively). The Polish Socialists in each of the occupied areas cooperated in one or another fashion with the Socialist parties of the partitioning powers, more closely though with the German Social Democratic Party and the Austrian Social Democratic Party (until 1898 there was no Russian Socialist Party).

   Proletariat, founded in 1882 by Ludwik Warynski, was called the first Polish Socialist Party. It signed an agreement with the Russian *Narodnaya Volya* (People's Will). After the destruction of *Proletariat* in the late 1880s, three small groups continued to function, the so-called "Second *Proletariat,*" (Marcin Kasprzak), the *Union of Polish Workers* (Julian Marchlewski, Adolf Warszawski, Bronislaw Wesolowski), and the *Association of Workers.* Simultaneously with the *Proletariat,* the *Polish People* was organized by Bronislaw Limanowski in Portsmouth in 1881.

   In 1892, the leaders of the Polish Socialist groups of Austrian Galicia and German Silesia formed distinct and separate Polish parties in their territories. In November 1892, a congress of all Polish

Socialists in exile created the united Polish Socialist Party (PPS). PPS covered the Russian territories of Poland and was closely related to the German–Polish Socialist Party and to the Polish Social Democratic Party in Austrian Galicia. Until the foundation of the Social Democracy of the Kingdom of Poland (SDKP) by Rosa Luxemburg, Julian Marchlewski, Adolf Warszawski, and Leo Jogiches in 1893, the Poles appeared as one unit at international congresses.

The SDKP saw itself as the direct successor to *Proletariat*. Its immediate aim was a liberal constitution for the entire Russian empire with territorial autonomy for Poland; Polish independence was specifically rejected. Up to the First World War, the Polish Socialist movement remained sharply divided on the issue of Polish independence.

After the fusion of SDKP and the Lithuanian Social Democrats (1899), the new party took the name of Social Democracy of the Kingdom of Poland and Lithuania (SDKPiL).

In 1911, the SDKPiL split into two factions: the Zarzadowcy faction included Rosa Luxemburg, Leo Jogiches–Tyszka, Marchlewski, and Felix Dzherzhynski, while the Roslamowcy faction had as members Hanecki, Radek, the Brothers Stein, and Bronski. Both factions passed out of existence with the formation of the Polish Communist Party in 1918. This party was shortly declared illegal; it was almost totally purged by Stalin in 1937. The direct successor of the Polish Communist Party was the Polish Workers' Party (*Polska Partia Robotnicza*), founded in 1942.

The PPS ceased to exist in 1948 when it was united with the PPR. The fusion of these two gave birth to the present Polish United Workers' Party (PZPR), the ruling party in the Polish People's Republic.

4. Józef Szujski (1835–1883), Polish historian and statesman, spokesman for a conciliatory, pro-Austrian policy, co-author of *Teka Stańczyka*—a political pamphlet opposing the independence movement in Poland.

   Tadeusz Kościuszko (1746–1817), Polish general, supreme commander of the so-called Kościuszko Insurrection of 1794. Directed against Russia and Prussia—the main beneficiaries of Poland's partitions of 1776 and 1793—the abortive insurrection was followed by the third partition in 1795, which wiped Poland from the map of Europe until she regained independence in 1918.

   The November Insurrection, 1830-31, in Russia-occupied Poland, was caused by an intensified Russianizing policy. The pro-Russian

Polish nobility and upper military class were opposed by revolutionary intellectuals and the lower-ranking army officers. When the sejm dethroned the tsar, an armed conflict erupted which ended in Russia's ultimately liquidating the sovereignty of the rump Kingdom of Poland.

The January Insurrection; 1863–64, was directly caused by the draft of Poles into the tsarist army. Supported by peasants and civilians, the insurrection spread to the Prussia- and Austria-occupied territories of Poland. It ended in defeat, and the commander in chief, Romuald Traugutt, was hanged by the Russians.

5. Actually, the articles were written by Engels. But Marx submitted them, and it is perfectly correct for Rosa Luxemburg to cite them as illustrating Marx's technique of analysis.
6. Friedrich Engels, "Der Schweizer Bürgerkrieg," in *Nachlass*, II, 448.

2. The Nation-State and the Proletariat

The question of nationality cannot be solved merely by presuming that socialists must approach it from the point of view of the class interests of the proletariat. The influence of theoretical socialism has been felt indirectly by the workers' movement as a whole, to such an extent that at present there is not a socialist or workers' party which does not use at least the Marxist terminology, if not the entire Marxist way of thinking. A famous example of this is the present Social Revolutionary Party of Russia, in whose theory—as far as one can speak of such—there are at least as many elements borrowed from the Marxist School as there are elements inherited from the *Narodniki* and the People's Will. In like manner, all socialist groups of the petit bourgeois and nationalistic type in Russia have their own fancies which are solely "in the interest of the proletariat and socialism." The Polish Social Democracy, now in decline, had especially distinguished itself in comparison with the naive, patriarchal —let us say—national socialism of Mr. Limanowski, particularly in that the "goodhearted" Mr. Limanowski never even used the name of Karl Marx, while social patriotism, from the beginning, sought to legitimize its program with Marxist terminology as a "class interest of the proletariat."

But it is obvious that the class character of any particular demand is not established by merely incorporating it mechanically into the program of a socialist party. What this or any other party considers a "class interest" of the proletariat can only be an imputed interest, concocted by subjective reasoning. It is very easy, for instance, to state that the workers' class interest demands the establishment of a minimum-wage law. Such a law would protect the workers against the pressures of competition, which might come from a less developed locality. It would assure them of a certain minimum standard of living, etc. Such demands have been presented repeatedly by socialist circles; however, the principle has not yet been accepted by the socialist parties in general, for the valid reason that the universal regulation of wages by means of legislation is but a utopian dream under today's anarchistic conditions of private economy. This is because workers' wages, like the prices of any kind of commodity, are set up in the capitalistic system under the operation of "free competition" and the spontaneous movement of capital. Therefore, the legal regulation of wages can be achieved only in exceptional, clearly defined areas, e.g., in small communities. And since the general establishment of a minimum-wage law clashes with the current conditions of capitalism, we must admit that it is not a true proletarian interest, but rather a fabricated or imputed one, in spite of the fact that it can be supported by a completely logical argument.

Likewise, one can, in a purely abstract way, figure out various "class interests" for the proletariat, which, however, would have to remain as mere clichés in the socialist program. This is especially so, as, the more that other social elements attach themselves to the workers' movement, the stronger is the tendency to suggest various sincere but unrealistic demands of these foreign elements as class interests of the proletariat. The other social elements referred to here include those members of society who have been deprived of political shelter by the failure of the bourgeois parties; in this category are the bourgeois and petit bourgeois intelligentsia. If the socialist parties had no objective criterion by which to establish just what fits the class interests of the proletariat, but were only directed by what certain people might think would be good or useful for the workers, then socialist programs would be a motley collection of subjective, and often completely utopian, desires.

Basing itself on historical foundations—on the foundations of the development of capitalist society—today's Social Democracy derives its immediate interests (the demands of today's proletariat) as well as its long-range goals, not merely from subjective reasoning about what would be "good" or "useful" for the proletariat, but from examining the objective development of society for a verification of its actual interests, as well as for material means for their realization. It is from this standpoint that the main alternatives for a practical solution to the question of nationality should be examined—those which are suggested by historical examples as well as those which correspond to the slogans popular in socialist circles.

We should first consider the idea of a *nation-state.* In order to evaluate this concept accurately, it is first necessary to search for historical substance in the idea, to see what is actually hiding behind the mask.

In his article on the struggles of nationalities and the social-democratic program in Austria, published over ten years ago, Kautsky enumerates three factors, which, according to him, make up the "roots of the modern national idea," as found in the rise of the modern state in all of Europe. These factors are: the desire of the bourgeoisie to assure for itself an internal or domestic market for its own commodity production; second, the desire for political freedom—democracy; and finally, expansion of the national literature and culture to the populace.[1]

In Kautsky's theory one can see, above all, his basic

position, his own view of nationality as a *historical category*. According to his reasoning, the idea of the nation is intimately connected with a definite era of modern development. The market interests of the bourgeoisie, democratic currents, culture of the people—these are typical aspects of a bourgeois society.

Naturally, we are not speaking here of a nationality as a specific ethnic or cultural group. Such nationality is, of course, separate and distinct from the bourgeois aspect; national peculiarities had already existed for centuries. But here we are concerned with national movements as an element of political life, with the aspirations of establishing a so-called nation-state; then the connection between those movements and the bourgeois era is unquestionable. The history of the national unification of Germany is a typical example of this connection, as the nucleus around which the later German Reich crystallized was the German *Zollverein* and *Zollparlament*. Their sponsor, Friedrich List, with his trivial theory of "national economy," can be more justifiably considered the real messiah of the national unity of Germany than the idealist Fichte, mentioned usually as the first apostle of German national rebirth. This "national" movement, which captured the imagination of the German "people and princes" during Fichte's time, and which the pseudo-revolutionary *Burschenschaften* loudly ushered in (in spite of Fichte's ardent sympathy for the Great French Revolution), basically represented only a medieval reaction against the seeds of the Revolution, which were brought to Germany by Napoleon, and against the elements of the modern bourgeois system. The sultry, romantic wind of "national rebirth" finally died out after the victorious return of Germany to feudal subdivision and to pre-March reaction. By contrast, the gospel of that vulgar agent of German industry, List, in the thirties and forties based the "national rebirth" on the elements of bourgeois development, on industry and trade, on the theory of the "domestic market." The material basis for this patriotic movement, which in the thirties and forties of the nineteenth century aroused such strong political, educational, philosophical, and literary currents in Germany, was, above all, the need to unify all the German territories (which were divided into several dozen feudal statelets and were crisscrossed by customs and tax barriers) into one great, integrated, capitalistic "fatherland," establishing a broad foundation for mechanized manufacturing and big industry.

The history of the industrial and commercial unification of Germany is so completely intertwined with the fate of Germany's political unification, that the history of the Customs Union [*Zollverein*], which reflected all the political developments and happenings in Germany, passes over, with perfect continuity, into the history of the birth of the present German Reich. In 1834, the Customs Union was born, grouping seventeen minor states around Prussia; and gradually, one after another, the remaining states also joined this Union. However, Austria remained altogether separate from the Union, and the Schleswig-Holstein War finally decided the matter in favor of Prussia. In 1867, the last renewal of the Customs Union became superfluous in the presence of the new national union; and the North German Union, after the Franco-Prussian War, transferred its customs rights and duties by inheritance to the newly formed Reich. In the place of the *Zollbundesrat* and the *Zollparlament* there were now the Bundesrat and Reichstag. In this example from modern history, Germany excellently demonstrates the true economic foundation of modern nation-states.

Although the bourgeois appetite for markets for "its own" commodities is so elastic and extensive that it always has the natural tendency to include the entire globe, the very essence of the modern bourgeois "national idea" is based on the premise that in the eyes of the bourgeoisie of every country, its own nation—their "fatherland"—is called and destined by nature to serve it [the bourgeoisie] as a field for the sale of products. It is as if this were an exclusive patrimony determined by the god Mercury. At least this is how the national question appears where the development of capitalism takes place "normally," without abrupt fluctuations, i.e., where production for the domestic market exceeds production for export. This is exactly what happened in Germany and in Italy.

However, it would be wrong to take Kautsky's formulation literally; we cannot assume that the material foundation of modern national movements is only the vaguely understood appetite of the industrial bourgeoisie for a "native" market for its commodities. Moreover, a capitalistic bourgeoisie needs many other conditions for its proper development: a strong military, as a guarantee of the inviolability of this "fatherland," as well as a tool to clear a path for itself in the world market; furthermore, it needs a suitable customs policy, suitable forms of administration in regard to communications, jurisdiction, school systems, and financial policy. In a word, capitalism demands for its proper development not only markets, but also the whole apparatus of a modern capitalistic state. The bourgeoisie needs for its normal existence not only strictly economic conditions for production, but also, in equal measure, political conditions for its class rule.

From all this it follows that the specific form of national aspirations, the true class interest of the bourgeoisie, is *state independence.* The nation-state is also simultaneously that indispensable historical form in which the bourgeoisie passes over from the national defensive to an offensive position, from protection and concentration of its own nationality to political conquest and domination over other nationalities. Without exception, all of today's "nation-states" fit this description, annexing neighbors or colonies, and completely oppressing the conquered nationalities.

This phenomenon becomes understandable only when one takes into consideration the fact that, according to the bourgeois way of thinking, it is possible to have a national movement for unification and defense of one's own nationality, and at the same time, to oppress another nationality (which is, of course, contrary to the very ideology of the "nation-state"). The German bourgeoisie in 1848 presents a striking example of this phenomenon in its attitude toward the Polish question. As is known, during the revolution [of 1848], when German national patriotism was most evident, Karl Marx and his circle advocated Polish independence; however, he proved to be but a prophet crying in the wilderness. The German "nation-state," from its first stages of development, did not conform at all with the accepted understanding of a nation-state in regard to nationalities. The borders of the Reich actually split the German nation, dividing it between Austria and the new "national" state of Germany, and putting together the Germans and the racially distinct peoples in territories annexed from Poland, Denmark, and France.

An even more striking example is Hungary, whose struggle for national independence was so much admired in its time. Even our own Polish revolutionary leaders—Bem, Wysocki, and Dembicki—had "tilted their lances" to assist them. But when examined from the viewpoint of nationality, this struggle was nothing more than an attempt to assure class rule of the Magyar minority over a country of nine nationalities, with the Magyars oppressing the other nationalities. The national "independence" of the Hungarians was bought by severing the Carpathian Slovaks from their brothers, the Sudeten Czechs; separating the Germans of Bratislava, Temesvar, and Transylvania from the Austrian Germans; and the Croats and Dalmatian Serbs from Croatia and the Slovenians.[2]

The aspirations of the Czechs are characterized by the same dichotomy. These aspirations arouse distrust among the Germans because, among other things, they are directed clearly at separating the German population of Sudetenland from the Germans of the Alpine countries. The primary objective of the Czechs was to force the Germans, as a minority group under the crown of Wenceslaus (Vaclav), into complete dependence on the Czechs in matters of culture and administration. As if this were not enough, the division of the Czech lands created a nationality division for the Czechs themselves by uniting five and one-third million Czechs with three million Germans and nearly two hundred thousand Poles. Still separated from this "national" Czech state were two million Carpathian Slovaks, a group closely related to the Czechs and left at the mercy of the Magyars. Therefore, these Slovaks are also loudly advocating their cause, which has been completely neglected by the Czech nationalists.*

Finally, and we do not have to go far for an example, Polish bourgeois nationalism is directed as much against the Ruthenians as against the Lithuanians. The very nationality which had to endure the bitter policy of extermination by the partitioning powers—Prussia and Russia—now refuses the right of independent existence to other nationalities. According to the Stanczyk[3] policy in Galicia, the Poles oppressed the Ruthenians, whose struggle for nationality runs like a red thread through the political history of the development of Galicia in the second half of the last century. The recent

* At a press convention of Slavic journalists in June 1898, the Slovak delegate, *Karol Salva,* from Liptov, called to the Czechs: "If harmony is to exist between us, then not only do we have to bestir ourselves, but you also! I know the reason for your lack of interest in us, up to this time. The region of the Slovaks has been up to now (with a few glorious exceptions) regarded as a *foreign country* by the Czech people!"

movement for national rebirth of the Lithuanians was met with similar hostility in Polish nationalistic circles.*

This strange double-edged character of bourgeois patriotism, which is essentially based on the conflicting interests of various nationalities rather than on harmony, becomes understandable only when one takes into consideration the fact that the historical basis of the modern national movements of the bourgeoisie is nothing more than its aspirations to class rule, and a specific social form in whose aspirations this

* For example, prompted by such an innocent undertaking as the establishment of an association for the restoration of the right to use the Lithuanian language in the Catholic Church in Lithuania, the Vilna *Lithuanian Courier* wrote in the summer of 1906:

> How many times already have the groundless accusations against the Poles of forced Polonization of Lithuanian lands been refuted! How many times were claims of Lithuanians against Poles proven to have no sound basis—claims that historical developments happened to take one course and not another! The Poles are not to be accused of Polonization tendencies, but, on the contrary, the Lithuanians should be accused of attempts at Lithuanization. If the perspectives, reached by way of mutual concessions and peaceful conventions, of living side by side peacefully do not please the Lithuanians, if they insist on taking advantage of every means of harassing and annihilating the Poles, then let them remember that they were the first to cast down the gauntlet before the Poles and that on them will fall the responsibility for this.

This reference to the "historical development," which insured the superiority of one nationality over another (accusing of chauvinism those who are fighting for the existence of their own nationality), along with the obscure threats against the other, call to mind the Prussian HKT, which defended the threatened Germans against the "attempts of Polonization," of Count Stanislaw Tarnowski, who derided the Ruthenians as being concerned primarily with the malicious "harassment" of the Poles.

The HKT, or Hakata, were German chauvinists, organized in 1894 for the purpose of eradicating the Polish elements in Poznan province. The leaders of the group were Hahnemann, Kennemann, and Tiedemann.—*Ed.*

expression is found: the modern *capitalistic state*—"national" in the sense of the dominance of the bourgeoisie of a certain nationality over the entire mixed population of the state. A democratic organization, together with general education of the people—these distinctly ideological elements of the nation mentioned by Kautsky—are merely details of a modern bourgeois state, easily attainable by the bourgeoisie within the framework and spirit of the state. Therefore, independence and state unification constitute the real axis around which the national movements of the bourgeoisie rotate.*

This matter appears quite different from the point of view of the interests of the proletariat. The contemporary proletariat, as a social class, is the offspring of the capitalist economy and the bourgeois state. The capitalist society and bourgeois state—taking them not as an abstract idea, but in tangible form as history has created them in each country—were already, from the very beginning, a frame of activity for the proletariat. A bourgeois state—national or not national—is just that foundation, together with capitalistic production as the ruling form of social economy, on which the working class grows and thrives. In this respect, there is a basic historical difference between the bourgeoisie and the proletariat. The bourgeoisie develops and is carried in the womb of the feudal class system. Aspiring to assure triumph for capitalism as the form of production, and for itself as the ruling class, the bourgeoisie *creates* the modern state on the ruins of the feudal system. Within the bounds of the development of capitalism and the rule of the bourgeoisie,

* The majority of the bourgeois legal theorists, therefore, recognize the independent existence of a state as an indispensable attribute of the "national idea." Messrs. Bluntschli and Co., the ideologists of their own class, achieve nothing else by using abstract definitions and subdivisions, than what has been already achieved by the power-hungry bourgeoisie in the course of history.

the proletariat is next to make itself heard politically—still as part of the bourgeois state. But the state was already from the beginning its natural womb, just as the shell of an egg is for the chicken. Therefore, historically speaking, the idea that the modern proletariat could do nothing as a separate and conscious class without first creating a new nation-state, is the same as saying that the bourgeoisie in any country should first of all establish a feudal system, if by some chance it did not come about normally by itself, or had taken on particular forms, as for instance in Russia. The historical mission of the bourgeoisie is the creation of a modern "national" state; but the historical task of the proletariat is the abolition of this state as a political form of capitalism, in which they themselves, as a conscious class, come into existence to establish the socialist system. The proletariat, as part of the whole society, can take part in national movements of the bourgeoisie, where the bourgeois development demands the creation of a "nation-state," as was the case, for example, in Germany. But then it follows the lead of the bourgeoisie, and does not act as an independent class with a separate political program. The national program of the German socialists in the forties advanced two ideas, directly opposing the national program of the bourgeoisie: unification with borders which would be based strictly on divisions of nationalities, and a republican form of government.

The interests of the proletariat on the nationality question are just the opposite of those of the bourgeoisie. The concern about guaranteeing an internal market for the industrialists of the "fatherland," and of acquiring new markets by means of *conquest*, by colonial or military policies—all these, which are the intentions of the bourgeoisie in creating a "national" state, cannot be the aims of a conscious proletariat.

The proletariat, as a legitimate child of capitalistic development, takes this development into account as a necessary historical background of its own growth and political maturation. Social Democracy itself reflects only the evolutionary side of capitalist development, whereas the ruling bourgeoisie looks after this development on behalf of reaction. Social Democracy nowhere considers its task to be the active support of industry or trade; rather it struggles against military, colonial, and customs protection, just as it combats the whole basic apparatus of the existing class state—its administration, legislature, school systems, etc.*

The national policy of the proletariat, therefore, basically clashes with the bourgeois policy to the extent that in its essence it is only defensive, never offensive; it depends on the harmony of interests of all nationalities, not on conquest and subjugation of one by another. The conscious proletariat of every country needs for its proper development peaceful existence and cultural development of its own nationality,

* "It is correct," says Kautsky, "that Social Democracy is the party of social development; its aim is the development of society beyond the capitalist stage. Evolution, as is known, does not exclude revolution, which is but an episode of evolution. The ultimate goal of Social Democracy is the destruction of the proletariat in such a way that the proletariat will take over and control social production, as a result of which the workers will cease being proletarians and constituting a separate class of society. This outcome depends on certain economic and political preconditions. It presupposes a certain level of capitalist development. Therefore, the proletariat has for its task the support of economic development; but its task is hardly to actively support the expansion of capitalism—in other words, it is not to support the growth of capitalist profits. This latter is the historic task of the capitalist class, to which it is loyally attending. We have no need to help them in this and we can help them the less, the more we fight against capitalist methods of development. . . . We do not need to take a position in favor of replacement of workers by machines, nor of the expropriation of handworkers by factories, etc. Our task in economic development is organization and support of the proletariat in its class struggle."—*Die Neue Zeit, 1898–1899*, Vol. I, pp. 292-93.

And this same argument, Kautsky adds, applies in an even greater degree to the field of political relations.

but by no means does it need the dominance of its nationality over others. Therefore, considering the matter from this point of view, the "nation"-*state,* as an apparatus of the domination and conquest of foreign nationalities, while it is indispensable for the bourgeoisie, has no meaning for the class interests of the proletariat.

Therefore, of these "three roots of the modern national idea" which Kautsky enumerated, for the proletariat as a class only the last two are important: democratic organization, and education of the populace. Vital for the working class, as conditions of its political and spiritual maturity, are the freedom of using its own native language, and the unchecked and unwarped development of national culture (learning, literature, the arts) and normal education of the masses, unimpaired by the pressures of the nationalists–so far as these can be "normal" in the bourgeois system. It is indispensable for the working class to have the same equal national rights as other nationalities in the state enjoy.[4] Political discrimination against a particular nationality is the strongest tool in the hands of the bourgeoisie, which is eager to mask class conflicts and mystify its own proletariat.

The advocates [Polish nationalists] of the "very best" social condition state at this point that, whatever the situation, the surest guarantee of cultural development and of the rights of every nationality is precisely the independence of the state, their own nation-state, and that therefore the nation-state is finally also an indispensable class interest of the proletariat. We are hardly concerned with determining what is or would be "the best" for the proletariat. Such observations have no practical value. Moreover, once the subject of "what would be the best" from the standpoint of the proletariat is approached in an abstract way, we would have to conclude that "the best" cure for national pressure, as well as for all types of disorders of a social nature, is undoubtedly the socialist system. A utopian argument must always lead to a utopian solution, if only by leaping to the "state of the future," whereas actually the problem should be solved within the framework of existing bourgeois reality.

Moreover, from the point of view of *methods,* the above reasoning contains still another historical misunderstanding. The argument that an independent nation-state is, after all, "the best" guarantee of national existence and development involves operating with a conception of a nation-state as a completely *abstract* thing. The nation-state as seen only from a national point of view, only as a pledge and embodiment of freedom and independence, is simply a remnant of the decaying ideology of the petite bourgeoisie of Germany, Italy, Hungary—all of Central Europe in the first half of the nineteenth century. It is a phrase from the treasury of disintegrated bourgeois liberalism. Since then, the development of the bourgeoisie has proved unequivocally that a modern nation-state is more real and tangible than the vague idea of "freedom" or national "independence"; that it is indeed a definite historical reality, neither very alluring nor very pure. The substance and essence of the modern state comprise not freedom and independence of the "nation," but only the class dominance of the bourgeoisie, protectionist policy, indirect taxation, militarism, war, and conquest. The bourgeoisie used to use the obvious technique of trying to cover up this brutal historical truth with a light ideological gauze, by offering the purely negative happiness of "independence and national freedom." For a time this technique paid off. But today it is only necessary to recall the circumstances under which this contention was advanced, to understand that it is simply opposed to what can and should be the class position of the *proletariat.*

In this case, as in many others, *anarchism,* the supposed antagonist of bourgeois liberalism, proved to be its worthy child. Anarchism, with characteristic "revolutionary" seriousness, accepted at face value the phraseology of the liberal ideology and, like the latter, showed only contempt for the historical and social content of the nation-state, which it set down as nothing else than an embodiment of "freedom," of the "will of the people," and of similar empty words. Bakunin, for example, wrote in 1849 about the national movements of Central Europe:

> The first sign of life in the Revolution [of 1848] was the cry of hatred toward the old oppression, a cry of sympathy and love for all oppressed nationalities. . . . "Away with the oppressors!" reverberated as if from one breast; "Salvation for the oppressed Poles, Italians, and all! No more wars of conquest; just one more war should be carried through to its end—a glorious revolutionary struggle with the purpose of eventual liberation for all peoples! Down with the artificial boundaries which have been forcibly erected by despotic congresses according to so-called historical, geographical, strategic necessities! There should no longer be any other barriers between the nations but those corresponding to nature, to justice, and those drawn in a democratic sense which the sovereign will of the people themselves traces on the basis of their national characteristics!" Such was the cry which rang out among all the peoples.[5]

To these dithyrambics on the subject of national independence and "the will of the people," Marx answered:

> Here there is no mention of reality, or insofar as it is considered at all, it is represented as something falsely, artificially established by "despots" and "diplomats." Against this wicked reality is pitted the alleged will of the people with its categorical imperative of an absolute demand for "freedom," "justice," and "humanity." . . . They can demand "freedom" of this or that a thousand times; if the thing is impossible, it will not take place, and in spite of everything it will remain an "empty dream." . . . Just a word about the "universal brotherhood of peoples" and the establishment of boundaries

> which are traced by "the sovereign will of the people themselves on the basis of their national characteristics." The United States and Mexico are two republics; in both of them the people are sovereign. Then how did it happen that between these republics, which, according to the moralistic theory should be "brotherly" and "federated," a war broke out over Texas: that the "sovereign will" of the American people, supported by the bravery of American volunteers, moved the American borders (established by nature itself) a few hundred miles further south, claiming this action to be from "geographic, commercial, and strategic necessities"?[6]

Marx's answer to this ironic question is clear. "Nation-states," even in the form of republics, are not products or expressions of the "will of the people," as the liberal phraseology goes and the anarchist repeats. "Nation-states" are today the very same tools and forms of class rule of the bourgeoisie as the earlier, non-national states, and like them they are bent on conquest. The nation-states have the same tendencies toward conquest, war, and oppression—in other words, the tendencies to become "not-national." Therefore, among the "national" states there develop constant scuffles and conflicts of interests, and even if today, by some miracle, all states should be transformed to "national," then the next day they would already present the same common picture of war, conquest, and oppression. The example given by Marx is typical in this regard. Why and over what did the war between the United States and Mexico arise?[7] California was indispensable for the capitalistic development of the United States, first, as a gold treasury in the literal sense, second, as a gateway to the Pacific Ocean. Only by the acquisition of this land could the capitalism of the United States extend from ocean to ocean, entrenching itself and opening for itself an outlet to the West as well as to the East. For the backward

Mexicans, California was just a simple territorial possession. The interests of the bourgeoisie were decisive. The "nation-state," worshiped and idealized by the anarchists as the "will of the people," served as an efficient tool of conquest in the interests of capitalism.

But even more striking examples of this kind are produced by the history of modern South America. We have already mentioned the double-edged character of the "national" liberation of the Spanish and Portuguese colonies at the dawn of the nineteenth century. Here their further political history, already as independent "nation-states," interests us as a colorful illustration of anarchistic phrases of "national freedom" and the "will of the people."

Brazil gained her freedom from Portugal after a hard struggle in 1825. In that same year a war broke out between Brazil and Argentina (which had just been liberated from under the scepter of Spain) over the province of Banda Oriental. Both of these new "nation"-states wanted to scoop up this province, which finally won independence itself as the Republic of Uruguay, but thanks only to the armed intervention of European states which had colonial interests in South America. France and other European countries issued an ultimatum to Argentina, which obstinately refused to recognize the independence of Uruguay and Paraguay. As a consequence, in 1845 another war broke out with the participation of Paraguay, Uruguay, and Brazil. In 1850, again a war was unleashed between Brazil and Argentina, in which Brazil, with the help of Paraguay and Uruguay, first defeated Argentina and then actually conquered Uruguay. In 1864, she formally forced this "independent" Uruguay to submission by armed action. Paraguay rose up against this action and declared war on Brazil, which was joined by Argentina and Uruguay. This war, lasting from 1865 to 1870, finally assured Brazil, where there ruled not so much "the will of the people" as the will and interests of the coffee plantation owners, the position of a dominant Great Power in South America. History does not touch upon the rule of the whites in Brazil (who make up less than one-third of the population) over the Negroes and the mixed population. Only after internal struggles was the emancipation of the slaves announced in 1871, but with compensation to be paid to their owners from state funds. Parliament, however, being the instrument of the plantation owners, did not vote these funds and slavery was still practiced. In 1886 the freeing of slaves over seventy years of age was declared; the rest were supposed to wait another seventeen years for freedom. But in 1888 the dynastic party, struggling to hold the throne, forced through parliament the general abolition of slavery without compensation, and this was decisive for the future of the republican movement. The plantation owners stood behind the republican banner en masse, and in the military *coup* of 1889, Brazil was declared a republic.*

This is how idyllic the internal conditions and events in South America look since the time of the rising of the "nation-states" and the establishment of the "will of the people." A beautiful complement to this picture is offered by the United States of Australia. Hardly had these states emerged from the position of English colonies and gained their freedom—the republican form of government or the federal system, the very ideal of Bakuninist phraseology—when

* The extent of the influence of the "coffee" interests on the "national will" in this "national" republic, even after the formal abolition of slavery (which is, moreover, still practiced to this very day), is proved by this next incident. When the coffee plantations caused a great crisis last year [1907] by releasing unlimited amounts of coffee on the international coffee market, thereby causing a drastic fall in prices, the Brazilian plantation owners forced the government to purchase the entire surplus of coffee with state funds. Naturally, a violent shake-up of the finances and entire material existence of the whole population has resulted from this original experiment.

they began an offensive policy in regard to New Hebrides, next door to New Guinea, and in skillful imitation of the United States of America, declared their own particular "national" doctrine: that "Australia should belong to the Australians." At the same time, the growing navy of the Australian Union is an emphatic commentary on this doctrine.

If, on the one hand, political independence, i.e., the nation-state, is necessary for capitalism and the class interest of the bourgeoisie just because a nation-state is a tool of domination (or control) and conquest, on the other hand, the working class is interested in the *cultural* and *democratic* content of nationalism, which is to say that the workers are interested in such political systems as assure a free development of culture and democracy in national life by means of defense, not conquest, and in the spirit of solidarity and cooperation of various nationalities which belong historically in the same bourgeois state. Equality before the law for nationalities and political organizations, and the assurance of national cultural development—such are the general forms of the program of the proletariat, a natural program resulting from its class position, in contrast to the nationalism of the bourgeoisie.

II

The classical confirmation and proof of these general principles is the most famous nationality problem within the framework of the Russian state—the Polish question.

In Poland, the national movement, right from the beginning, took on a completely different character from that of Western Europe. Those who search for a historical analogy for the Polish national idea in the history of today's Germany and Italy, betray their own misunderstanding of the true historical substance of the national movements in Germany and Italy as well as in Poland. With us Poles the national idea was a class idea of the nobility, never of the *bourgeoisie.* The material base of Polish national aspirations was determined, not as in Central Europe in the nineteenth century, by modern capitalist development, but, on the contrary, by the nobility's idea of its social standing, rooted in the natural-feudal economy.

The national movements of Poland vanished together with these feudal relations; whereas the bourgeoisie, as the historical spokesman of capitalistic development, was with us, from the very beginning, a clearly antinational factor. This was due not only to the specific origin of the nineteenth-century bourgeoisie, alien and heterogeneous, a product of colonization, an alien body transplanted into the Polish soil. Also decisive was the fact that Polish industry from its beginning, already in the 1820s and 1830s, was an export industry, even before it managed to control or even to *create* a domestic market within Poland. We will not quote here all the statistics of the industrial development of our country, but rather refer the reader to our treatise, *Die Industrielle Entwicklung Polens* [The Industrial Development of Poland] (published also in Russian), as well as to the work *Kwestja polska a ruch socjalistyczny* [The Polish Question and the Socialist Movement], Cracow, 1905. Here we shall recall only the most important outlines of this development.

Export to Russia, especially of the basic branches of capitalist industry, i.e., the production of textiles, became the basis for the existence and development of Polish capitalism from its beginnings, and furthermore, also the basis of the Polish bourgeoisie. As a consequence, our bourgeoisie from the first showed political leanings, not toward the west, to the national unification of Galicia with the Crown, but toward the east: toward Russia. These leanings, after the withdrawal of the customs barrier between the Empire and the Polish Kingdom, increased with *the development of big industry.* However, the real rule of the bourgeois class in society began after the abortive January Insurrection [1863]. The new rule was inaugurated by the "program of organic work"[8] which meant a renunciation of national independence. Moreover, the class rule of the bourgeoisie in Poland not only did not demand the creation of a united nation-state, as in Germany and Italy, but, on the contrary, it arose on the foundations of the conquest and division of Poland. The idea of unification and national independence did not draw its vital juices from capitalism; on the contrary, as capitalism developed, this idea became historically outlived. And that very circumstance, that particular historical relationship of the capitalistic bourgeoisie to the national idea in our country, became decisive also for the fate of that idea and defined its social character. In Germany, in Italy, as one half-century before in South America, the "national rebirth" carried with it all the traits of a revolutionary, progressive spirit. Capitalistic development embraced this national idea, and historically speaking, elevated it with the political ideals of the revolutionary bourgeoisie: democracy and liberalism. Exactly in this historical sense, the national idea was only a detail of the general class program of the bourgeoisie—of the modern bourgeois state. In Poland there arose an opposition between the national idea and the bourgeois development, which gave the former not only a utopian but also a reactionary character. This opposition is reflected in the three phases of the history of the idea of Polish national independence.

The first is the failure of the armed struggle of the Polish nobility. Not even the most ardent advocates of the theory of "violence and force" in the philosophy of history will explain the defeat of Polish insurrectionist movements as mere superiority of the Russian bayonets. Whoever knows anything about the modern economic and social history of

Poland knows that the defeat of the military insurrectionists was prepared by the same capitalistic market interest which elsewhere, in the words of Kautsky, comprised one of the main elements of the modern national idea. The endeavors of the bourgeoisie to secure for themselves conditions of large-scale capitalistic production did not involve the demand for a nation-state; on the contrary, the bourgeoisie sought to exploit the annexation, and to paralyze the national movement of the nobility. Thus [in Poland], the idea of a nation-state, an idea essentially bourgeois, was sabotaged by the bourgeoisie, and met defeat in the January [1863] uprising.

The second phase was the inheritance of the Polish national idea by the petite bourgeoisie. In this incarnation, the national idea changed from an armed struggle to a policy of neutrality, and at the same time, began to show its weakness. After vegetating for twenty years away from society—in the eighties and nineties petit bourgeois nationalism lingered in emigration in the form of a half-dozen "all-Polish patriots"—finally, with the opening of the present revolutionary era, it has emerged as an active party on the political scene.

The National Democracy proclaimed its entrance into a politically active phase with a public renunciation of the program of national independence as an unrealizable utopia, and with writing into its program instead the double slogan of autonomy of the country and counter-revolution. Now, after throwing off the ballast of the traditional national program, "National Democracy" quickly becomes the true political force in the society. Having failed in its second petit bourgeois form, the program of the nation-state is replaced by a program which is practical and realizable on the basis of a bourgeois Poland—a program of autonomy.

Finally, the third and last phase in the history of the Polish national idea is its attempt to join the class movement of the proletariat. The twenty-year, social-patriotic experiment of the PPS was the only case in the history of the international workers' movement where the slogan of the nation-state was made part of a socialist program. And this singular experiment ended after twenty years in exactly the same kind of crisis and in the same manner as the petit bourgeois experiment. . . . At the time of the outbreak of the Workers' Revolution [1905] in Russia, the PPS, so as to secure for itself a part in active politics and in the life of the society, publicly renounced the program of rebuilding Poland. The National Democracy renounced this program so as to take an active part in the middle-class counter-revolution; the PPS did so to exert pressure for the proletarian revolution.

The crisis, decline, and fall of the PPS, brought on by this renunciation, constituted the third and last bankruptcy of the idea of the Polish nation-state—this time wearing the mantle of the proletariat. The current revolution, that mightiest social upheaval of modern times, which is calling all embryos of life to growth and maturity, and simultaneously tearing up the entire foundation of society with a giant plow, rejected the last trace of the idea of the Polish nation-state, as if it were an empty shell from which historical development had removed all content, and which could only roll about among the rubble of social traditions during the troubles of a period of reaction.

The historical career of Polish nationalism, however, has not yet come to an end. Indeed, it has ended its life as the idea of the nation-state, but it has simultaneously transformed itself from a utopian specter to a realistic factor of social life. The Polish bourgeois-capitalistic development fettered Poland to Russia and condemned the idea of national independence to utopianism and to defeat. But the other side of this bourgeois process is the revolutionary development of Polish society. All the manifestations and factors of social progress in Poland, above all its principal factor, the Polish proletariat and its part in the general revolution in the Tsarist Empire, have grown out of the foundations of this same bourgeois-capitalistic development. The social progress and revolutionary development of Poland are in this way united with the capitalistic process by unbreakable historical ties, which united Poland and Russia, and which buried the Polish national idea. Consequently, all separatist aspirations directed at raising an artificial barrier between Poland and Russia, are by nature directed against the interests of social progress and revolutionary development; or in other words, they are manifestations of reaction. But at the same time, the national idea, after the final failure of the program of the nation–state and national independence, was reduced to a general and undefined idea of national separation, and, as such, Polish nationalism became a form of social reaction blessed by tradition. The national idea became a collective ideological shield for the reactionary aspirations of the whole camp of bourgeois classes, nobility, middle class, and petite bourgeoisie. Historical dialectics also proved to be far more imaginative, supple, and inclined to variety than the minds of the politicians, caught in the grip of stereotypes, and speculating in the abstract wilderness of the "rights of nations." So many Russian, German, and other revolutionaries were, and still are, inclined to regard "national tradition" as a historic vessel, destined by nature for all times, to absorb and carry all sorts of revolutionary currents, as a sea conch, which, according to legend, when carried ashore and lifeless, will always repeat the distant roar of the sea waves when placed close to the ear. This "national tradition," in these concrete historical and social conditions which created today's Poland, becomes just the opposite: a vessel for all types of reaction, a natural shield for counter-revolution. Under the slogan of "national tradition" there took place the elections of the National Democracy to the first Duma, protected by the Cossacks from the criticisms and protests of the Polish proletariat. In the name of the "national idea" the National Democrats used bullets to chase away the Social Democratic workers from the pre-election meetings, and even killed several dozen workers in Warsaw, Lodz, and Pabianice.[9] Under the national slogan, workers' "national unions" were organized by the National Democracy for counteraction against the economic struggle and the revolutionary action of the proletariat. Under the national slogan, National Democratic railroad workers broke the railroad strike, which had been started in December 1905 in Poland, forcing the striking workers to return to work at gun point. Under the national slogan, the National Democracy began a crusade against the general strike and other forms of strikes, claiming they were ruining the "country's industry and the national wealth." Under the national slogan, the Polish Circle in the Duma renounced participation in the Vyborg Manifesto deliberations, and in the declaration of the Vyborg Manifesto itself, after the dispersion of the Duma.

Under the national slogan, the National Democracy organized so-called "Polish Falcons,"[10] or, rather, armed fighting squads destined for murdering socialists, making strikes impossible, and so on. Mr. Dmowski, the leader of the National Democracy, declared in its official organ that "socialists are outsiders" and are thus "foreign enemies," thereby justifying in advance the "national" murders of the socialists. And finally, in the name of the national idea, the future of the nation, and national defense, the Polish bourgeoisie, with the National Democracy at the head, publicly stood behind the banner of "neo-pan-Slavism," in the ranks of the hirelings of absolutism and the Russian "national idea," "with no reservations." The last vestige of the political "national" program—Poland's autonomy—was thus given up on the altar of counter-revolution. Mistreated by history, the Polish national idea moved through all stages of decline and fall. Having started its political career as a romantic, noble insurgent, glorified by international revolution, it now ends as a national hooligan—a volunteer of the Black Hundreds of Russian absolutism and imperialism.

Notes

1. *Die Neue Zeit, 1897–1898,* Vol. I, p. 517.
2. The numerical relationship of nationalities in Hungary at that time was more or less as follows:

Hungarians	5,000,000
Rumanians	2,300,000
Slovaks	1,670,000
Germans	1,500,000
Croats	900,000
Serbs	830,000
Ruthenians	443,000

3. Stanczyk was a nickname for conservatives in Galicia.
4. The working class in Poland was composed of various nationalities intermingled with each other, whereas the ruling class was quite solidly Polish (or German). The author is advocating for the working class—presumably for each of its nationalities—the same rights *as nationalities* that were enjoyed by the "other" nationalities, of the ruling class, that is.
5. Mikhail Bakunin, "Aufruf an die Slawen," Köthen, 1848, in *Zwei Schriften aus den 40er Jahren des XIX. Jahrhunderts,* Internationale Bibliothek für Philosophie, Bd. II, nos. 11-12 (Prague: 1936), p. 27.
6. It was Engels, not Marx, who penned this answer, in the *Neue Rheinische Zeitung,* February 15, 1849, no. 222. See Marx-Engels, *Werke,* VI, 271.
7. In the original the author has put "Texas" for "Mexico," which is obviously a slip.
8. "Return to organic work"—a slogan coined in the 1860s (after the abortive 1863-64 January Insurrection) by the so-called positivists in the Kingdom of Poland, and the Galicia conservatives. Rejecting romanticism and its lofty notions of insurgency and conspiracy, it called for a scientific approach in education, industry, trade, and

agriculture as the only means for Poland's survival.

9. Pabianice—an industrial city about 10 miles southwest of Lodz.
10. The Falcons (Sokõl) were a youth association in Galicia, founded in 1867 under the political guidance of the National Democracy.

3. *Federation, Centralization, and Particularism*

We must turn next to another proposed form of the solution of the nationality question, i.e., federation. Federalism has long been the favorite idea of revolutionaries of anarchic hue. During the 1848 revolution Bakunin wrote in his manifesto: "The revolution proclaimed by its own power the dissolution of despotic states, the dissolution of the Prussian state . . . Austria . . . Turkey . . . the dissolution of the last stronghold of the despots, the Russian state . . . and as a final goal—a universal federation of European Republics." From then on, federation has remained an ideal settlement of any nationality difficulties in the programs of socialist parties of a more or less utopian, petit bourgeois character; that is, parties which do not, like Social Democracy, take a historical approach but which traffic in subjective "ideals." Such, for example, is the party of Social Revolutionaries in Russia. Such was the PPS in its transitional phase, when it had ceased to demand the creation of a national state and was on the way to abandoning any philosophical approach. Such, finally, are a number of socialist groups in the Russian Empire, with which we will become acquainted more closely at the end of the present chapter.

If we ask why the slogan of federation enjoys such wide popularity among all revolutionaries of anarchistic coloring, the answer is not difficult to find: "Federation" combines—

at least in the revolutionary imagination of these socialists—"independence" and "equality" of nations with "fraternity." Consequently, there is already a certain concession from the standpoint of the law of nations and the nation-state in favor of hard reality, it is a *sui generis*, ideological, taking into account the circumstance, which cannot be overlooked, that "nations" cannot live in the vacuum of their "rights" as separate and perfectly self-sufficient "nation-states," but that there exist between them some links. Historically developed connections between various nationalities, the material development which welded whole areas, irrespective of national differences, the centralization of bourgeois development—all this is reflected in the heads of those revolutionary improvisers; in place of "brute force" they place "voluntarism" in relations between nations. And since republicanism is self-evident in this because the very same "will of the people" which restores independence and equality to all nations obviously has so much good taste as to throw simultaneously with contempt to the dump of history all remnants of monarchism, consequently the existing bourgeois world is transformed at one stroke into a voluntary union of independent republics, i.e., federation. Here we have a sample of the same "revolutionary" historical caricature of reality by means of which the appetite of Tsarist Russia for the southern Slavs was transformed, in Bakunin's phraseology, into the pan-Slavic ideal of anarchism, "a federation of Slavic peoples." On a smaller scale, an application of this method of "revolutionary" alterations of reality was the program of the PPS adopted at its Eighth Congress in 1906: a republican federation of Poland with Russia. As long as the social-patriotic standpoint—in the prerevolutionary period—was maintained in all its purity and consistency, the PPS recognized only the program of nation-states, and rejected with contempt and hatred the idea of federation offered, for instance, by the Russian Social Revolutionaries. When the outbreak of revolution all at once demolished its presuppositions, and the PPS saw itself forced to follow the road of concessions in favor of reality which could no longer be denied, in view of the obvious fact that Poland and Russia form one social entity, a manifestation of which was precisely the common revolution, the program of federation of Poland with Russia, previously held in contempt, became the form of that concession. At the same time, the PPS, as is usual with "revolutionaries" of this type, did not notice the following fact: when Social Democracy took for the historical basis of its program and tactics the joint capitalistic development of Poland and Russia, it merely stated an objective, historical fact, not depending on the will of the socialists. From this fact, the revolutionary conclusion should have been drawn in the form of a united class struggle of the Polish and Russian proletariat. The PPS, however, putting forward the program of federation of Poland with Russia, went much further: in place of the passive recognition of historical fate, it itself actively proposed a union of Poland with Russia and assumed responsibility for the union, and in lieu of the objective historical development, it placed the subjective consent of socialists in "revolutionary" form.

But federalism as a form of political organization has, like the "nation-state" itself, its definite historical content, quite different from, and independent of, the subjective ideology attached to that form. Therefore, the idea of federation can be evaluated from the class standpoint of the proletariat only when we examine the fate and role of that idea in modern socialist development.

II

An outstanding tendency of capitalistic development in all countries is indisputably an internal, economic, and capitalist centralization, i.e., an endeavor to concentrate and weld into one entity the state territory from the economic, legislative, administrative, judicial, military, etc. viewpoints. In the Middle Ages, when feudalism prevailed, the link between the parts and regions of one and the same state was extremely loose. Thus, each major city with its environs, itself produced the majority of objects of daily use to satisfy its needs; it also had its own legislation, its own government, its army; the bigger and wealthier cities in the West often waged wars on their own and concluded treaties with foreign powers. In the same way, bigger communities lived their own closed and isolated life, and each area of land of a feudal lord or even each area of knightly estates constituted in itself a small, almost independent state. The conditions of the time were characterized by a diminution and loosening of all state norms. Each town, each village, each region had different laws, different taxes: one and the same state was filled with legal and customs barriers separating one fragment of a state from another. This decentralization was a specific feature of the natural economy and the nascent artisan production of the time.

Within the framework of the pulverization of public life, connected with the natural economy, and of the weak cohesion between the parts of the state organism, territories and whole countries passed incessantly from hand to hand in Central and Western Europe throughout the Middle Ages. We note also the patching together of states by way of purchase, exchange, pawnings, inheritance, and marriage; the classical example is the Hapsburg monarchy.

The revolution in production- and trade-relations at the close of the Middle Ages, the increase of goods production and moneyed economy, together with the development of international trade and the simultaneous revolution in the military system, the decline of knighthood and the rise of standing armies, all these were factors that, in political relations, brought about the increase of monarchical power and the rise of absolutism. The main tendency of absolutism was the creation of a centralized state apparatus. The sixteenth and seventeenth centuries are a period of incessant struggle of the centralist tendency of absolutism against the remnants of feudalist particularism. Absolutism developed in two directions: absorbing the functions and attributes of the diets and provincial assemblies as well as of the self-governing municipalities, and standardizing administration in the whole area of the state by creating new central authorities in the administration and the judiciary, as well as a civil, penal, and commercial code. In the seventeenth century, centralism triumphed fully in Europe in the form of so-called "enlightened despotism," which soon passed into unenlightened, police-bureaucratic despotism.

As a result of the historical circumstance that absolutism was the first and principal promoter of modern state centralism, a superficial tendency developed to identify centralism in general with absolutism, i.e., with reaction. In reality, absolutism, insofar as, at the close of the Middle Ages, it combated feudal dispersion and particularism, was undoubtedly a manifestation of historical progress. This was perfectly well understood by Staszic, who pointed out that the [Polish] gentry commonwealth could not survive "in the midst of autocracies." On the other hand, absolutism itself played only the role of a "stirrup drink" [parting good wishes] with regard to the modern bourgeois society for which, politically and socially, it paved the way by toppling feudalism and founding a modern, uniform, great state on its ruins. Indeed, independent of absolutism, and after its historical demise, bourgeois society continued to carry through with undiminished force and consistency the centralist tendency. The present centralism of France as a political area is the work of the Great Revolution. The very name, "Great Revolution," exerted, everywhere its influence reached in Europe, a centralizing influence. Such a product of the Revolution's centralism was the "République Helvétique," in which, in 1798, suddenly the previously loosely confederated Swiss cantons were compressed. The first spontaneous action of the March [1848] revolution in Germany was the destruction by the popular masses of the so-called customs houses [Mauthäuser], the symbols of medieval particularism.

Capitalism, with its large-scale machine production, whose vital principle is concentration, swept away and continues to sweep away completely any survivals of medieval economic, political, and legal discrimination. Big industry needs markets and freedom of untrammeled trade in big areas. Industry and trade, geared to big areas, require uniform administration, uniform arrangement of roads and communications, uniform legislation and judiciary, as far as possible in the entire international market, but above all in the whole area inside each respective state. The abolition of the customs, and tax autonomy of the separate municipalities and gentry holdings, as well as of their autonomy in administering courts and law, were the first achievements of the modern bourgeoisie. Together with this went the creation of one big state machinery that would combine all functions: the administration in the hands of one central government; legislation in the hands of a legislative body—the parliament; the armed forces in the form of one centralized army subject to a central government; customs arrangements in the form of one tariff encompassing the entire state externally; a uniform currency in the whole state, etc. In accordance with this, the modern state also introduced in the area of spiritual life, as far as possible, a uniformity in education and schools, ecclesiastical conditions, etc., organized on the same principles in the entire state. In a word, as comprehensive a centralization as possible in all areas of social life is a prominent trend of capitalism. As capitalism develops, centralization increasingly pierces all obstacles and leads to a series of uniform institutions, not only within each major state, but in the entire capitalistic world, by means of international legislation. Postal and telegraphic services as well as railway communication have been for decades the object of international conventions.

This centralist tendency of capitalistic development is one of the main bases of the future socialist system, because through the highest concentration of production and exchange, the ground is prepared for a socialized economy conducted on a world-wide scale according to a uniform plan. On the other hand, only through consolidating and centralizing both the state power and the working class as a militant force does it eventually become possible for the proletariat to grasp the state power in order to introduce the dictatorship of the proletariat, a socialist revolution.

Consequently, the proper political framework in which the modern class struggle of the proletariat operates and can conquer is the big capitalistic state. Usually, in the socialist ranks, especially of the utopian trend, attention is paid only to the economic aspect of capitalistic development, and its categories—industry, exploitation, the proletariat, depressions—are regarded as indispensable prerequisites for socialism. In the political sphere, usually only democratic state institutions, parliamentarianism, and various "freedoms" are regarded as indispensable conditions of this movement. However, it is often overlooked that the modern big state is also an indispensable prerequisite for the development of the modern class struggle and a guarantee of the victory of socialism. The historical mission of the proletariat is not "socialism" applicable on every inch of ground separately, not dictatorship, but world revolution, whose point of departure is big-state development.

Therefore, the modern socialist movement, legitimate child of capitalist development, possesses the same eminently centralist characteristic as the bourgeois society and state. Consequently, Social Democracy is, in all countries, a determined opponent of particularism as well as of federalism. In Germany, Bavarian or Prussian particularism, i.e., a tendency to preserve Bavaria's or Prussia's political distinctiveness, their independence from the Reich in one respect or another, is always a screen for gentry or petit bourgeois reaction. German Social Democracy also combats, with full energies, the efforts, for instance, of South German particularists to preserve a separate railroad policy in Bavaria, Baden, Württemberg; it also energetically combats particularism in the conquered provinces of Alsace-Lorraine, where the petite bourgeoisie tries to separate itself, by its French nationalism, from political and spiritual community with the entire German Reich. Social Democracy in Germany is also a decided opponent of those survivals of the federal relationship among the German states inside the Reich which have still been preserved. The general trend of capitalist development tends not only toward the political union of the separate provinces within each state, but also toward the abolition of any state federations and the welding of loose state combinations into homogeneous, uniform states; or, wherever this is impossible, to their complete breakup.

An expression of this is the modern history of the Swiss Confederacy, as well as of the American Union; of the German Reich, as well as of Austria-Hungary.

III

The first centralist constitution of the integrated republic of Switzerland, created by the great revolution, was obliterated without a trace by the time of the Restoration, and reaction, which triumphed in Switzerland under the protection of the Holy Alliance, quickly returned to the independence of the cantons, to particularism and only a loose confederation. Domestically, this implementation of the ideal "of voluntary union of independent groups and state units" in the spirit of anarchists and other worshipers of "federation," involved the adoption of an aristocratic constitution (with the exclusion of the broad working masses) as well as the rule of Catholic clericalism.

A new opposition trend, toward the democratization and the centralization of the Swiss federation, was born in the period of revolutionary seething between the July [1830] and March [1848] revolutions, which was manifested in Switzerland in the form of a tendency to create a close state union in place of federation, and to abolish the political rule of noble families and of the Catholic clergy. Here, centralism and democracy initially went hand in hand, and encountered the opposition of the reaction which fought under the slogan of federation and particularism.

The first constitution of the present Swiss Confederation of 1848 was born out of a bitter struggle against the so-called "Sonderbund," i.e., a federation of seven Catholic cantons which, in 1847, undertook a revolt against the general confederation in the name of saving the independence of the cantons and their old aristocratic system, and clericalism. Although the rebels proudly waved the banner of "freedom and independence" of the cantons against the "despotism" of the Confederacy, in particular of "freedom of conscience" against Protestant intolerance (the ostensible cause of the conflict was the closing of the convents by the Democratic Radical parties), democratic and revolutionary Europe, undeceived by this, applauded wholeheartedly when the Confederacy, by brutal armed force, i.e., by "violence," forced the advocates of federalism to bow and surrender to the Confederate authority. And when Freilingrath, the bard of the *Neue Rheinische Zeitung,* triumphantly celebrated the victory of the bayonets of Swiss centralism as a reveille to the March revolution—"In the highlands the first shot was fired, in the highlands against the parsons"—it was the absolutist government of Germany, the pillar of Metternich's reaction, that took up the cause of the federalists and the defenders of the old independence of the cantons. The later development of Switzerland up until the present has been marked by constant, progressive, legal and political centralization under the impact of the growth of big industry and international trade, railroads, and European militarism. Already the second Constitution of 1874 extended considerably the attributes of the central legislation, the central government authority, and particularly of a centralized judiciary in comparison with the Constitution of 1848. Since the Constitution was thoroughly revised in 1874, centralization has progressed continuously by the addition of ever new individual articles, enlarging the competence of the central institutions of the Confederacy. While the actual political life of Switzerland, with its development toward a modern capitalist state, is increasingly concentrated in the federal institutions, the autonomous life of the canton declines and becomes increasingly sterile. Matters have gone even further. When the federal organs of legislation and uniform government, originating from direct elections by the people (the so-called Nazionalrat and the so-called Bundesrat), assume increasingly more prestige and power, the organ of the federal representation, i.e., of the cantons (the so-called Ständerat), becomes more and more a survival, a form without content, condemned by the development of life to slow death.* At the same time, this process of centralization is supplemented by another parallel process of making the cantonal constitutions uniform by means of constant revisions in the legislatures of the respective cantons and the mutual imitation and borrowing among them. As a result, the former variety of cantonal particularisms rapidly disappears. Until now, the main safeguard of this political separateness

* Characteristic is the antipathy, general among the Swiss population, against the Ständerat as a "do-nothing" institution. This is only a subjective expression of the fact that this organ of federalism has been deprived of its functions by the objective course of historical development.

and independence of the cantons was their local civil and penal law which preserved the entire medley of its historical origin, tradition, and cantonal particularism. At present, even this stubbornly defended fortress of the cantons' independence has had to yield under the pressure of Switzerland's capitalist development—industry, trade, railroads and telegraphs, international relations—which passed like a leveling wave over the legal conditions of the cantons. As a result, the project of one common civil and penal code for the entire confederation has been already elaborated, while portions of the civil code have already been approved and implemented. These parallel currents of centralization and standardization, working from above and below and mutually supplementing each other, encounter, almost at every step, the opposition of the socially and economically most backward, most petit bourgeois French and Italian cantons. In a significant manner, the opposition of the Swiss decentralists and federalists even assumes the forms and colors of a nationality struggle for the French Swiss: the expansion of the power of the Confederacy at the expense of cantonal particularism is tantamount to the increase of the preponderance of the German element, and as such they, the French Swiss, openly combat it. No less characteristic is another circumstance, viz., the same French cantons which, in the name of federation and independence, combat state centralism, have internally the least developed communal self-government, while the most democratic self-governing institutions, a true rule of the people, prevail in those communes of the German cantons which advocate centralization of the Confederation. In this way, both at the very bottom and at the top of state institutions, both in the latest results of the development of present-day Switzerland and at its point of departure, centralism goes hand in hand with democracy and progress, while federalism and particularism are linked with reaction and backwardness.

In another form the same phenomena are repeated in the history of the United States of America.

The first nucleus of the Union of the English colonies in North America, which until then had been independent, which differed greatly from one another socially and politically, and which in many respects had divergent interests, was also created by revolution. The revolution was the advocate and creator of the process of political centralization which has never stopped up to the present day. Also, here, as in Switzerland, the initial, most immature form of development, was the same "voluntary federation" which, according to the conscious and unconscious adherents of anarchistic ideas, stands at the apex of modern social development as the crowning summit of democracy.

In the first Constitution of the United States, elaborated in the period 1777–1781, there triumphed completely the "freedom and independence of the several colonies, their complete right of self-determination." The union was loose and voluntary to such an extent that it practically did not possess any central executive and made possible, almost on the morrow of its establishment, a fratricidal customs war among its "free and equal" members, New York, New Jersey, Virginia, and Maryland, while in Massachusetts, under the blessing of complete "independence" and "self-determination," a civil war, an uprising of debt-encumbered farmers broke out, which aroused in the wealthy bourgeoisie of the states a vivid yearning for a strong central authority. This bourgeoisie was forcibly reminded that in a bourgeois society the most beautiful "national independence" has real substance and "value" only when it serves the independent utilization of the fruits of "internal order," i.e., the undisturbed rule of private property and exploitation.

The second Constitution of 1787 already created, in place of federation, a unified state with a central legislative authority and a central executive. However, centralism had still, for a long time, to combat the separatist tendencies of the states-righters which finally erupted in the form of an open revolt of the Southern states, the famous 1861 war of secession. Here we also see a striking repetition of the 1847 Swiss situation. As advocates of centralism, the Northern states acted, representing the modern, big-capital development, machine industry, personal freedom and equality before the law, the true corollaries of the system of hired labor, bourgeois democracy, and bourgeois progress. On the other hand, the banner of separatism, federation, and particularism, the banner of each hamlet's "independence" and "right of self-determination" was raised by the plantation owners of the South, who represented the primitive exploitation of slave labor. In Switzerland as in America, centralism struggled against the separatist tendencies of federalism by means of armed force and physical coercion, to the unanimous acclaim of all progressive and democratic elements of Europe. It is significant that the last manifestation of slavery in modern society tried to save itself, as reaction always does, under the banner of particularism, and the abolition of slavery was the obverse of the victory of centralist capitalism. After the victorious war against the secessionists, the Constitution of the American Union underwent a new revision in the direction of centralism; the remainder was, from then on, achieved by big capital, big power, imperialist development: railroads, world trade, trusts, finally, in recent times, customs protectionism, imperialist wars, the colonial system, and the resulting reorganization of the military, of taxation, and so on. At present, the central executive in the person of the President of the Union possesses more extensive power, and the administration and judiciary are more centralized than in the majority of the monarchies of Western Europe. While in Switzerland the gradual expansion of the central functions at the expense of federalism takes place by means of amendments to the constitution, in America this takes place in a way of its own, without any constitutional changes, through a liberal interpretation of the constitution by the judicial authorities.

The history of modern Austria presents a picture of incessant struggle between a centralist and federalist trend. The starting point of this history, the 1848 revolution, shows the following division of roles: the advocates of centralism are the German liberals and democrats, the then leaders of the revolution, while the obstruction under the banner of federalism is represented by the Slavic counter-revolutionary parties: the Galician nobility; the Czech, Moravian, and Dalmatian diets; the pan-Slavists; and the admirers of Bakunin, that prophet and phrasemaker of the anarchist "autonomy of free peoples." Marx characterized the policy and role of the Czech federalists in the 1848 revolution as follows:

> The Czech and Croat pan-Slavists worked, some deliberately and some unknowingly, in accordance with the clear interests of Russia. They betrayed the cause of revolution for the shadow of a nationality which, in the best case, would have shared the fate of the Polish one. The Czech, Moravian, Dalmatian, and a part of the Polish delegates (the aristocracy) conducted a systematic struggle against the German element. The Germans and a part of the Poles (the impoverished gentry) were the main adherents of revolutionary progress; fighting against them, the mass of the Slavic delegates was not content to demonstrate in this way the reactionary tendencies of their entire movement, but even debased itself by scheming and plotting with the very same Austrian government which had dispersed their Prague congress. They received a well-deserved reward for their disgraceful behavior. They had supported the government during the October uprising, the outcome of which finally assured a majority to the Slavs. This now almost exclusively Slavic assembly was dispersed by the Aus-

> trian soldiery exactly as the Prague congress had been, and the pan-Slavists were threatened with imprisonment if they dared to complain. They achieved only this: that the Slavic nationality is now everywhere threatened by Austrian centralism.[1]

Marx wrote this in 1852 during the revival of absolutist rule in Austria after the final collapse of the revolution and of the first era of constitutionalism—"a result which they owe to their own fanaticism and blindness."

Such was the first appearance of federalism in the modern history of Austria.

In no state did the sociohistorical content of the federalist program and the fallacy of the anarchist fantasies concerning the democratic or even revolutionary character of that slogan appear so emphatically also in later times, and, so to speak, symbolically, as in Austria. The progress of political centralization can be directly measured here by the program of the right to vote for the Vienna parliament, which, passing successively through four phases of gradual democratization, was increasingly becoming the main cement binding together the state structure of the Hapsburg monarchy. The October Patent of 1860, which inaugurated the second constitutional era in Austria, had created in the spirit of federalism a weak central legislative organ, and given the right of electing the delegations to it not to the people, but to the diets of the respective crownlands. However, already in 1873, it proved indispensable for breaking the opposition of the Slavic federalists, to introduce voting rights not by the diets, but by the people themselves, to the Central Parliament [Reichsrat] —although it was a class, unequal, and indirect voting system. Subsequently, the nationality struggle and the decentralist opposition of the Czechs, which threatened the very existence and integrity of the Hapsburg monarchy, forced, in 1896, the replacement of their class voting right by a universal one, through the addition of a fifth curia (the so-called universal-election curia). Recently we witnessed the final reform of the electoral law in Austria in the direction of universal and equal voting rights as the only means of consolidating the state and breaking the centrifugal tendencies of the Slavic federalists. Especially characteristic in this respect is the role of Galicia. Already from the first session of the Viennese Reichsrat and the Galician Diet in April 1861, the Galician nobility came forward as an extreme opposition against the liberal cabinet of Schmerling, violently opposing the liberal reforms in the name of "national autonomy" and the right of nations to "self-determination," i.e., in the name of the autonomous rights of the Provincial Diet.

Soon the policy became crystallized in the Stanczyk program of the so-called Cracow party, the party of such men as Tarnowski, Popiel, Wodzicki, and Kozmian, and found its expression in the notorious "resolution" of the Galician Diet of September 28, 1868, which is a kind of Magna Carta of the "separation of Galicia." The resolution demanded such a broadening of the competence of the Provincial Diet that for the Central Parliament there remained only the most important all-monarchy matters; it completely abolished the central administration, handing it over exclusively to the crownland authorities, and in the end completely separating also the crownland judiciary. The state connection of Galicia with Austria was reduced here to such a flimsy shadow that sanguine minds, who did not yet know the flexibility of Polish nationalism, would be ready to see in this ideal program of federalism, "almost" national independence or at least a bold striving toward it. However, to prevent any such illusions, the Stanczyk party had announced its political credo and begun its public career in Austria not with the above program of federation but with the notorious address of the Diet of December 10, 1866, in which it proclaimed its classical formula: "Without fear of deserting the national idea and with faith in the mission of Austria we declare from the bottom of our hearts that we stand and wish to stand by Your Majesty." This was only a concise aphoristic formulation of the sanguinary crusade which the nobility party around *Przeglad Polski* [Polish Review] waged, after the January uprising, against the insurrection and the insurgents, against the "conspiracy," "illusions," "criminal attempts," "foreign revolutionary influences," "the excesses of social anarchy," liquidating with cynical haste the last period of our national movements under the slogan of "organic work" and public renunciation of any solidarity with Russian-dominated Poland. Federalism and political separatism were not in reality an expression of national aspirations but were, rather, their simple negation and their public renunciation. The other harmonious complement of the Stanczyk program of federation (read: separation) was opposition and obstruction in coalition with Czech and Moravian federalists and the German clerical-reactionary party against any liberal reforms in Austria: against the liberal communal law, against the liberal law concerning elementary schools, against the introduction of the law concerning direct elections by the people to the Central Parliament; on the other hand it supported the government in all reactionary projects, e.g., support of the military laws starting with Taaffe's Law, etc. This development has been coupled with extreme reaction also in provincial policies, the most glaring expression of which is the adamant opposition against the reform of elections to the Provincial Diet.

Finally, the third component of Galician federalism is the policy of the Polish nobility toward the Ruthenians. Quite analogous to the French federalists of Switzerland, the Galician advocates of a potential decentralization of the Austrian state have been strict centralists internally in relation to the Ruthenian population. The Galician nobility has from the beginning stubbornly combated the demand of autonomy for the Ruthenians, the administrative division of Galicia into

Eastern and Western, and the granting of equal status to the Ruthenian language and script along with the Polish language. The program of "separation" and federalism suffered a decisive defeat in Austria as early as 1873, when direct elections to the Central Parliament were introduced, and from then on the Stanczyk party, in keeping with its opportunistic principles, abandoned the policy of obstruction and acquiesced in Austrian centralism. However, Galician federalism from then on appears on the stage if not as a program of realistic politics then as a means of parliamentary maneuvers each time that serious democratic reforms are considered. The last memorable appearance of the program of "separating" Galicia in the public arena is connected with the struggle of the Galician nobility against the most recent electoral reform, against the introduction of universal and equal voting rights for the Vienna Parliament. And as if to put stronger emphasis on the reactionary content of the federalist program, the deputies of Austrian Social Democracy, in April 1906, voted unanimously against the motion concerning the separation of Galicia. At their head in his character as representative of the Austrian Workers' Party, a representative of the all-monarchy proletarian policy spoke and voted against the separation of Galicia: this was Mr. Ignacy Daszynski, who, as a leader in the three parts of the patriotic PPS, considers the separation of the Kingdom of Poland from Russia as his political program. The Austrian Social Democracy is a determined and open advocate of centralism, a conscious adherent of the state consolidation of Austria and consequently a conscious opponent of any separatist tendencies.

"The future of the Austrian state"—says Kautsky—"depends on the strength and influence of Social Democracy. Precisely because it is revolutionary, it is in this case a party upholding the state [*eine staatserhaltende Partei*] in this sense; although this sounds strange, one may apply to the Red revolutionary Social Democracy the words which half a century ago Grillparzer addressed to the hero of the Red Yellow reaction, General Radetzky: 'In your camp is Austria.' " [*"In deinem Lager ist Oesterreich"*].[2] Therefore, just as in the matter of the "separation" of Galicia, Austrian Social Democracy decisively rejects the program of the Czech federalists, that is, the separation of Bohemia. Kautsky writes:

> The growth of the idea of autonomy for Bohemia is only a partial manifestation of the general growth of reaction in all big states of the Continent. The program of "autonomy" would not yet make Bohemia an autonomous state. It would still remain a part of Austria. The Central Parliament would not be abolished by this. The most important matters (military affairs, customs, etc.) would remain in its competence. However, the separation of Bohemia would break the power of the Central Parliament, which today is very weak. It would break it not only in relation to the diets of the several nations but also in relation to the central government, on the model of the delegations. [The reference here is to delegations of Austria and Hungary which were elected by the Vienna and Budapest parliament and had as their task the arrangement of the so-called Austro-Hungarian compromise, that is, the mutual relationship or proportion contributed by both countries for the common expenses of the state and the settlement of certain matters affecting both.] The state council, that is, the Central Parliament of Austria, would have to be reduced to a miserable idol nodding its head to everything. The power of the central government in military and customs affairs, as well as foreign policy, would then become unrestricted. The separation of Bohemia would signify the strengthening of the rule of bourgeois peasant clericalism in the Alpine lands of the nobility and in Galicia; also that of the capitalist magnates in Bohemia. As long as these three strata must exercise their authority in the Central Parliament jointly, they

> cannot develop all their power because their interests are not identical; holding them together is no easy matter. Their strength will be increased if each of these strata can concentrate on a certain defined area. The clericals in Innsbrück and Linz, the Galician nobility in Cracow and Lemberg, the Bohemian Tories in Prague are more powerful separately than all together in Vienna. Just as in Germany, the reaction draws its strength from the particularism and weakness of the Central Parliament; here, just as there, giving one's moral support to particularism means working in favor of reaction. Here, just as there, we are obligated to resist strongly the present current tending to the weakening of the Central Parliament. [Kautsky ends with these words:] We must combat Bohemian states' rights [the program of separating off Bohemia] as a product of reaction and a means of its support. We must combat it since it means splitting the proletariat of Austria. The road from capitalism to socialism does not lead through feudalism. The program of separating off Bohemia is just as little a preliminary to the autonomy of peoples as anti-Semitism (that is, a unilateral struggle against Jewish capital) is a preliminary to Social Democracy.[3]

Where the remnants of feudalism have been preserved to this day in Europe, they are everywhere a protection of monarchy. In Germany, a striking manifestation of this is the fact that the unity of the Reich is based on a universal equal voting right to Parliament, while all German states taken individually have much more reactionary state constitutions, from Prussia, with its (as Bismarck expressed it) "most monstrous" tri-class electoral law, up to Mecklenburg, which is still in general a medieval state with a purely class constitution.

The city of Hamburg itself is an even more striking example if we believe that progress and democracy are connected with centralism, and reaction with particularism and federalism. The city of Hamburg, which forms three electoral districts of the German Reich, is represented in Parliament, on the basis of a universal voting right, exclusively by Social Democratic deputies. On the basis of the Constitution of the Reich as a whole, the Workers' Party is, therefore, in Hamburg, the unique ruling party. But the very same city of Hamburg, as a separate little state, on the basis of its distinction, separateness, introduced for itself a new electoral law even more reactionary than the one in force until now, which makes it almost impossible to elect Social Democrats to the Hamburg Diet.

In Austria–Hungary we see the same. On the one hand, a federal relationship between Hungary and Austria is an expression not of freedom and progress but of monarchical reaction because it is known that the Austro-Hungarian dualism is maintained only by the dynastic interest of the Hapsburgs, and Austrian Social Democracy clearly declared itself in favor of the complete dissolution of that federation and the complete separation of Hungary from Austria.

However, this position resulted by no means from the inclinations of Austrian Social Democracy for decentralization in general, but just the reverse: it resulted from the fact that a federal connection between Hungary and Austria is an obstacle to an even greater political centralization inside Austria for the purpose of restoring and consolidating the latter, and here the very same Social Democratic Party is an advocate of as close a union of the crownlands as possible, and an opponent of any tendencies to the separation of Galicia, Bohemia, Trieste, the Trentino, and so on. In fact, the only center of political and democratic progress in Austria is her central policy, a Central Parliament in Vienna which, in its development, reached a universal equal-voting right, while the autonomous Diets—Galician, Lower Austrian, Bohemian—are strongholds of the most savage reaction on the part of the nobility or bourgeoisie.

Finally, the last event in the history of federal relationships, the separation of Norway from Sweden, taken up in its time eagerly by the Polish social-patriotic parties (see the Cracow *Naprzód* [Forward]) as a joyous manifestation of strength and the progressiveness of separatist tendencies, soon changed into a new striking proof that federalism and state separations resulting from it are by no means an expression of progress or democracy. After the so-called Norwegian "revolutions," which consisted in the dethronement and the expulsion from Norway of the King of Sweden, the Norwegians quietly elected another king for themselves, having even formally, in a popular ballot, rejected the project of introducing a republic. That which superficial admirers of all national movements and all semblances of independence proclaimed as a "revolution" was a simple manifestation of peasant and bourgeois particularism, a desire to possess for their own money a "king of their own" instead of one imposed by the Swedish aristocracy, and, therefore, a movement which had nothing in common whatever with a revolutionary spirit. At the same time, the history of the disintegration of the Swedish–Norwegian union again proved how far, even here, the federation had been an expression of purely dynastic interests, that is, a form of monarchism and reaction.

IV

The idea of federalism as a solution of the nationality question, and in general, an "ideal" of the political system in international relations, raised sixty years ago by Bakunin and other anarchists, finds at present refuge with a number of socialist groups in Russia. A striking illustration of that idea, as well as of its relation to the class struggle of the proletariat at the present time, is given by the congress of those federalist groups of all Russia held during the recent [1905] revolution and whose deliberations have been published in a detailed report.*

First of all, a characterization of the political *complexion* and of the "socialism" of these groups is interesting. In the Congress, there participated Georgian, Armenian, Byelorussian, Jewish, Polish, and Russian federalists. The Georgian Socialist Federalist Party operates mainly—according to its own report—not among the urban population but in the countryside, because only there does there exist in a compact mass the national Georgian element; these number about 1.2 million and are concentrated in the gubernias of Tiflis, Kutai, and partially, Batum. This party is almost completely recruited from peasants and petty gentry. "In its striving for an independent regulation of its life"—declares the delegate of the Georgian Socialist Federalist Party—"without counting on the centralist bureaucracy, whether this be absolutistic or constitutional or even social-democratic (!), the Georgian peasantry will probably find sympathy and help on the part of that petty Georgian gentry which lives on the land and by the size of its possessions and also its way of life differs little from the peasantry." Therefore, the party considers that "even independently of considerations of a basic (!) nature, merely the practical conditions of Georgian agriculture demand the treatment of the agrarian question as a class question, peasant or gentry only as an over-all national question, as a social (!) problem, as a problem of work(!)." Starting with these assumptions, the Georgian Federalists, in harmony with the Russian Social Revolutionaries, strive for the "socialization of land which is to be achieved under the rule of the capitalistic or bourgeois system." A beautiful addition to this program is the reservation that "socialization" cannot be extended to orchards, vineyards and other "special cultiva-

* See the *Proceedings of the Russian National Socialist Parties, April 16-20, 1907,* Knigoi Izdatielstvo, Sejm (St. Petersburg: 1908).

tions," or to farms, because these are areas "demanding a certain contribution of work and material means which cannot be returned in one year or in several years" and which "would be difficult for a Georgian peasant to renounce." Consequently, there remains private property for "cultivations," and "socialism" for grain-planting—of which there is little in the Caucasus—as well as for dunes, marginal lands, bogs, and forests.

The main thing on which the Socialist Federalists put emphasis is the reservation that the agricultural question in Georgia should be decided not in a constituent assembly nor in a central parliament, but only in autonomous national institutions, because "however life will decide this question, in principle, only this is unquestionable, that the land in a Georgian territory should belong first of all to the Georgian people." The question, how it happens that the "socialist" party is joined, en masse, by the petty gentry and bourgeoisie, the delegates of the Georgian Federalists explained by saying that this happens only because "there is no other party which would formulate the demands of these strata."

The Armenian Revolutionary Federation, that is, Dashnaktsutyun, founded at the beginning of the 1890s for the purpose of liberating the Armenians from Turkey, was exclusively concerned with "militarizing the people," i.e., the preparation of fighting detachments and armed expeditions into Turkey, the import of weapons, the direction of attacks on Turkish troops, etc. Only recently, at the beginning of the current century, the Armenian Revolutionary Federation expanded its activity into the Caucasus and assumed at the same time a social aspect. The cause for the revolutionary outburst of the movement and the terroristic action in the Caucasus was the confiscation of the estates of the Armenian clergy for the [tsarist] treasury in 1903. Besides its main "combat" action, the party began, against the background of those events, a propaganda among the rural population in the

Caucasus as well as a struggle against tsardom. The agrarian program of Dashnaktsutyun demands the expropriation of gentry estates without compensation, and surrendering them to the communes for equal distribution. This reform is to be based on the still rather general communal property in the central part of the Transcaucasus. Recently, there arose a "young" trend among the Armenian Federalists maintaining that the Dashnaktsutyun party is simply a bourgeois, nationalistic organization of a rather doubtful socialistic aspect–an organization linking within itself completely heterogeneous social elements, and in its activity and action on completely heterogeneous sociopolitical territory, such as Turkey on the one side and the Caucasus on the other. This party recognizes, according to its own report, the principle of federalism both as a basis of nation-wide relations and the basis on which should be thoroughly reconstructed the conditions in the Caucasus, and finally, as an organizing principle for the party.

A Byelorussian organization was formed in 1903 under the name of the Byelorussian Revolutionary Hromada. Its cardinal programmatic demand was separation from Russia, and in the sphere of economics, the nationalization of the land. In 1906, this program underwent a revision and from then on the party has been demanding a federal republic in Russia, with territorial autonomy for Lithuania and a diet in Vilna, as well as a nonterritorial national cultural autonomy for the remaining nationalities inhabiting Lithuania, while on the agrarian question the following demands were adopted: lands held by the treasury, by the church, and by the monasteries, as well as big landed property above eighty to one hundred dessiatins are to be confiscated and turned into a land fund out of which, first of all, the landless and small peasants should be supplied on the basis of hereditary property, with the aim of eliminating pauperism as well as developing the productive forces of the country. The socialization of land cannot yet be mentioned because of the low intellectual level of the Byelorussian peasant. Thus, the task of the party is the creation and maintenance of a peasant farm in a normal size of eight dessiatins, as well as the consolidation of lands. Further, forests, bodies of water, and bogs are to be nationalized. Hromada carries on its activity among the Byelorussian peasants who inhabit, to the number of about seven millions, the gubernias of Vilna, Minsk, Grodno, and part of Witebsk.

The Jewish Federalist group, "Sierp" ["The Sickle"], organized only a few years ago by Jewish dissidents from the Russian Social Revolutionary Party, demands nonterritorial autonomy for all nationalities in the Russian state; out of them would be created voluntary state political associations combining together into a state federation, in order to strive in that way for its ultimate goal, territorial (!) autonomy for the Jews. It directs its activity mainly to the organizing of Jewish workers in Witebsk, Ekaterinoslav, Kiev, etc., and it expects the implementation of its program to arise from the victory of the socialist parties in the Russian state.

It is superfluous to characterize the remaining two organizations, the PPS "revolutionary faction," and the Russian Party of Social Revolutionaries, since they are sufficiently known by origin and character.

Thus appears that Diet of Federalists cultivating at present that antiquated idea of federation rejected by the class movement of the proletariat. It is a collection of only petit bourgeois parties for whom the nationalist program is the main concern and the socialist program an addition; it is a collection of parties mainly representing—with the exception of the revolutionary fraction of the Polish Socialist Party and the Jewish Federalists—the chaotic aspirations of a peasantry in opposition, and the respective class proletarian parties that came into being with the revolutionary storm, in clear opposition to the bourgeois parties. In this collection of petit bourgeois elements, the party of the Russian terrorists is a trend, not only the oldest one, but also the one furthest left. The others manifest, much more clearly, that they have nothing in common with the class struggle of the proletariat.

The only common ground which links this variegated collection of nationalists has been the idea of federation, which all of them recognize as a basis of state and political, as well as party, relations. However, out of this strange harmony, antagonism arises immediately from all sides the moment the question turns to practical projects of realizing that common ideal. The Jewish Federalists bitterly complain of the "haughtiness" of the nations endowed by fate with a "territory" of their own, particularly the egoism of the Polish Social Patriots, who presented the greatest opposition to the project of nonterritorial autonomy; at the very same time, these Jewish nationalists questioned in a melancholy way whether the Georgian Federalists would admit any other nationality to their territory, which they claimed as the exclusive possession of the Georgian nationality. The Russian Federalists, on the other hand, accuse the Jewish ones, saying that, from the standpoint of their exceptional situation, they want to impose on all nationalities a nonterritorial autonomy. The Caucasian, Armenian, and Georgian Federalists cannot agree concerning the relationship of the nationalities in a future federal system, specifically on the question of whether other nationalities are to participate in the Georgian territorial autonomy, "or whether such counties as Akhalkalak, inhabited mainly by Armenians, or Barchabin, with a mixture of population, will form individual autonomous territories, or will create an autonomy for themselves according to the composition of their population." The Armenian Federalists, on their part, demand the exclusion of the city of Tiflis from the autonomous Georgian territory, inasmuch as it is a center primarily inhabited by Armenians. On the other hand, all the Georgian and Armenian Federalists recognize that at present, since the Tatar-Armenian slaughter, the

Tatars must be excluded from the federation of autonomous Caucasian peoples as "a nationality immature from the cultural point of view"! Thus, the conglomeration of nationalists agreeing unanimously to the idea of federation changes into as many contradictory interests and tendencies; and the "ideal" of federalism, which constitutes in the theoretical and superhistorical abstraction of anarchism the most perfect solution of all nationality difficulties, on the first attempt at its implementation appears as a source of new contradictions and antagonisms. Here it is strikingly proved that the idea of federalism allegedly reconciling all nationalities is only an empty phrase, and that, among the various national groups, just because they don't stand on a historical basis, there is no essentially unifying idea which would create a common ground for the settlement of contradictory interests.

But the same federalism separated from the historical background demonstrates its absolute weakness and helplessness not only in view of the nationality antagonisms in practice but also in view of the nationality question in general. The Russian Congress had as its main theme an evaluation and elucidation of the nationality question and undertook it unrestricted by any "dogmas" or formulae of the "narrow doctrine of Marxism." What elucidation did it give to one of the most burning questions of present political life? "Over the whole history of mankind before the appearance of socialism"—proclaimed the representative of the Social Revolutionary Party in his speech at the opening of the Congress—"one may place as a motto the following words from the Holy Scripture: 'And they ordered him to say "shibboleth" and he said "sibboleth" and they massacred him at the ford of the river.' Indeed, the greatest amount of blood spilled in international struggle was spilled because of the fact that one nation pronounced 'shibboleth' and the other 'sibboleth.' " After this profound introduction from the philosophy of history, there followed a series of speeches maintained at the same level, and the debates about the nationality questions culminated in the memorandum of the Georgian Federalists, which proclaimed:

"In primitive times, when the main task of people was hunting wild animals as well as creatures like themselves, there were neither masters nor slaves. Equality in social relations was not violated; but later, when people came to know the cultivation of the soil, rather than killing and eating their captives they began to keep them in captivity. What, therefore, was the reason out of which slavery arose? Obviously not only material interests as such, but also this circumstance: that man was by his physical nature a hunter and a warrior(!). And despite the fact that man has already long since become an industrial animal, he is to this very day a predator, capable of tearing apart his neighbor for minor material considerations. This is the source of unending wars and the domination of classes. Naturally the origin of class domination was influenced also by other causes, for instance, man's ability to become accustomed to dependence. But undoubtedly if man were not a warrior, there would be no slavery." There follows a bloody picture of the fate of the nationalities subject to tsardom and then again a theoretical elucidation: "Somebody may tell us that bureaucratic rule rages not only in the borderlands but in Russia itself. From our point of view this is completely understandable. A nation subjugating other nations eventually falls into slavery itself. For instance, the more Rome expanded its domination, the more the plebeians were losing their freedom. Another example: during the great French Revolution the military victories of the Republican Army annihilated the fruit of the revolution—the Republic(!). The Russians themselves enjoyed incomparably greater freedom before they united in one powerful state, that is, at the time of the rule of the separate princes." Thus, the memorandum ends its historio-philosophical lecture; freedom does not agree with the clatter of arms. Conquest was the main cause which brought into being both slavery as well as the rule of some social classes over others.

This is all that the Federalists of the present time are able to say about the nationality question. It is literally the same phraseology from the standpoint of "justice," "fraternity," "morality," and similar beautiful things which already, sixty years ago, was proclaimed by Bakunin. And just as the father of anarchism was blind to the Revolution of 1848, its inner springs, its historical tasks, the present last of the Mohicans of federalism in Russia stand helpless and powerless before the revolution in the tsarist system.

The idea of federation, by its nature and historical substance reactionary, is today a pseudo-revolutionary sign of petit bourgeois nationalism, which constitutes a reaction against the united revolutionary class struggle of the proletariat in the entire Empire.

Notes

1. Friedrich Engels and Karl Marx, *Revolution und Konterrevolution in Deutschland* (Weimar: 1949), pp. 77, 78-79.
2. *Die Neue Zeit, 1897–1898,* Vol. I, p. 564.
3. *Die Neue Zeit, 1898–1899,* pp. 293, 296, 297, 301.

4. Centralization and Autonomy

We have noted the general centralizing tendency of capitalism in the bourgeois states. But local autonomy also grows simultaneously out of the objective development and out of the needs of bourgeois society.

Bourgeois economy requires as great a uniformity as possible in legislation, the judiciary, administration, the school system, etc., in the entire area of the state, and as far as possible, even in international relations. But the same bourgeois economy, in carrying out all these functions, demands accuracy and efficiency quite as much as uniformity. The centralism of the modern states is of necessity connected with a bureaucratic system. In the medieval state, in a serf economy, public functions were connected with landed property; these were the "concrete rights," a kind of land tax. The feudal lord of estates was at the same time and by the same token a civil and criminal judge, the head of the police administration, the chief of military forces in a certain territory, and collector of taxes. These functions connected with owning real estate were, like the land itself, the object of transactions, gift, sale, inheritance, and so on. Absolutism, which increased toward the end of the Middle Ages, paving the way for capitalism by its struggle against feudal dispersal of state authority, separated public functions from land ownership and created a new social category for the execution of these functions, namely crown officials. With the development of modern capitalistic states, the performance of public functions passed completely into the hands of paid hirelings. This social group increased numerically and created the modern state bureaucracy. On the one hand, the transfer of public functions to hired personnel—completely devoted to their work and directed by one powerful political center—corresponds with the spirit of bourgeois economy, which is based on specialization, division of labor, and a complete subordination of manpower to the purpose of maintaining the social mechanism; on the other hand, however, the centralist bureaucracy has serious drawbacks hampering the economy.

Capitalist production and exchange are characterized by the highest sensitivity and elasticity, by the capacity and even the inclination for constant changes in connection with thousands of social influences which cause constant fluctuations and undulations in market conditions, and in the conditions of production themselves. As a result of these fluctuations, the bourgeois economy requires subtle, perceptive administration of public services such as the centralized bureaucracy, with its rigidity and routine, is not able to afford. Hence, already as a corrective to the centralism of the modern state, there develops, in bourgeois society, along with legislation by representative assemblies, a natural tendency toward local autonomy, giving the possibility of a better adjustment of the state apparatus to social needs. For local autonomy takes into account the manifold variety of local conditions and also brings about a direct influence and cooperation of society through its public functions.

However, more important than the deficiencies inseparable from the rule of bureaucracy, by which the theory of bourgeois liberalism usually explains the necessity for autonomy, there is another circumstance. The capitalist economy brought forth, from the moment of the inception of mass factory production, a whole series of entirely new social needs imperiously demanding satisfaction. Above all, the penetration of big capital and the system of hired labor, having undermined and ruined the entire traditional social structure, created a plague unknown before, namely mass unemployment and pauperization for the proletariat. Since capital needs a reserve labor force and since public security must be preserved, society, in order to hold in check the proletarian masses deprived of means of livelihood and employment, cannot but take care of them. In this way, modern public welfare comes into being as a social function within the framework of capitalistic production.

The agglomeration of big masses of industrial proletarians in the worst material conditions in the modern industrial centers created for the adjacent bourgeois classes a threat of infectious diseases and brought about another urgent social need: public concern for health, and in connection with this, the whole management of the sewage system and supply of water as well as public regulation of building construction.

The requirements of capitalist production and of bourgeois society brought about for the first time the problem of popular education. The system of schools accessible to broad masses, not only in the big cities but also in the provinces and among the rural population, brought the idea that the creation and regulation of schools was a public function.

The movement of goods and persons in the whole area of the state as a normal phenomenon and a condition of the existence of capitalist production brought forth the need for constant public conern about roads and means of communication, not only in the form of trunk-line railroads and maritime traffic, important from the point of view of military strategy and world trade, but also of vehicular roads, highways, bridges, river navigation, and subsidiary railroads. The creation and maintenance of these indispensable conditions of internal communication became one of the most urgent economic needs of bourgeois society.

Finally, public safety of persons and property as a matter of general concern and social need is also a clearly modern product, connected with the requirements of capitalist economy. In medieval society, safety was guaranteed by some special areas of legal protection: for the rural population, the area of the respective feudal dominion, for the burghers, the protective walls of the city and the statutes and "freedoms" of each city separately. The knights were supposed to guarantee their own safety. Modern society, based on the production of goods, needs safety of persons and property as a universal social guarantee for everybody in the entire territory of the state without discrimination. The central government cannot satisfy all these needs. There are some the government cannot take care of at all, like the local affairs in the remote parts of the country; understandably, the government tends to transmit the expenses of managing such affairs to the local population.

Local autonomy, therefore, originates in all modern states very early, above all in the form of transferring the material burden of a series of social functions to the population itself.

On the other hand, capitalism stratifies and links into one economic and social organism the biggest state areas, and, to a certain extent, the entire world. At the same time, however, in order to promote its interests, to perfect and integrate the bourgeois economy, capitalism splits the [autonomous] states and creates new centers, new social organisms, as, for instance, big cities and provincial regions, etc. A contemporary modern city is tied by numberless economic and political bonds not only to the state but to the entire world. The accumulation of people, the development of municipal transportation and economy, turns the city into a separate small organism; its needs and public functions are more numerous and varied than were those of a medieval city, which with its handicraft production, was almost entirely independent both economically and politically.

The creation of different states and of new urban areas provided the framework for the modern municipal government—a product of new social needs. A municipal or provincial government is necessary in order to comply with the needs of these specific social organisms into which capitalism, following the economic principle of the contradictory interests of the city and the village, transformed the city on the one hand and the village on the other. Within the framework of the special capitalistic connection between industry and agriculture, that is, between city and village, within the framework of the close mutual dependence of their production and exchange, a thousand threads linking the daily interests of the population of each major city with the existence of the population of the neighboring villages there goes, in a natural way, a provincial autonomy as in France—departmental, cantonal, or communal. Modern autonomy in all these forms is by no means the abolition of state centralism but only its supplementation; together they constitute the characteristic form of the bourgeois state.

Besides political unification, state sovereignty, uniform legislation, and centralized state government, local autonomy became, in all these countries, one of the basic policy issues both of the liberals and of the bourgeois democracy. Local autonomy, growing out of the modern bourgeois system in the manner indicated, has nothing in common with federalism or particularism handed down from the medieval past. It is even its exact opposite. While the medieval particularism or federalism constitutes a separation of the political functions of the state, modern autonomy constitutes only an adaptation of the concentrated state functions to local needs and the participation in them of the people. While, therefore, communal particularism or federalism in the spirit of

Bakunin's ideal is a plan for splitting the territory of a big state into small areas partly or completely independent of each other, modern autonomy is only a form of democratization of a centralized big state. The clearest illustration of this point is the history of modern autonomy, which grew in the chief modern states on the grave of the former particularism and in clear opposition to it.

II

State administrative and bureaucratic centralism was initiated in France by absolutism during the *ancien régime.* By the suppression of communal independence in the cities, especially in Paris, by subjugating the largest feudal possessions and incorporating them into the crownlands, finally by concentrating administration in the hands of the state council and royal supervisors, there was created already in the time of Richelieu a powerful apparatus of state centralism. The former independent feudal fiefs were reduced to the condition of provinces; some of them were governed by assemblies whose power, however, was more and more of an illusion.

The Great Revolution undertook its work in two directions. On the one hand, continuing the tendency toward political centralization, it completely abolished the territorial remnants of feudalism; on the other, in place of the provincial administration of bureaucrats assigned by the government, it created a local administration with representatives elected by the people. The Constituent Assembly wiped from the map of France the historical division of the country into provinces, as well as the medieval division into administratively diverse cities and villages. On the *tabula rasa* which was thus left the Constituent Assembly, following the idea of Siéyès, introduced a new, simple, geometrical division into square departments. The departments, in turn, are subdivided into *arrondissements,* cantons, and communes, each governed by a body elected by public vote. The constitution of the Directory of the Year III made certain changes in details, maintaining however, the foundations of the great reform effected by the Constituent Assembly; it was this reform which had given to modern history an epoch-making model of modern autonomy, which grew up on the grave of feudal decentralization and was imbued with an entirely new idea, namely, democratic representation by election.

There followed a hundred years of change in the history of autonomy in France. This history and the whole political fate of democracy in the country oscillated, in a characteristic manner, between two poles. The slogan of the aristocratic, monarchical reaction is, throughout this time, decentralization, in the sense of returning to the independence of the former historical provinces, while the slogan of liberalism and democracy is close adherence to political centralism and at the same time, the rights of representation of the local population, especially in the commune. The first blow to the work of the Revolution in that field was dealt by Napoleon, who was crowned by the so-called Statute of Pluvois 28 of the year VIII (Feb. 17, 1800), his *coup d'état* of 18th Brumaire. This statute, taking advantage of the general confusion and chaos caused especially in the provinces by the counter-revolution during the time of the Directory, for which the democratic autonomy was blamed, hastily compressed the work of the Revolution into the framework of bureaucracy. Maintaining the new territorial division of France in line with political centralism, Napoleon abolished, by one stroke of the pen, any participation of the people in local autonomy and gave over the entire power into the hands of officials assigned by the central government: prefect, subprefect, and mayor. In the department, the Napoleonic prefect was, in a considerable measure, a resurrection of the supervisor from the happy times of the *ancien régime.* Napoleon expressed this reversion with characteristic frankness when he said, *"Avec mes préfets, mes gens d'armes et mes prêtres, je ferai tout ce que je voudrai."* ["With the help of my prefects, police, and priests, I will do whatever I like."]

The Restoration kept the system of its predecessor in general; according to a current expression, "The Bourbons slept on a bed that had been made by Napoleon." However, as soon as the aristocratic emigration returned home its battle cry was decentralization, a return to the system of the provinces. The notorious *chambre introuvable* had scarcely assembled when one of the extreme Royalists, Barthe Lebastrie, at a meeting of January 13, 1816, solemnly announced the indispensability of decentralization. On many later occasions the leaders of the right, Corbière, De Bonald, La Bourdonnaye, de Villèle, Duvergier de Hauranne, argued "the impossibility of reconciling the monarchy with republican uniformity and equality." Under this standard, the aristocracy fought simply for a return to its former position in the provinces from the economic and political point of view. At the same time, it denounced political centralism as "a ground for revolution, a hotbed of innovations and agitation." Here we already hear literally the same arguments under cover of which the right, half a century later, tried to mobilize the provincial reaction against the revolutionary Paris Commune.

Therefore, the first timid attempt at the reform of the local administration with application of the principle of election, that is, the project of Martignaque, called forth a storm in the honorable pre-July assembly and was rejected clearly as the "beginning of revolution." The enraged representatives of the landed aristocracy demanded only the broadening of the competence of the prefect and subprefect and making them dependent on the central authority. However, the days of the Restoration were already numbered and the defeat of Martignaque's project became the prologue of the July Revolution. The July Monarchy, which was only an improved edition of the Restoration in the spirit of the rule of the richest bourgeoisie, introduced insignificant changes in local autonomy; it provided a shadow of the system of election. The law of 1831 on the communes and the law of 1833 on the departments gave the right of suffrage for municipal and departmental councils to a small minority of the most highly taxed as well as to the bureaucracy and bourgeois intelligentsia, without, however, any broadening of the attributes of these councils.

The revolution of 1848 restored the work of its great predecessor, introduced universal suffrage for departmental councils, and made the meetings of the councils public. After the June days, the party of the aristocratic-clerical right violently demanded the return to decentralization as a weapon against the hydra of socialism. In 1849–1851, the departmental councils unanimously demanded the extension of their competence and extraordinary powers in case of civil war, for use against Paris. Thiers, at that time still a liberal, on the contrary, insisted on centralism as the most certain preventive means against socialism. (The very same Thiers, it is true, in 1871, himself waved the banner of federalism and decentralization to mobilize the provinces against the Paris Commune.) The Second Republic, in liquidating the work of the February Revolution, prepared in 1851 a project for the reform of local administration which restored completely the system of Napoleon I, with an all-powerful prefect, and in this way built here, as in general, a bridge on which Napoleon III entered. The latter undertook an even more thorough revision of the February achievements, put local administration even further back than the reforms of Napoleon I, and abolished the openness of the meetings of the departmental councils and their right to elect their own cabinet; from then on the government appointed mayors quite arbitrarily, i.e., not from within the communal council. Finally,

Napoleon III expanded the power of the prefects (by the laws of 1852 and 1861) to such an extent that he made them completely independent of the government. These omnipresent departmental satraps, dependent directly on Louis Napoleon, became, by virtue of their function of "directors" of elections to Parliament, the main pillars of the Second Empire.

The course of the above history until the beginning of the Second Empire was characterized by Marx in broad strokes in his *The Eighteenth Brumaire of Louis Bonaparte* in the following way:

> This executive power with its enormous bureaucratic and military organization, with its ingenious state machinery, embracing wide strata, with a host of officials numbering half a million, besides an army of another half-million, this appalling parasitic body, which enmeshes the body of French society like a net and chokes all its pores, sprang up in the days of the absolute monarchy, with the decay of the feudal system, which it helped to hasten. The seignorial privileges of the landowners and towns became transformed into so many attributes of the state power, the feudal dignitaries into paid officials, and the motley pattern of conflicting medieval plenary powers into the regulated plan of a state authority whose work is divided and centralized as in a factory. The first French Revolution, with its task of breaking all separate local, territorial, urban, and provincial powers in order to create the civil unity of the nation, was bound to develop what the absolute monarchy had begun: centralization, but at the same time the extent, the attributes, and the agents of governmental power. Napoleon perfected this state machinery. The Legitimist Monarchy and the July Monarchy added nothing but a greater division of labor, growing in the same measure as the division of labor within bourgeois society created new groups of in-

> terests, and, therefore, new material for state administration. Every *common* interest was straightaway severed from society, counterposed to it as a higher, *general* interest, snatched from the activity of society's members themselves and made an object of governmental activity, from a bridge, a schoolhouse, and the communal property of a village community to the railways, the national wealth, and the national university of France. Finally, in its struggle against the revolution, the parliamentary republic found itself compelled to strengthen, along with the repressive measures, the resources and centralization of governmental power. All revolutions perfected this machine instead of smashing it. The parties that contended in turn for domination regarded the possession of this huge state edifice as the principal spoils of the victor.
>
> But under the absolute monarchy, during the first Revolution, under Napoleon, bureaucracy was only the means of preparing the class rule of the bourgeoisie. Under the Restoration, under Louis Philippe, under the parliamentary republic, it was the instrument of the ruling class, however much it strove for power of its own.
>
> Only under the second Bonaparte does the state seem to have made itself completely independent. As against civil society, the state machine has consolidated its position so thoroughly that the chief of the Society of December 10 suffices for its head, an adventurer blown in from abroad, raised on the shield by a drunken soldiery, which he has bought with liquor and sausages, and which he must continually ply with sausage anew.[1]

The bureaucratic system of Napoleon III stirred up, especially toward the end of his reign, a strong opposition; this opposition comes through clearly in the statements of certain local administrations. The most striking example was the famous "Nancy Manifesto," which demanded extreme decentralization and under whose banner there rallied, in 1865, the whole legitimist-clerical opposition of the last phase of the

Empire. In the name of "freedom and order" the Manifesto demanded the liberation of the Commune from the supervision of the prefect, the appointment of the mayor from among the communal councilors, and the complete elimination of the *arrondissement* councils. On the other hand, the Manifesto demanded establishing cantonal councils and assigning to them the distribution of taxes, and finally, revising the boundaries between departments in the spirit of returning to the historical boundaries of the provinces and making the departments so revised independent concerning budget and the entire administration. This program, which aimed "to create preventive measures against revolutions," to save "freedom compromised by three revolutions," was accepted by all liberal conservatives of the Odilon Barrot type, and its advocates were headed by all the leaders of legitimism, i.e., the Bourbon party: Béchard, Falioux, Count Montalembert, and finally, the Pretender to the crown himself, Count Chambord, who, in his Manifesto of 1871 raised "administrative decentralization" to the role of a leading programmatic demand on the banner of the white lilies.

The Nancy program provoked sharp resistance from two sides—from the Empire and from the extreme Left, Republicans, Democrats, and Socialists. The latter, condemning the counter-revolutionary tendency of legitimist "decentralization," said, in the words of Victor Hugo: "Gentlemen, you are forging a chain and you say: 'This is freedom.' " "Therefore," they exclaimed, "we do not want your departmental councils as a legislative authority, nor your permanent departmental commissions as administrative authority in which a triple feudalism would prevail: the landed interest, the church, and industry, interested in keeping the people in ignorance and misery."* Under the pretext of freedom,

* Quoted in Avalov, *Decentralization and Self-government in France. Departmental Councils from the Reform of Bonaparte to Our Days,* p. 246.

France was to be handed over as prey to bishops, landed aristocracy, and factory owners—this is the opinion of contemporary democracy and socialists about the 1865 program. Louis Blanc was an especially inflexible opponent of decentralization, even to the departments, which he considered an artificial creation, though he fervently encouraged the widest self-government of the Commune as the natural historical organization and the foundation of the state.

In the revolutionary camp the advocates of decentralization, who indeed went further than the legitimists, were only adherents of Proudhon, such as Desmaret, who distinctly proclaimed the slogan of federalism both in application to "the United States of Europe" and to communes and districts within the state, as an ideal solution of the social question because it was a way of "annihilating power by dividing it." That the adherents of this anarchistic manner of disposing of the bourgeois state have not yet died out in France is proved by the book which appeared in 1899, *Le principe sauveur par un girondin,** in which the author sharply polemicizes against the centralism and homogeneity of the modern state, advocating, instead of departmental autonomy, the complete dissolution of the state in the spirit of federation. New voices in the same spirit have been heard even in later years—and enthusiasts for "historical" decentralization still crop up from the camp of the Royalists, as is demonstrated by the legitimist pamphlet from the time of the Dreyfus affair, *La décentralization et la monarchie nationale.*

The opposition between the views of the contemporary socialists and the anarchistic Proudhon was formulated as early as 1851 by Louis Blanc in his pamphlet, *La République une et indivisible,* in which in a thunderous voice he warned the republic against the danger of federalism, opposing to the

* Cited by Avalov, p. 228.

antagonisms of thirty-seven thousand tiny parliaments "*la grande tradition montagnarde en fait de centralization politique,*" and "*une administration surveillée.*" As a matter of fact, France at that moment was less threatened by the danger of federalism than by its opposite: the *coup d'état* of Louis Bonaparte and the absolute rule of his prefects.

The same grouping of parties with regard to local administration was also reflected in the notorious national assembly in Bordeaux after the fall of the Empire. After the destruction of the Paris Commune the main question concerning decentralization was whether it could serve as a preventive against the revolutionary movements of the proletariat. First of all, the Third Republic hastened to expand the competence of the departments, equipping them—in accordance with the leading idea of reaction since the time of the Restoration—with special powers against the revolution. The so-called "Loi Tréveneuc" of February 15, 1872, bears the significant title "Loi relative au rôle éventuel des conseils généraux dans des circonstances exceptionnelles." On the other hand, the powers of the communes were, after a temporary expansion, again restricted: whereas in 1871 the communal councils had received the power of electing their mayor, after three years they were again deprived of this right, and the government of the Third Republic appointed thirty-seven thousand mayors through its prefects, thus showing itself a faithful exponent of the monarchical traditions.

However, in the foundation of the Third Republic there occurred certain social changes which, despite all external obstacles, pushed the matter of local autonomy on to completely new paths. Although the independence of the urban and rural communes might have been abhorrent to the bourgeois reaction, intimidated by the great traditions of the Paris Commune from 1793 to 1871, it eventually became an indispensable need, especially since the inception of big industry under the wings of the Second Empire. It was then that railroads began to be built on a large scale. The artificially fostered and protected big industry not only flourished in Paris but in the fifties and sixties it spread into the provinces and suburban areas where capitalism sought cheap factory sites and cheap labor. Enterprises, industrial centers, financial fortunes mushroomed in the hothouse temperature of the Empire, suppressing small industry and introducing mass factory labor of women and children. The Paris Stock Exchange occupied second place in Europe. Together with this explosion of "original accumulation," as yet unbridled by any protective law—there was still no factory inspection—or by labor organization and struggle, there took place in France an unparalleled accumulation of mass poverty, disease, and death. Suffice it to mention that there were cases when female factory workers were paid one sou, i.e., five centimes per day, in a period of general unparalleled high prices of the prime necessities of life.* The short period of this exploiting economy made bourgeois society painfully aware of the lack of any public activity to prevent glaring poverty, infectious diseases, danger to life and property on public roads, etc. As early as 1856, much was written and spoken about the necessity of an official inquiry concerning pauperism in France. In 1858, such an inquiry "confidentially" ordered by the government predictably came to naught.

The state of public education corresponded more or less with these economic conditions. School courses for adults, subsidized by the government under Louis Philippe by the tiny sum of 478 francs on the average annually, were, during the Empire, deprived of this subsidy and neglected. A certain historian described the state of elementary schools in 1863 as follows:

* This fact is quoted by G. Weill, *Histoire du mouvement social en France* (1904), p. 12.

> Thousands of communes are without schools for girls; villages are deprived of any schools at all; a large number of others stay briefly in school and do not learn anything useful; there are no schools for adults and not a single library in the villages; the annual figures show that there is more than 27 percent illiteracy; that living conditions of the male and female teachers are miserable; that 5000 female teachers receive less than 400 francs annual wages, some receive seventy-five francs per year. Not a single one is entitled to retirement pay. Not a single male teacher enjoys a retirement pay which would assure him of one franc daily subsistence.*

Among the workers in Paris, the inquiry ordered by the Chamber of Commerce in 1860 ascertained that fifty thousand, i.e., about 13 percent of the working population, was completely illiterate. The Third Republic, whose mission it was to build a durable home for the bourgeoisie and first of all to liquidate the bankrupt estate taken over from the Empire, found itself faced with a number of new tasks: military reform, and in connection with this, a health reform; also a reform, or rather creation of public education; reform of transportation, completely neglected by the Empire, which was solely occupied with decorating and reforming Paris to turn it into a model capital of the Monarchy. Moreover, the Third Republic faced the task of acquiring means for these reforms. This meant an increase of taxes. However, these went primarily for military expenditures, for colonial policy, and especially for the maintenance of the bureaucratic apparatus. Without the participation of the local population, above all of the communes, the Third Republic would never have been able to solve these tasks.

At the same time, big industry's revolutionizing of conditions under the Empire completely changed the role of the department. When Louis Blanc, in the national assembly in

* Ibid., p. 11.

1871, declared that the department is an artificial product of administrative geometry, this was doubtless an anachronistic view. Indeed, in their beginning, emerging from the hands of the constituent assembly, the departments were an entirely "free improvisation" of the genius of the Revolution, a simple network of symmetrical figures on the map of France; and it was exactly in this abolition of all historical boundaries of the provinces that the powerful innovating thought, that great *"tradition montagnarde"* consisted, which, on the ruins of the medieval system, created a politically unified modern France. For decades, during the Restoration and later, the departments did not have any life of their own; they were used by the central government only as branch offices, as the sphere of action of the clerk-prefect whose only palpable expression was the obligatory *"hôtels de préfecture."* However, in modern France, new local needs have brought, in the course of time, new institutions surrounding these fortresses of the central bureaucracy. The new "departmental interests" which have gained increasing recognition are centered around shelters, hospitals, schools, local roads, and the procurement of "additional centimes" necessary to meet the costs.

The originally empty framework of the departments, drawn on the grave of the medieval particularism of the provinces, became in the course of time, through the development of bourgeois France, filled with new social content: the local interests of capitalism. The local administration of France by all-powerful prefects could suffice in the second half of the nineteenth century only for the artificial maintenance of the Empire. The Third Republic was eventually forced, in its own interests, to admit the local population to participation in this administration and to change the communes and departments from exclusive instruments of the central government into organs of democratic autonomy.

However, this shift could be effected only within the Third Republic. In the same way that the republican form of government was consolidated in France ultimately thanks only to circumstances which permitted the social nucleus of this clearly bourgeois political form to be husked from its ideological cocoon, from the illusion of "social republic" created by three revolutions in the course of almost half a century, so the local self-government had first to be liberated from the traditional ideology hostile to it. As late as the 1871 National Assembly, some advocates of liberalism abhorred the "reactionary" idea of autonomy which they persistently identified with feudal decentralization. The Monarchist, d'Haussonville, warned his party, reminding it that already during the Great Revolution the appearance of adhering to federalism was sufficient to send people to the guillotine, while Duvergier de Hauranne declared that France was faced with a dilemma: either uniform administration represented in each department by a prefect, or a federation of autonomous departments. These were the last reverberations of an opinion which weighed on people's minds for three-quarters of a century. Only when, with the fall of the Second Empire and the triumph of the Third Republic, the attempts of the aristocratic clerical reaction were defeated once and for all and the phantom of the federalism of the "historic provinces" was relegated to the realm of disembodied spirits did the idea of the relative independence of the departments cease to give an impression of federalism which frightened away bourgeois liberalism and democracy. And only when the last flicker of the Paris Commune revolutionary tradition died out in the cinders of the 1871 Commune and under the withered lawn of the "Confederates' Wall" ["Mur des Fédérés"] at Père Lachaise, where the corpses and half-dead bodies of the Commune's heroes were dumped, only then did the idea of communal self-government cease to be synonymous with social upheaval in the minds of the bourgeoisie, and the Phrygian cap cease to be the symbol of the City Hall. In a word, only when both departmental and communal autonomy were able to demonstrate their proper historical social value as genuinely modern institutions of the bourgeois state, growing out of its own needs and serving its interests, did the progressive development of local autonomy in France become possible. The organic statute of 1871, supplemented by the law of 1899, at last authorized representatives of departments chosen by general elections of the people to participate in the administration with a determining voice, and the statute of 1884 gave a similar right to the communal councils, returning to them the power of choosing their own mayor. Slowly and reluctantly, and only in recent times, the modern autonomy of France has liberated itself from the iron bonds of bureaucracy.

The history of self-government in England followed entirely different paths. Instead of the revolutionary changeover from medieval to modern society, we see here, on the contrary, an early compromise which has preserved to this day the old remnants of feudalism. Not so much by the shattering of old forms as by gradually filling them with new content, bourgeois England has carved out a place for itself in medieval England. And perhaps in no other area is this process so typical and interesting as in the area of local self-government. At first glance, and according to a commonplace expression, England appears as the country with the oldest local self-government, nay, as the cradle, the classical homeland of self-government, on which the liberalism of the continent sought to model itself. In reality, that age-old self-government of England belongs to the realm of myths, and the famous old English self-government has nothing in common with self-government in the modern sense. Self-government was simply a special system of local administration which originated at the time of the flowering of feudalism and bears all the hallmarks of its origin. The centers of that system are the county, a product of the feudal conditions after the Norman Conquest, and the parish, a product of medieval, ecclesiastical conditions; while the main person, the soul of the whole county administration, is the justice of the peace, an office created in the fourteenth century along with the three other county offices: the sheriff, conducting the elections to parliament, administering judgments in civil lawsuits, etc.; the coroner, conducting inquests in cases of violent death; and finally, the commander of the county militia. Among these officials only the secondary figure of the coroner is elective; all other officers are appointed by the Crown from among the local landed aristocracy. Only landed proprietors with a specified income could be appointed to the office of justice of the peace. All these officers fulfilled their duties without remuneration, and the purely medieval aspect is further indicated by the fact that in their competence they combined judicial and executive power. The justice of the peace did everything in the county as well as in the parish, as we shall presently see. He ran the courts, assigned taxes, issued administrative ordinances, in a word, he represented in his person the whole competence of public authority entirely in accordance with the feudal attributions of the landed proprietor; the only difference here was his appointment by the Crown. The justice of the peace, once appointed, became an omnipotent holder of public power: justices of the peace were entirely independent of the central government, and in general, not responsible, because the old system of English self-government obviously knows nothing of another basic feature of modern administration: the judicial responsibility of officials and the supervision by the central authority over local offices. Any participation of the local population in this administration was out of the question. If, therefore, the ancient English self-government may be regarded as a kind of autonomy, this can be done only in the sense that it was a system of unrestricted autonomy of the landed aristocracy, who held in their hands the complete public power in the county.

The first undermining of this medieval system of administration coincides with the reign of Elizabeth, i.e., the period of that shattering revolution in rural property relations which inaugurated the capitalistic era in England. Violent expropriations of the peasantry by the aristocracy on the broadest scale, the supersession of agriculture by sheep-herding, the secularization of church estates which were appropriated by the aristocracy, all this suddenly created an immense rural proletariat, and in consequence, poverty, beggary, and public robbery. The first triumphal steps of capital shook the foundations of the whole society and England was forced to face a new threat–pauperism. There began a crusade against vagrancy, beggary, and looting, which extends in a bloodstained streak until the middle of the nineteenth century. Since, however, prisons, branding with hot irons, and even the gallows proved an entirely insufficient medicine against the new plague, summary convictions came into being in England and also "public philanthropy"; next to the gallows at the crossroads arose the parish workhouse. The modern phenomenon of mass pauperism was the first problem transcending the powers and means of the medieval system of administration as carried out by the self-government of the aristocracy. The solution adopted was to shift the new burden to new shoulders–of the middle classes, the wealthy bourgeoisie. Now the mold-covered church parish was called to a new role–care of the poor. In the peculiar English administration, the parish is not only a rural but also an urban organization, so that to this day the parish system overlaps the modern administrative network in the big cities, creating a great chaos of competences.

At the end of the sixteenth century, a tax for the poor was introduced in the parish, and this tax gradually became the cornerstone of the tax system of the commune. The poor rates grew from £900,000 sterling at the end of the seventeenth century to £7,870,801 sterling in 1881. The collection and administration of these funds, the organization of assistance and workhouses, called forth a new organization of the communal office; and to it there also fell presently another important public function which was likewise caused by the needs of the nascent capitalist economy: supervision of roads. This organization also comprised, from then on, besides the rector who was at the head and two church wardens elected by the commune, two overseers of the poor, designated by the justice of the peace, and one surveyor of the highways, also designated by the justice of the peace. As we see, this was still the use of the old self-government apparatus for modern purposes. The landed aristocracy in the persons of the justices of the peace preserved power in their hands; only the material burden fell on the bourgeoisie. The commune had to carry the burden of the poor tax; however, it didn't have any voice in the apportionment of the tax. The latter function was an attribute of the justice of the peace and of the communal overseers subject to him.

In such a state the local administration survived until the nineteenth century. A few attempts at admitting the population to participation in this administration were undertaken at the beginning of that century but came to nothing.

In the meantime, capitalism in England entered new paths; big machine industry celebrated its triumphal entry and undertook an assault on the old fortress of self-government, which the crumbling structure could not withstand.

The violent growth of factory industry at the end of the eighteenth and the beginning of the nineteenth century caused a complete upheaval in the conditions of England's social life. The immense influx of the rural proletariat to the cities soon brought about such a concentration of people and such a housing shortage in the industrial cities that the workers' districts became abhorrent slums, dark, stinking, filthy, plague-ridden. Sickness among the population assumed terrifying proportions. In Scotland and Ireland an outbreak of typhoid took place regularly after each price increase and each industrial crisis. In Edinburgh and Glasgow, for instance, as stated by Engels in his classic work, *The Condition of the Working Class in England in 1844,* in the year 1817, 6,000 persons fell ill; in 1826 and 1837, 10,000 each; in 1842, in Glasgow alone, 32,000, i.e., 12 percent of the entire population. In Ireland, in 1817, 39,000 persons fell ill with typhoid, in 1819, 60,000; in the main industrial cities of Counties Cork and Limerick, one-seventh and one-fourth respectively of the entire population fell victim in those years to the epidemic. In London and Manchester, malaria was endemic. In the latter city, it was officially stated that three-quarters of the population needed medical help every year, and mortality among children up to five reached, in the industrial city of Leeds in 1832, the terrifying figure of 5,286 out of a population of 100,000. The lack of hospitals and medical help, housing shortages, and undernourishment of the proletariat became a public threat.

In no less a degree, the intellectual neglect of the mass of the people became a public plague when big industry, having concentrated immense crowds of the proletariat under its command, made them a prey of spiritual savages. The textile industry especially, which was the first to introduce mass labor of women and children at the lowest age and which made impossible any home education, however rudimentary, made the filling of this gap, i.e., the creation of elementary schools, a public need. However, the state performed these tasks to a minimal degree. At the beginning of the fourth decade [of the century], out of the budget of England amounting to £55 million, public education is allotted the ridiculous sum of £40,000. Education was left mainly to private initiative, especially of the church, and became mostly an instrument of bigotry and a weapon of sectarian struggle. In Sunday schools, the only ones accessible to working-class children, the latter were often not even taught reading and writing, as occupations unworthy of Sunday; while in the private schools, as was demonstrated by a parliamentary inquiry, the teachers themselves often did not know how to read or write. In general, the picture revealed by the famous Children Employment Commission showed the new capitalistic England as a scene of ruin and destruction, a wreckage of the entire antiquated, traditional, social structure. The great social reform was accomplished for the purpose of establishing tolerable living conditions for the new host, i.e., for the capitalistic bourgeoisie. The elimination of the most threatening symptoms of pauperism, the provision of public hygiene, elementary education, etc. became an urgent task. However, this task could be achieved only when both in state policy and in the entire administration the exclusive rule of the landed aristocracy was abolished and yielded to the rule of the industrial bourgeoisie. The election reform of 1832, which broke the political power of the Tories, is also the date from which begins self-government in England in the modern sense, i.e., self-government based on the participation of the population in the local administration, and on paid, responsible officials in the role of executor of its will under the supervision and control of the central authority. The medieval division of the state into counties and parishes corresponded to the new grouping of the population and local needs and interests as little as the medieval offices of the justice of the peace and parish councils. But while the revolutionary French liberalism swept from the country the historic provinces and in their place erected a homogeneous France with new administrative divisions, the conservative English liberalism created only a new administrative network—inside, beside, and through the old divisions, without formally abolishing them. The peculiarity of English self-government consists in the fact that, unable to utilize the completely inadequate framework of traditional self-government, it created a new kind of base: special communal associations of the population for each of the basic functions of self-government.

Thus, the law of 1834 establishes new "poor law unions" comprising several parishes whose population jointly elects, on the basis of a six-class electoral law, in accordance with the taxes paid, a separate board of guardians for each union. This body decides the whole matter of welfare, building of workhouses, issuing doles, etc.; it also hires and pays the officials who carry out its decisions. The old office of the parish overseer of the poor changed from an honorary to a paid one, and was reduced to the function of imposing and collecting taxes assigned by the board.

According to the same model, but quite independently, the law of 1847 created a new, broad organization to take care of public health and supervision of buildings, cleanliness of streets and houses, water supply, and food marketing. Also for this purpose new associations of the local population with representatives elected by it were established. On the basis of the Public Health Act of 1875, England—with the exception of the capital—is divided into urban and rural sanitary districts. The organ of representation is, in the urban districts, the city council; in the boroughs, special local boards of health; and in the rural districts health is supervised by the board of guardians. All these boards decide all matters pertaining to health and hire salaried officers who carry out the resolutions of the board.

The administration of local transportation also followed the same lines but independently of the two bodies mentioned above. For this purpose, highway districts were created, composed of several parishes whose population elects separate highway boards. In many rural districts, transportation is the concern of the local board of health, or the board of guardians which administers both transportation and poor relief. The highway boards or the boards of guardians decide about transportation enterprises and hire a paid district surveyor as the official carrying out their orders. And so the office of the former honorary highway surveyor vanished.

Finally, education was also entrusted to a special self-governing organization. Individual parishes, cities, and the capital form as many school districts. However, the board of education of the council of state has the right to combine several urban parishes into one district. Every district elects a school board entrusted with supervision of elementary education; it makes decisions concerning tuition-free schooling and the hiring of officials and teachers.

In this way there came into being, quite independently from the old organization of self-government, new, multiple, autonomous organizations which, precisely because they originated not by way of a bold revolutionary reform but as discrete patchwork, formed an extremely complex and involved system of often overlapping areas of competence. However, it is characteristic for the classic country of capitalist economy that the axis around which this modern self-government was crystallized—so far clearly on the lowest level in the rural commune—was the organization of public welfare, the organization for combating pauperism: the "poor" was, in England, to the middle of the nineteenth century, the official synonym for the worker, just as in a later time of orderly and modernized conditions, the sober expression "hands" became such a synonym. Beside this new organization of self-government, the old counties with their justices of the peace became a relic. The justice of the peace fell to the subordinate role of participant in the local council, and supervision of administration was left him only to a certain extent in matters of highways. When, however, the local administration passed from the hands of the justice appointed by the Crown to the elected representatives of the local population, the administrative decentralization by no means increased, but on the contrary, was eliminated. If, in the old days, the justice of the peace was an all-powerful master in the council, entirely independent of the central government, at present, the local government is subject on the one hand to the uniform parliamentary legislation, and on the other to strict control by the central administrative authorities. The Local Government Board specially created for this purpose controls the activity of the local boards of guardians and boards of health through visiting inspectors, while the school boards are subject to the board of education of the state council.

Also, urban self-government in England is a product of most recent times. Only slight traces survived to modern times of the communal independence of the medieval city. The modern city, an outcome of the capitalist economy of the nineteenth century, made a new urban organization indispensable: initiated by the law of 1835, it was not finally established until 1882.

The history of self-government in Germany and Austria lacks such distinctive features as that of France or England; however, it generally followed the same lines. In both countries, the division into cities and rural communes resulting from the medieval development brought about a highly developed self-government of the cities and their political independence, and also created the political split, perhaps the greatest in Europe, of the state territory into independent feudal areas. After the sixteenth century, and especially in the eighteenth century, during the time of enlightened absolutism, the cities completely lost their independence and fell under the authority of the state. At the same time, the rural communes lost their traditional self-governing institutions, having completely fallen, through the growth of serfdom, under the authority of landowners. Although much later than in France, absolutism nevertheless, as the creator of a unified state authority and territory, triumphed in Germany in the eighteenth century. At the beginning of the nineteenth century, bureaucratic centralism is everywhere victorious.

However, before long, in connection with the rising big-industrial production and the aspiration of the bourgeoisie to introduce modern conditions into the state, the development of local self-government on new principles begins. The first general law of this kind originated in Austria during the March Revolution. Actually, however, the foundations of the present self-government were laid in Austria by the statute of 1862; in the respective crownlands, particular communal laws came into being later through legislation of the Diet.

In Germany, there prevails French law, partly derived from Napoleonic times, which does not distinguish between the urban and rural commune: for instance, in the Rhineland, in the Bavarian Palatinate, Hesse, Thuringia, etc. On the other hand, the Prussian model prevailing in western and eastern Germany is an independent product. Although the Prussian urban law dates already from 1808, the actual period of the development of the present self-government in Prussia fell in the sixties and the main reforms in the seventies and eighties. Among the main areas of urban administration—province, district (*Kreis*), and commune—only the last has well-developed, self-governing institutions, i.e., extensive power of the representatives elected by the population; in the remaining ones, representative bodies (*Kreistag, Provinzallandtag*) exist but they are rather modernized, medieval class diets and their competence is extremely limited by the competence of officials appointed by the Crown, such as *Regierungspräsident* in the province, and *Landrat* in the district.

Local self-government in Russia constitutes one of the most outstanding attempts of absolutism which, in the famous "liberal reforms" after the Sebastopol catastrophe, aimed at adjusting the institutions of oriental despotism to the social needs of modern capitalist economy. Between the peasant reform and the reform of the courts at the threshold of the "renewed" Russia of Alexander II, stands the law which created the territorial institutions. Modeled on the newly established self-governing institutions of Prussia, the system of the Russian *"zemstvo"* is a parody of English self-government; it entrusts the entire local administration to the wealthy nobility, and at the same time subjects this self-government of the nobility to strict police supervision and the decisive authority of tsarist bureaucracy.

The law governing elections to the county and gubernial territorial councils happily combines, in the tri-curial system and indirect elections, the class principle with the census principle. It makes the county marshal of the nobility the exofficio chairman in the district council, and securing in it to the nobility curia half of the seats suspends over all resolutions of the council, like a Damocles sword, the threatening veto of the governor.

As a result of this peculiarity of Russia's social development, which, in the period before 1905 made not the urban bourgeoisie, but certain strata of the nobility the advocates of "liberal dreams" however pale, even this parody of self-governing institutions represented by the Russian *zemstvos* has become, in the hands of the nobility, a framework for serious social and cultural activity. However, the sharp clash that immediately arose between liberalism, nestling in the territorial administration, on the one hand, and the bureaucracy and government on the other, glaringly illuminated the genuine contradiction between modern self-government and the medieval state apparatus of absolutism. Beginning a few years after the introduction of the *zemstvos,* the collision with the power of the governors extends like a red thread through the history of self-government in Russia, oscillating between the deportation of recalcitrant council chairmen to more or less distant regions; and the boldest dreams of

Russian liberals in the form of an all-Russian Congress of *zemstvos* which was supposed to be transformed into a constituent assembly that would abolish absolutism in a peaceful manner.

The few years of the action of the [1905] revolution solved this historical collision, violently moving the Russian nobility to the side of reaction and depriving the parody of territorial self-government of any mystifying resemblances to liberalism. Thus was clearly demonstrated the impossibility of reconciling the democratic self-government indispensable in a bourgeois society with the rule of absolutism, as well as the impossibility of grafting modern bourgeois democracy onto the class action of the territorial nobility and its institutions. Local self-government in the modern sense is only one of the details of the general political program whose implementation in the entire state constitutes the task of the revolution.

In particular, the Kingdom of Poland and Lithuania must participate in this political reform. This Kingdom is at present a unique example of a country with a highly developed bourgeois economy which, however, is deprived of any traces of local self-government.

In ancient Poland, a country of natural economy and gentry rule, there obviously was no local self-government. Polish district and provincial councils possessed only functions connected with elections to the sejm. Although cities possessed their Magdeburg laws, imported from Germany and standing outside the national law, in the seventeenth and eighteenth centuries, with the complete decline of cities, the majority of them fell under the law of serfdom or regressed to the status of rural settlements and communes, and in consequence urban self-government disappeared.

The Duchy of Warsaw, which was an experiment of Napoleon, was endowed with a system of self-government bodily transferred from France, not the one which was the product of revolution, but a self-government squeezed in the clamps of the Statute of Pluvois 28. The Duchy was divided into departments, counties, and communes with "municipal" self-governments and "prefects" who appointed municipal councilors from a list of candidates elected at county diets, which was a slavish copy of the Napoleonic "*listes de confiance*" in the department. These bodies, destined mainly to impose state taxes, had only advisory functions otherwise, and lacked any executive organs.

In the Congress Kingdom, the French apparatus was completely abolished; only the departments remained, renamed "voyvodship." However, they still had no self-governing functions, only a certain influence on the election of judges and administrative officials. After the November Insurrection [1830], even this remnant of self-governing forms was abolished, and with the exception of the short period of Wielopolski's experiment in 1861, when provincial and county as well as urban councils were created on the basis of indirect, multilevel elections and without any executive organs, the country to this day remains without any form of self-government. A weak class commune crippled by the government is the only relic in this field. Consequently, the Kingdom of Poland represents at present, after a hundred years of the operation of Russian absolutism, some analogy to that *tabula rasa* which the Great Revolution created in France in order to erect on this ground a radical and democratic reform of self-government unrestricted by any historical survivals.

III

Karl Kautsky characterizes the basic attitude of Social Democracy to the question of autonomy as follows:

> The centralization of the legislative process did not by any means involve the complete centralization of

administration. On the contrary. The same classes which needed unification of the laws were obliged thereafter to bring the state power under their control. However, this took place only incompletely under the parliamentary form of government, in which the government is dependent on the legislature. The administration, with the whole bureaucratic apparatus at its disposal, was nominally subordinate to the central legislature, but the executive often turned out to be stronger in practice. The administration influences the voters in the legislature through its bureaucracy and through its power in local matters; it corrupts the legislators through its power to do them favors. However, the strongly centralized bureaucracy shows itself less and less able to cope with the increasing tasks of the state administration. It is overcome by them. The results are: fumbling, delays, postponing the most important matters, complete misunderstanding of the rapidly changing needs of practical life, massive waste of time and labor in superfluous pencil work. These are the rapidly increasing shortcomings of bureaucratic centralism.

Thus there arises, along with the striving for uniformity of legislation, after the several provincial legislatures have been superseded by a central parliament, a striving for decentralization of administration, for local administration of the provinces and communes. The one and the other are characteristic of the modern state.

"This self-government does not mean the restoration of medieval particularism. The commune [*Gemeinde*] (and likewise the province) does not become a self-sufficient entity as it once was. It remains a component part of the great whole, the nation,* and has to work for it and within the limits that it sets. The rights and duties of the individual communes as against the state are not laid down in special treaties. They are a product

* Here used as synonymous with "state."—Kautsky.

> of the general system of laws, determined for all by the central power of the state; they are determined by the interests of the whole state or the nation, not by those of the several communes."—K. Kautsky, *Der Parlamentarismus, die Volksgesetzgebung und die Sozialdemokratie,* p. 48.
>
> If Comrade Stampfer will keep separate the centralization of administration and the centralization of the legislative process, he will find that the paths being followed by German and Austrian Social Democracy respectively are not diverging at all, but are going in the same direction as the whole of modern democracy. Opposition to all special privileges in the country, strengthening of the central legislature at the expense of the provincial parliaments as well as of the government administration; weakening of the central administration both through the strengthening of the central legislature and through the devolution of self-administration to the communes and provinces—this latter process taking, in Austria, in accordance with its own local conditions, the form of self-administration of the nationalities—but a self-administration regulated for the whole country by the central legislature along uniform lines: that is, in spite of all historical and other social differences, in Germany and Austria the position of Social Democracy on the question of centralism and particularism.[2]

We have quoted the above extensive argument of Kautsky on the question we are examining but not because we unreservedly share his views. The leading idea of this argument: the division of modern state centralism into administrative and legislative, the rejection of the former and the absolute reognition of the latter, appears to us somewhat too formalistic and not quite precise. Local autonomy—provincial, municipal, and communal—does not at all do away with administrative centralism; autonomy covers only strictly local matters, while the administration of the state as a whole remains in the hands of the central authority, which, even in such democratic states as Switzerland, shows a constant tendency to extend its competence.

An outstanding feature of modern administration in contradistinction to medieval particularism is precisely the strict supervision by central institutions and the subordination of the local administration to the uniform direction and control of the state authorities. A typical illustration of this arrangement is the dependence of the modern self-governing officials in England on the central offices and even the special creation over them of a central Local Government Board which eliminates genuine administrative decentralization represented by the old system in which, it will be recalled, the all-powerful justices of the peace were entirely independent of the central government. In the same way, the most recent development of self-government in France paves anew the way to democratization, and at the same time gradually eliminates the independence of the prefect from the central ministries, a system that had characterized the government of the Second Empire.

The above phenomenon also completely corresponds to the general direction of political development. A strong central government is an institution peculiar not only to the epoch of absolutism at the dawn of bourgeois development but also to bourgeois society itself in its highest stage, flowering, and decline. The more external policy—commercial, aggressive, colonial—becomes the axis of the life of capitalism, the more we enter into the period of imperialistic "global" policy, which is a normal phase of the development of bourgeois economy, and the more capitalism needs a strong authority, a powerful central government which concentrates in its hands all the resources of the state for the protection of its interests outside. Hence, modern autonomy, even in its widest application, finds definite barriers in all those attributes of power which are related to the foreign policy of a state.

On the other hand, autonomy itself puts up barriers to legislative centralization, because without certain legislative competences, even narrowly outlined and purely local, no self-government is possible. The power of issuing within a certain sphere, on its own initiative, laws binding for the population, and not merely supervising the execution of laws issued by the central legislative body, constitutes precisely the soul and core of self-government in the modern democratic sense—it forms the basic function of municipal and communal councils as well as of provincial diets or departmental councils. Only when the latter in France acquired the right of deciding in the last instance about their problems instead of submitting their opinions in a consultative capacity, and particularly when they acquired the right of drafting their independent budget, only from that time dates the real beginning of the autonomy of the departments. In the same way, the foundation of urban self-government in Germany is the right of establishing the budget of the towns, and in connection with this the independent fixing of supplements to the state taxes and also the introduction of new communal taxes (although within limits fixed by state law). Further, when, for instance, the city council of Berlin or Paris issues binding regulations concerning the building code, insurance duties for home industry, employment and unemployment aid, the city sewage-disposal system, communications, etc., all these are legislative activities. The axis of the incessant struggle between local representatives and organs of the central administration is the democratic tendency constantly to expand the legislative competence of the elected organs and to reduce the administrative competence of the appointed organs.

The attitude to local autonomy—its legislative and administrative functions—constitutes the theoretical basis of the political fight which has been going on for a long time between Social Democracy on the one hand and the government and the bourgeois parties on the other. The latter hold a uniform view on the matter in question except for a small group of extreme-left progressives. While the theory of bourgeois reaction maintains that local self-government is, by its nature, only a localization of state administrations, that the commune, district, or province as a financial unit is called to administer the state property, Social Democracy defends the view that a commune, district, or province is a social body called upon to take care—in a local sphere—of a number of social matters and not only financial ones. The practical conclusion of these two theories is that the bourgeois parties insist that electoral rights to self-governing bodies should be limited by a property qualification, while Social Democracy calls for a universal and equal electoral right for the whole population. Generally speaking, the progress of modern self-government toward democracy can be measured by the expansion of the groups of population which participate in self-government by way of elections, as well as by the degree to which their representative bodies extend their competence. The transfer of some activities from the administration to the legislative, representative bodies is a measure extending the latter's competence. It seems therefore that the centralized state apparatus can be separated from local self-government, and modern self-government from feudal and petit bourgeois particularism. This can be done, in our opinion, not by a formalistic approach, whereby the legislative and the administrative powers are separated, but by separating some spheres of social life—namely those which constitute the core of a capitalist economy and of a big bourgeois state—from the sphere of local interests.

In particular, Kautsky's formula including national autonomy under the general heading of local self-government would, in view of his theory about legislative centralization, lead Social Democracy to refuse to recognize regional diets on the ground that they were a manifestation of legislative decentralization, i.e., medieval particularism. Kautsky's arguments are in their essence extremely valuable as an indication concerning the general tendency in Social Democratic policy, concerning its basic standpoint toward centralism and big-power policy on the one hand and particularistic tendencies on the other. But precisely from the same foundations from which, in all capitalistic states, grows local self-government, there also grows in certain conditions national autonomy, with local legislation as an independent manifestation of modern social development, which has as little in common with medieval particularism as the present-day city council has with a parliament of the ancient Hanseatic republic.

5. *The National Question and Autonomy*

Capitalism transforms social life from the material foundations up to the top—the cultural aspects. It has produced a whole series of entirely new economic phenomena: big industry, machine production, proletarization, concentration of property, industrial crises, capitalist monopolies, modern industry, labor of women and children, etc. Capitalism has produced a new center of social life: the big city, as well as a new social class: the professional intelligentsia. Capitalist economy with its highly developed division of labor and constant progress of technology needs a large specialized staff of employees with technical training: engineers, chemists, architects, electricians, etc. Capitalist industry and commerce need a whole army of lawyers: attorneys, notaries, judges, etc. Bourgeois management, especially in big cities, has made health a public matter and developed for its service large numbers of physicians, pharmacists, midwives, dentists, as well as public hospitals with appropriate staffs. Capitalist production requires not only specially trained production managers but universal, elementary, popular education, both to raise the general cultural level of the people which creates ever-growing needs, and consequently demand for mass articles, and to develop a properly educated and intelligent worker capable of operating large-scale industry. Hence, for bourgeois society everywhere, popular education and vocational training are indispensable; consequently we see public schools and numerous elementary, secondary, and college teachers, libraries, reading rooms, etc.

Capitalistic production and participation in the world market are impossible without appropriately extensive, speedy, and constant communication—both material and cultural. Bourgeois society has thus created on the one hand railroads and modern postal and telegraph services, and on the other—based on these material foundations—a periodical press, a social phenomenon which before was entirely unknown. To work for the press there has come into being in bourgeois society a numerous category of professional journalists and publicists. Capitalism has made any manifestation of human energy, including artistic creativity, an object of commerce, while on the other hand, by making art objects accessible to the broad masses of the people through mass production, it has made art an everyday need of at least urban society. Theater, music, painting, sculpture, which, in the period of natural economy had been a monopoly and private luxury of individual, powerful sponsors, are in bourgeois society a public institution and part and parcel of the normal daily life of the urban population. The worker's cultural needs are met in the taverns or beer gardens and by cheap book illustrations and junky ornaments; he adorns his person and his lodging with artistic tawdriness, while the bourgeoisie has at its disposal philharmonics, first-rate theaters, works of genius, and objects of elegance. However, the one and the other kind of consumption calls forth a numerous class of artists and artistic producers.

In this way capitalism creates a whole new culture: public education, development of science, the flowering of learning, journalism, a specifically geared art. However, these are not just mechanical appendages to the bare process of production or mechanically separated lifeless parts. The culture of bourgeois society itself constitutes a living and to some extent autonomous entity. In order to exist or develop, this society not only needs certain relationships of production, exchange, and communication, but it also creates a certain set of intellectual relations within the framework of contradictory class interests. If the class struggle is a natural product of the capitalist economy then its natural needs are the conditions that make this class struggle possible; hence not only modern political forms, democracy, parliamentarianism, but also open public life, with an open exchange of views and conflicting convictions, an intense intellectual life, which alone makes the struggle of classes and parties possible. Popular education, journalism, science, art–growing at first within the framework of capitalist production–become in themselves an indispensable need and condition of existence of modern society. Schools, libraries, newspapers, theaters, public lectures, public discussions grow into the normal conditions of life, into the indispensable intellectual atmosphere of each member of the modern, particularly urban society, even outside the connection of these phenomena with economic conditions. In a word, the vulgar material process of capitalism creates a whole new ideological "superstructure" with an existence and development which are to some extent autonomous.

However, capitalism does not create that intellectual spirit in the air or in the theoretical void of abstraction, but in a definite territory, a definite social environment, a definite language, within the framework of certain traditions, in a word, within definite national forms. Consequently, by that very culture it sets apart a certain territory and a certain population as a cultural national entity in which it creates a special, closer cohesion and connection of intellectual interests.

Any ideology is basically only a superstructure of the material and class conditions of a given epoch. However, at the same time, the ideology of each epoch harks back to the ideological results of the preceding epochs, while on the other hand it has its own logical development in a certain area. This is illustrated by the sciences as well as by religion, philosophy, and art.

The cultural and aesthetic values created by capitalism in a given environment not only assume a certain national quality through the main organ of cultural production, i.e., the language, but merge with the traditional culture of society, whose history becomes saturated with its distinct cultural characteristics; in a word, this culture turns into a national culture with an existence and development of its own. The basic features and foundations of modern culture in all bourgeois countries are common, international, and the tendency of contemporary development is doubtless toward an ever greater community of international culture. However, within the framework of this highly cosmopolitan, bourgeois culture, French is clearly distinguished from English culture, German from Dutch, Polish from Russian, as so many separate types.

The borderlines of historical stages and the historical "seams" are least detectable in the development of an ideology.* Because the modern capitalist culture is an heir to and continuator of earlier cultures, what develops is the continuity and monolithic quality of a national culture which, on the surface, shows no connection with the period of capitalist economy and bourgeois rule. For the phrasemonger of the "National Democracy," or mindless "sociologist" of social patriotism, the culture of present-day Poland is, in its core, the same unchanged "culture of the Polish nation" as at the time of Batory or Stanislas Augustus, while Straszewicz,

* Incidentally, this is the only reason why histories of philosophy such as those of Zeller or Kuno Fischer are possible, in which the development of "ideas" takes place in a void, with no relation to the prosaic history of society.

Swiatochowski, and Sienkiewicz are direct-line spiritual heirs of Rey of Nagtowice, Pasek, and Mickiewicz. In fact, however, the literature and the press in modern, bourgeois Poland are appallingly trivial; Polish science and the entire Polish culture are appallingly poor; they belong in a new historical stage completely alien in spirit and content to the old culture of feudal Poland, mirrored in its last monumental work, *Pan Tadeusz.* Present-day Polish culture, in all its destitution, is a modern product of the same capitalist development that chained Poland to Russia and placed at the head of society, in the role of ruling class, a rabble of heterogeneous moneymakers without a past, without a revolutionary tradition, and professional traitors to the national cause. The present-day bourgeois learning, art, and journalism of Poland are in spirit and content ideological hieroglyphs from which a materialist historian reads the history of the fall of gentry Poland, the history of "organic work," conciliation, National Democracy, deputations, memoranda, up to the "national" elections to the tsarist Duma under a state of emergency, and "national" teams to murder Polish Socialist workers. Capitalism created modern Polish national culture, annihilating in the same process Polish national independence.

Capitalism annihilated Polish national independence but at the same time created modern Polish national culture. This national culture is a product indispensable within the framework of bourgeois Poland; its existence and development are a historical necessity, connected with the capitalistic development itself. The development of capitalism, which chained Poland to Russia by socioeconomic ties, undermined Russian absolutism, united and revolutionized the Russian and Polish proletariat as a class called upon to overthrow absolutism, and in this way created, under the Tsars, the indispensable preconditions for achieving political freedom. But within the framework and against the background of this general tendency toward the democratization of the state, capitalism at the same time knit more closely the socioeconomic and cultural-national life of the Polish kingdom, thus preparing the objective conditions for the realization of Polish national autonomy.

As we have seen, the requirements of the capitalist system lead with historic necessity in all modern states to the development of local self-government through the participation of the people in carrying out sociopolitical functions on all levels, from the commune to the district and province. Where, however, inside a modern state there exist distinct nationality districts constituting at the same time territories with certain economic and social distinctions, the same requirements of the bourgeois economy make self-government on the highest, country-wide level, indispensable. On this level, local self-government is also transformed, as a result of a new factor, national-cultural distinctness, into a special type of democratic institution applicable only in quite specific conditions.

The Moscow–Vladimir industrial district, with its economic achievements, local specific interests, and concentration of population, differs certainly as much from the vast Russian space surrounding it as does the Kingdom of Poland. However, the factor distinguishing our country from the central district of Russia in a decisive way, is the distinctness of the cultural-national existence, which creates a whole sphere of separate common interests besides purely economic and social ones. Just as an urban or village commune, district, department or gubernia, province or region must possess, in keeping with the spirit of modern self-government, a certain range of local legislation contained within the framework of state laws, national self-government, in the spirit of democracy, must be based on the representation of the people and their power of local legislation within the framework of state laws, to satisfy the national socioeconomic and cultural-national needs.

The entire modern culture is, above all, a class, bourgeois culture. Learning and art, school and theater, professional intelligentsia, the press—all primarily serve the bourgeois society, are imbued with its principles, its spirit, its tendency. But the institutions of the bourgeois system, like the capitalist development itself, are, in the spirit of the historical dialectic, twofold, double-edged phenomena: the means of class development and rule are at the same time so many means for the rise of the proletariat as a class to the struggle for emancipation, for the abolition of bourgeois rule. Political freedom, parliamentarianism are, in all present-day states, tools for building up capitalism and the interests of the bourgeoisie as the ruling class. However, the same democratic institutions and bourgeois parliamentarianism are, at a certain level, an indispensable school of the proletariat's political and class maturity, a condition of organizing it into a Social Democratic party, of training it in open class struggle.

The same applies to the sphere of the intellect. The basic school, elementary education, is necessary for bourgeois society in order to create appropriate mass consumption as well as an appropriate contingent of able working hands. But the same school and education become the basic tools of the proletariat as a revolutionary class. The social, historical, philosophical, and natural sciences are today the ideological products of the bourgeoisie and expressions of its needs and class tendencies. But on a certain level of its development the working class recognizes that for it also "knowledge is power"—not in the tasteless sense of bourgeois individualism and its preachings of "industriousness and diligence" as a means of achieving "happiness," but in the sense of knowledge as a lever of class struggle, as the revolutionary consciousness of the working masses. Finally, socialism, which links the interest of the workers as a class with the development and future of mankind as a great cultural brotherhood, produces a particular affinity of the proletarian struggle with the interests of culture as a whole, and causes the seemingly contradictory and paradoxical phenomenon that the conscious proletariat is today in all countries the most ardent and idealistic advocate of the interests of learning and art, the same bourgeois culture of which it is today the disinherited stepchild.

The national autonomy of the Kingdom of Poland is primarily necessary for the Polish bourgeoisie to strengthen its class rule and to develop its institutions in order to exploit and oppress with no restrictions whatsoever. In the same way as the modern state-political parliamentary institutions, and, as their corollary, the institutions of local self-government are on a certain level an indispensable tool of bourgeois rule and a close harmonization of all state and social functions with the interests of the bourgeoisie, in a narrower sense, national autonomy is an indispensable tool of the strict application of the social functions in a certain territory to the special bourgeois interests of that territory. Absolutism, which safeguarded the crudest although the most important vital interest of the ruling classes, viz., the limitless exploitation of the working strata, naturally, at the same time, sacrificed to its own interests and working methods all subtle interests and forms of bourgeois rule, i.e., treated them with Asiatic ruthlessness. Political liberty and self-government will eventually give the Polish bourgeoisie the possibility of utilizing a number of presently neglected social functions—schools, religious worship, and the entire cultural-spiritual life of the country—for its own class interests. By manning all offices of the administration, judiciary, and politics, the bourgeoisie will be able to assimilate genuinely these natural organs of class rule with the spirit and home needs of bourgeois society, and so turn them into flexible, accurate, and subtle tools of the Polish ruling classes. National autonomy, as a part of all-state political freedom, is, in a word, the most mature political form of bourgeois rule in Poland.

However, precisely for this reason, autonomy is an indispensable class need of the Polish proletariat. The riper the bourgeois institutions grow, the deeper they penetrate the social functions, the more ground they cover within the variegated intellectual and aesthetic sphere, the broader grows the battlefield and the bigger the number of firing lines wherefrom the proletariat conducts the class struggle. The more unrestrictedly and efficiently the development of bourgeois society proceeds, the more courageously and surely advances the consciousness, political maturity, and unification of the proletariat as a class.

The Polish proletariat needs for its class struggle all the components of which a spiritual culture is made; primarily, its interests, essentially based on the solidarity of nations and striving toward it, require the elimination of national oppression, and guarantees against such oppression worked out in the course of social development. Moreover, a normal, broad, and unrestricted cultural life of the country is just as indispensable for the development of the proletariat's class struggle as for the existence of bourgeois society itself.

National autonomy has the same aims as are contained in the political program of the Polish proletariat: the overthrow of absolutism and the achievement of political freedom in the country at large; this is but a part of the program resulting both from the progressive trends of capitalist development and from the class interests of the proletariat.

II

The national separateness of a certain territory in a modern state is not by itself a sufficient basis for autonomy; the relationship between nationality and political life is precisely what calls for closer examination. Theoreticians of nationalism usually consider nationality in general as a natural, unchangeable phenomenon, outside social development, a conservative phenomenon resisting all historical vicissitudes. In accordance with this view bourgeois nationalism finds the main sources of national vitality and strength not in the modern historical formation, i.e., urban, bourgeois culture, but, on the contrary, in the traditional forms of life of the rural population. The peasant mass with its social conservatism appears to the romantics of nationalism as the only genuine mainstay of the national culture, an unshakable fortress of national distinctness, the stronghold of the proper national genius and spirit. When, in the middle of the last century, there began to flourish, in connection with the nationalist trend in the politics of Central Europe, so-called folklorism, it turned above all to the traditional forms of peasant culture as to the treasury in which every nation deposits "the threads of its thoughts and the flowers of its feelings." In the same way at present, the recently awakened Lithuanian, Byelorussian, and Ukrainian nationalism bases itself entirely on the rural population and its conservative forms of existence, significantly starting the cultivation of this age-old and virgin national field with spreading primers and the Holy Scripture in the national language and national orthography. Already, in the 1880s, when the pseudosocialistic and pseudorevolutionary *Glos* [*Voice*] was published in Warsaw, the Polish National Democracy too, following its infallible reactionary instinct, turned its peculiar national sentiments, happily married to the anti-Semitism of the urban bourgeoisie, toward the rural population. Finally, in the same way, the most recent "nationalist" current in Russia, the party of Mr. Korfanty and Company, is based mainly on the conservatism of the rural population of Upper Silesia, exploited as a foundation for economic and political success by the reactionary Polish petite bourgeoisie.

On the other hand, the problem of which social strata constitute the proper guardians of national culture has recently caused an interesting exchange of views in the Social Democratic camp.

In the study of the "nationality question," quoted by us several times, Karl Kautsky, criticizing the work of the Austrian party publicist Otto Bauer on the same subject, says:

> Class differences lead Bauer to the paradoxical opinion that only those portions of a nation constitute a nation which participate in the culture; consequently, until now, only the ruling and exploiting classes.
>
> "In the period of the Staufers"—writes Bauer—"the nation existed only in the cultural community of knighthood. . . . A homogeneous national character produced by the homogeneity of cultural influences, was only the character of one class of the nation. . . . The peasant did not share in anything that united the nation. . . . Therefore the German peasants do not at all constitute the nation; they are the *Hintersassen* of the nation.—In a society based on the private ownership of the means of production, the ruling classes constitute the nation—formerly the knighthood, today the educated people, as a community of people in whom uniform education developed by the nation's history, with the help of a common language and national education, develops an affinity of characters. On the other hand the broad popular masses do not constitute the nation."*

According to Bauer only the socialist system, by making the masses of the working people participants in the entirety of the culture, will turn these masses into a nation. Kautsky replies to these arguments as follows:

> This is a very subtle thought with a very right core but in the nationality question it leads to a false road, for it

* Otto Bauer, *Die Nationalitaetenfrage und die Sozialdemokratie* (Vienna: 1907), pp. 49-50, 136.

treats the concept of nation in such a way as to make simply impossible the understanding of the force of the national thought in all classes in the present, and the bases of the present national contradictions of entire nations. Bauer conflicts here with the observation made by Renner* that it is precisely the peasant who is the preserver of nationality. Renner demonstrates that in Austria (including Hungary), during the last century, a number of cities changed their nationality, becoming Hungarian or Czech rather than German. On the other hand German cities, specifically Vienna, absorbed an immense influx of foreign nationalities and assimilated them to the German nation. However, in the countryside the linguistic boundaries have practically not shifted. Actually, in Austria's major cities, the process of Germanization has achieved its goal; at the beginning of the nineteenth century they had all been German cities, with the exception at the most of Galicia, Croatia, and the Italian towns. By contrast, the peasant population is the one that remained national; the tendencies toward making Austria a national state shattered against the peasantry. The peasant firmly adheres to his nationality as to any tradition, while the city dweller, especially the educated one, assimilates much more easily.**

In the course of his study, Kautsky is forced to considerably revise his reasoning. Examining more closely the foundations of modern national movements, he points out

* Another Austrian Social Democratic publicist who, under the pseudonym Springer, wrote a number of works on the nationality question in Austria: *Der Kampf der oesterreichischen Nationen um den Staat* (1902); *Grundlagen und Entwicklungsziele der oesterreichisch-ungarischen Monarchie* (1906).
** Kautsky, *Nationalität und Internationalität*, pp. 3, 4.

that precisely the bourgeois development calling into existence a new social class, the professional intelligentsia, creates in this form the main fact of the contemporary national idea and a pillar of national life. It is true that the same development simultaneously leads the social and cultural life of present-day nationalities, and particularly of the intelligentsia to international paths, and from this standpoint Kautsky rightly reverses the perspective outlined by Bauer, by explaining that the task of the great socialist reform in the future will not be the nationalization, i.e., the national separation of the working masses, but, on the contrary, blazing the trail for one universal, international culture in which distinct nationalities will disappear. However, in present-day conditions, the role of the urban, or strictly speaking, bourgeois element, is decisive for the fate of nationalities. If Kautsky in agreement with Renner points to a whole series of Slavic critics Germanized at the beginning of the nineteenth century in the Hapsburg monarchy as an example of the national nonresistance of the urban element, these facts may actually serve only as an illustration of the petit bourgeois conditions of the precapitalist era by which doubtless the urban life in the Slavic lands of Austria was characterized at the beginning of the nineteenth century. The further development of events, a definite swing of the same type of critics to their own nationality in the last few decades, which is confirmed by Kautsky and Renner, is, on the other hand, a striking example of how far the rise of its own bourgeois development in a country, its own industry, its own big city life, its own "national" bourgeoisie and intelligentsia, as it occurred for example in Bohemia, can form the basis for a resistant national policy and for an active political life connected with it.

The emphasis on the peasant element in connection with the fate of nationality is correct so far as the quite passive preservation of national peculiarities in the ethnic group is concerned: speech, mores, dress, and also, usually in close connection with this, a certain religion. The conservatism of peasant life makes possible the preservation of nationality within these narrow bounds and explains the resistance for centuries to any denationalization policy, regardless of either the ruthlessness of the methods or the cultural superiority of the aggressive foreign nationality. This is proved by the preservation of speech and national type among the South Slavic tribes of Turkey and Hungary, the preservation of the peculiarities of the Byelorussians, Ruthenians, Lithuanians in the Russian empire, of the Masurians and Lithuanians in East Prussia, or the Poles in Upper Silesia, etc.

However, a national culture preserved in this traditional-peasant manner is incapable of playing the role of an active element in contemporary political-social life, precisely because it is entirely a product of tradition, is rooted in past conditions, because—to use the words of Marx—the peasant class stands in today's bourgeois society outside of culture, constituting rather a "piece of barbarism" surviving in that culture. The peasant, as a national "outpost," is always and a priori a culture of social barbarism, a basis of political reaction, doomed by historical evolution. No serious political-national movement in present-day conditions is possible solely on a national peasant foundation. And only when the present urban classes—bourgeoisie, petite bourgeoisie, and bourgeois-intelligentsia—become the promoters of the national movement, will it be possible to develop, in certain defined circumstances, the seeming phenomenon of the national contradictions and national aspirations of "entire nations," referred to by Kautsky.

Passing in particular to the question of nationality self-government or autonomy, only from the standpoint of bourgeois nationalism is each "nationality" equally suitable material and a suitable basis for autonomous institutions. Such a view distinguishes in autonomy only certain cultural-national guarantees, i.e., treats autonomy in a negative and purely ideological aspect, as a certain minimal form of national "freedom," disregarding in it completely the positive social value, the specific historical function which constitutes the core of modern autonomy as distinct from medieval particularism. If, however, we transfer the concept of autonomy from this utopian-ideological area to the historical field and examine it as a specific indispensable result of the capitalist economy in a certain environment, as a form of satisfying certain social functions—material and spiritual—resulting from the needs of bourgeois society and its democratic development, we find that the functions of local autonomy within the framework of the modern constitutional state are indissolubly linked, like the entire political development of that state, with the forms of modern bourgeois life. The focus of autonomy and of the modern state in general, is the big city; its political level, the bourgeois class; its inseparable environment, the modern bourgeois intelligentsia, literary life, journalism, learning, and art.

Thus, local autonomy in the sense of the self-government of a certain nationality territory is only possible where the respective nationality possesses its own bourgeois development, urban life, intelligentsia, its own literary and scholarly life. The Congress Kingdom demonstrates all these conditions. Its population is nationally homogeneous because the Polish element has a decisive preponderance over other nationalities in the country's whole area, with the exception of the Suwałki gubernia in which the Lithuanians prevail. Out of the over-all population of 9,402,253 the Poles constitute 6,755,503, while of the remaining nationalities the Jews and Germans are mainly concentrated in the cities where, however, they do not represent a foreign bourgeois intelligentsia, but, on the contrary, are considerably assimilated by Polish cultural life, while the Russians, except in the Lublin and Siedlce regions, represent mainly the influx of bureaucratic elements alien to Polish society. The percentage of total population of these nationalities in the respective provinces, with the exception of Suwałki, appears, according to the census of 1897, as follows:

Gubernia	*Poles*	*Jews*	*Germans*	*Russians*
Kalisz	83.9%	7.6	7.3	1.1
Kielce	87.6	10.9	–	1.2
Lublin	61.3	12.7	0.2	21.0
Lomza	77.4	15.8	0.8	5.5
Piotrokow	71.9	15.2	10.6	1.6
Plock	80.4	9.6	6.7	3.3
Radom	83.8	13.8	1.1	1.4
Siedlce	66.1	15.5	1.4	16.5
Warsaw	73.6	16.4	4.0	5.4

Thus, in all the gubernias except two, and in the country as a whole, the Polish element constitutes more than 70 percent of the population; it is, moreover, the decisive element in the sociocultural development of the country.

However, the situation looks different when we turn to the Jewish nationality.

Jewish national autonomy, not in the sense of freedom of school, religion, place of residence, and equal civic rights, but in the sense of the political self-government of the Jewish population with its own legislation and administration, as it were parallel to the autonomy of the Congress Kingdom, is an entirely utopian idea. Strangely, this conviction prevails also in the camp of extreme Polish nationalists, e.g., in the so-called "Revolutionary Faction" of the PPS, where it is based on the simple circumstance that the Jewish nationality does not possess a "territory of its own" within the Russian empire. But national autonomy conceived in accordance with that group's own standpoint, i.e., as the sum of freedoms and rights to self-determination of a certain group of people linked by language, tradition, and psychology, is in itself a construction lying beyond historical conditions, fluttering in mid-air, and therefore one that can be easily conceived, as it were, "in the air," i.e., without any definite territory. On the other hand, an autonomy that grows historically together with local self-government, on the basis of modern bourgeois-democratic development, is actually as inseparable from a certain territory as the bourgeois state itself, and cannot be imagined without it to the same extent as "nonterritorial" communal or urban self-government. It is true that the Jewish population was completely under the influence of modern capitalistic development in the Russian empire and shares the economic, political, and spiritual interests of particular groups in that society. But on the one hand, these interests were never territorially separated so as to become specifically Jewish capitalist interests; rather, they are common interests of the Jewish and other people in the country at large. On the other hand, this capitalist development does not lead to a separation of bourgeois Jewish culture, but acts in an exactly opposite direction, leading to the assimilation of the Jewish bourgeois, urban intelligentsia, to their absorption by the Polish or Russian people. If the national distinctness of the Lithuanians or Byelorussians is based on the backward peasant people, the Jewish national distinctness in Russia and Poland is based on the socially backward petite bourgeoisie, on small production, small trade, small-town life, and—let us add parenthetically—on the close relation of the nationality in question to religion. In view of the above, the national distinctness of the Jews, which is supposed to be the basis of nonterritorial Jewish autonomy, is manifested not in the form of metropolitan bourgeois culture, but in the form of small-town lack of culture. Obviously any efforts toward "developing Jewish culture" at the initiative of a handful of Yiddish publicists and translators cannot be taken seriously. The only manifestation of genuine modern culture in the Russian framework is the Social Democratic movement of the Russian proletariat which, because of its nature, can best replace the historical lack of bourgeois national culture of the Jews, since it is itself a phase of genuinely international and proletarian culture.

Different, though no less complicated, is the question of autonomy in Lithuania. For nationalist utopians, obviously the existence of a certain territory inhabited by a population of distinct nationality is a sufficient reason to demand for the nationality in question, in the name of the right of all nationalities to self-determination, either an independent republic, or one federated with Russia, or the "broadest autonomy." Each of these programs was advanced in turn by the former "Lithuanian Social Democracy," then by the PPS in its federative phase, and finally by the recently organized "Byelorussian Socialist Commune" which, at its Second Congress in 1906, adopted a somewhat vague program of a "federal republic in Russia with a territorial-autonomous diet in Vilna for the territory of the Western country."* Whether the "Byelorussian Commune" demands the proclamation of the "Western country" as one of the republics into which the Russian Empire is to be split, or a "territorial autonomy" for that "Western country" is difficult to figure out; since an "autonomous" diet is demanded for Vilna, it would seem that the latter version is intended, or else, what is in complete harmony with the whole utopian-abstract treatment of the question, no basic distinctions are made between an independent republic, a federal system, and autonomy, but only qualitative distinctions. Let us examine the matter from the standpoint of territorial autonomy. The "Western country," according to the terminology in the Russian administrative division, is a preponderantly agrarian and small-industry district comprising areas with considerable variations in conditions. Apart from the local interests of the rural, municipal,

* *Proceedings of the Russian National Socialist Parties* (St. Petersburg: 1908), p. 92.

and provincial self-governments, this territory is much less of a distinct production and trading district, with a less distinctive character and a less distinct grouping of interests, than the Kingdom of Poland or the industrial Moscow district. On the other hand it is a distinct nationality district. But it is precisely with regard to this question of nationality that the greatest difficulties arise from the standpoint of potential autonomy. The "Western country," i.e., the territory of former Lithuania, is an area occupied by several different nationalities, and the first question that arises is: which nationality is to be served by the territorial-national autonomy that is at stake, which language, which nationality is to be decisive in the schools, cultural institutions, the judiciary, legislation, and in filling local offices? The Lithuanian nationalists obviously demand autonomy for the Lithuanian nationality. Let us look at the actual conditions of that nationality.

According to the census of 1897—the last one that has taken place and whose results in the area of nationality relations have been available to the public since 1905—the genuine Lithuanian nationality in the Russian empire numbers 1,210,510 people. This population inhabits mainly the Vilna, Kovno, Grodno, and Suwałki gubernias. Besides, there live almost exclusively in the Kovno gubernia, 448,000 persons of Samogitian nationality, who by no means identify with the Lithuanians. If we were to outline the territory that might serve as a basis for an autonomous Lithuania, we would have to eliminate part of the present "Western country," and on the other hand go beyond its borders and include the Suwałki gubernia which today belongs to the Congress Kingdom. We would obtain a territory approximately corresponding to the voyvodship of Vilna and Troki which, in prepartition Poland, constituted "Lithuania proper." The Lithuanian population is distributed in that territory as follows: out of the sum total of 1,200,000 Lithuanians almost half, i.e., 574,853, are concentrated in the Kovno gubernia. The second place with regard to the concentration of Lithuanians is occupied by the Suwałki gubernia, where 305,548 live; somewhat fewer are to be found in the Vilna gubernia, viz., 297,720 persons; finally, an insignificant number of Lithuanians, about 3,500, inhabit the northern portion of the Grodno gubernia. Actually, the Lithuanian population is doubtless more numerous, because in the census the language used by the respective populations was the main point taken into consideration, while a sizable proportion of Lithuanians use the Polish language in everyday life. However, in the present case, from the standpoint of nationality as a basis of national autonomy, obviously only the population wherein national distinctness is expressed in a distinct native language can be taken into account.

The distribution of the Lithuanian population becomes apparent only when we ascertain its numerical ratio to the remaining population in the same territory. The over-all population figure in the gubernias mentioned (always according to the 1897 census) is as follows:

		Percent Lithuanians
In the Kovno gubernia	1,544,569	37.0
In the Vilna gubernia	1,591,207	17.0
In the Grodno gubernia	1,603,409	0.2
In the Suwałki gubernia	582,913	52.0

Out of a total population of 5,322,093 in that territory, the Lithuanians constitute less than 23 percent. Even if we were to include, as do the Lithuanian nationalists, the entire Samogitian population with the Lithuanians, we would obtain the ratio of 31 percent, i.e., less than a third of the total population. Obviously, setting up the former "Lithuania proper" as the area of the Lithuanian nationality is, in present-day conditions, an entirely arbitrary and artificial construction.

The total population of the four "northwestern" gubernias included because of the Byelorussian nationality is as follows:

Minsk gubernia	2,147,621
Mogilev gubernia	1,686,764
Witebsk gubernia	1,489,246
Smolensk gubernia	1,525,279

Together with the population of the four gubernias inhabited by Lithuanians, this adds up to the considerable figure of 12,171,007. However, among this population, the Byelorussians constitute less than half, i.e., about 5.85 million (5,855,547). Even considering only the figures, the idea of fitting Lithuania's autonomy to the Byelorussian nationality seems questionable. However, this difficulty becomes much greater if we take into consideration the socioeconomic conditions of the respective nationalities.

In the territory inhabited by them the Byelorussians constitute an exclusively rural, agrarian element. Their cultural level is extremely low. Illiteracy is so widespread that the "Byelorussian Commune" was forced to establish an "Education Department" to spread elementary education among the Byelorussian peasants. The complete lack of a Byelorussian bourgeoisie, an urban intelligentsia, and an independent scholarly and literary life in the Byelorussian language, renders the idea of a national Byelorussian autonomy simply impractical.

The social conditions among the Lithuanian nationals are similar. To a preponderant degree farming is the occupation of the Lithuanians. In the cultural heart of Lithuania, the Vilna gubernia, the Lithuanians constitute 19.8 percent of the total population, and 3.1 percent of the urban population. In the Suwałki gubernia, the next with regard to Lithuanian concentration, the Lithuanians constitute as much as 52.2 percent of the gubernia population, but only 9.2 percent of the urban population. It is true that the cultural conditions among the Lithuanians are quite different from those in Byelorussia. The education of the Lithuanian population is on a relatively high level, and the percentage of illiterates is almost the lowest in the Russian Empire. But the education of Lithuanians is preponderantly a Polish education, and the Polish language, not the Lithuanian, is here the instrument of culture, which fact is closely connected with the fact that the possessing classes, the rural landed gentry, and the urban intelligentsia are genuinely Polish or Polonized to a high degree. The same situation prevails to a considerable degree in Ruthenia. Indeed, in Lithuania and Ruthenia the only nationality culturally fit to manage national autonomy is the Polish, with its urban population and its intelligentsia. Therefore, if the national autonomy of the "Western country" were to be considered, it would have to be neither a Lithuanian nor a Byelorussian autonomy, but a Polish one: the Polish language, the Polish school, Poles in public offices would be the natural expression of the autonomous institutions of the country.

Given this situation, culturally and nationally, Lithuania and Ruthenia would constitute only an extension of the Kingdom, not a separate autonomous region; they would form, with the Kingdom, a natural and historical region, with Polish autonomy over the Kingdom plus Lithuania.

Such a solution of the question is opposed by several decisive considerations. First of all, from the purely national point of view, this would be the rule of a small Polish minority over a majority of Lithuanians, Byelorussians, Jews, and others. In Lithuania and Ruthenia, the Jews and the Poles make up most of the urban population; together they occupy what would be the natural social centers of autonomous institutions. But the Jewish population decisively outnumbers the Polish, whereas in the Congress Kingdom there are 6,880,000 Poles (according to the 1897 census) and only 1,300,000 Jews. The percentage of each in the four gubernias of Lithuania proper in terms of the over-all population is as follows:

Gubernia	*Poles*	*Jews*
Suwałki	22.99	10.14
Kovno	9.04	13.73
Vilna	8.17	12.72
Grodno	10.08	17.37

Only in the Suwałki gubernia is the Jewish population smaller than the Polish, but even here this ratio is quite different when we take the towns into consideration: then the Poles constitute 27 percent, the Jews 40 percent of the urban population. It should also be taken into consideration that Jews in the Kingdom, if assimilated—more so in the urban areas—reinforce the Polish nationality; whereas in Lithuania the assimilation process, which is anyway much slower, occurs—when it does at all—among Jews who belong to the Russian culture; in both cases confusion among nationalities grows and the question of autonomy becomes more and more entangled. Suffice it to say that in the heart of Lithuania and the seat of the planned autonomous diet, Vilna, out of the 227 schools counted in 1900, 182 are Jewish!

Another consideration no less important is the circumstance that the Polish nationality is in Lithuania and Ruthenia precisely the nationality of the ruling strata: the gentry landowners and the bourgeoisie; while the Lithuanian and particularly the Byelorussian nationality is represented mostly by landless peasantry. Therefore, the nationality relationship is here—generally speaking—a relationship of social classes. Handing over the country's autonomous institutions to the Polish nationality would here mean the creation of a new powerful instrument of class domination without a corresponding strengthening of the position of the exploited classes, and would cause conditions of the kind that would be brought about by the proposed autonomy of Galicia for the Ruthenians.

Consequently, both for nationality and for social reasons the joining of Lithuania to the autonomous territory of the Kingdom or the separation of Lithuania and Ruthenia into an autonomous region with an unavoidable preponderance of the Polish element is a project which Social Democracy must combat in principle. In this form, the project of Lithuania's national autonomy altogether falls through as utopian, in view of the numerical and social relations of the nationalities involved.

III

Another outstanding example of the difficulties encountered by the problem of nationality autonomy in practice is to be found in the Caucasus. No corner of the earth presents such a picture of nationality intermixture in one territory as the Caucasus, the ancient historical trail of the great migrations of peoples between Asia and Europe, strewn with fragments and splinters of those peoples. That territory's population of over nine million is composed (according to the 1897 census) of the following racial and nationality groups:

	In Thousands
Russians	2,192.3
Germans	21.5
Greeks	57.3
Armenians	975.0
Ossetians	157.1
Kurds	100.0
Chechens	243.4
Circassians	111.5

Abkhaz		72.4
Lezgins		613.8
Georgians, Imeretins, Mingrels, etc.	Kartvelian	1,201.2
Jews		43.4
Tatars		1,139.6
Kumyks		100.8
Turks	Turco–Tatars	70.2
Nogays		55.4
Karaches		22.0
Kalmuks		11.8
Estonians Mordvinians		1.4

The territorial distribution of the largest nationalities involved is as follows: The Russians, who constitute the most numerous group in the whole Caucasus, are concentrated in the north, in the Kuban and Black Sea districts and in the northwest part of Tersk. Moving southward, in the western part of the Caucasus the Kartvelians are located; they occupy the Kutai and the southeastern part of the Tiflis gubernias. Still further south, the central territory is occupied by the Armenians in the southern portion of the Tiflis, the eastern portion of the Kars and the northern portion of the Erivan gubernias, squeezed between the Georgians in the north, the Turks in the west and the Tatars in the east and south, in the Baku, Elizabetpol and Erivan gubernias. In the east and in the mountains are located mountain tribes, while other minor groups such as Jews and Germans live, intermingled with the autochthonous population, mainly in the cities. The complexity of the nationality problem appears particularly in the linguistic conditions because in the Caucasus there exist, besides Russian, Ossetian, and Armenian, about a half-dozen languages, four Lezgin dialects, several Chechen, several Circassian, Mingrel, Georgian, Sudanese, and a number of others. And these are by no means dialects, but mostly independent languages incomprehensible to the rest of the population.

From the standpoint of the problem of autonomy, obviously only three nationalities enter into consideration: Georgians, Armenians, and Tatars, because the Russians inhabiting the northern part of the Caucasus constitute, with regard to nationality, a continuation of the state territory of the purely Russian population.

The relatively most numerous nationality group besides the Russians are the Georgians, if we include among them all varieties of Kartvelians. The historical territory of the Georgians is represented by the gubernias of Tiflis and Kutai and the districts of Sukhum and Sakatali, with a population of 2,110,490. However, the Georgian nationality constitutes only slightly more than half of that number, i.e., 1,200,000; the remainder is composed of Armenians to the number of about 220,000, concentrated mainly in the Akhalkalats county of the Tiflis gubernia, where they constitute over 70 percent of the population; Tatars to the number of 100,000; Ossetians, over 70,000; Lezgins represent half of the population in the Sakatali district; and Abkhazes are preponderant in the Sukham district; while in the Borchalin county of the Tiflis gubernia a mixture of various nationalities holds a majority over the Georgian population.

In view of these figures the project of Georgian nationality autonomy presents manifold difficulties. Georgia's historical territory, taken as a whole, represents such a numerically insignificant population—scarcely 1,200,000—that it seems insufficient as a basis of independent autonomous life in the modern sense, with its cultural needs and socioeconomic functions. In an autonomous Georgia, with its historical boundaries, a nationality that comprises only slightly more than half of the entire population would be called on to dominate in public institutions, schools, and political life. The impossibility of this situation is felt so well by the Georgian nationalists of revolutionary hue that they, a priori, relinquish the historical boundaries and plan to curtail the autonomous territory to an area corresponding to the actual preponderance of the Georgian nationality.

According to that plan, only sixteen of Georgia's counties would be the basis of the Georgian autonomy, while the fate of the four remaining ones with a preponderance of other nationalities would be decided by a "plebiscite" of those nationalities. This plan looks highly democratic and revolutionary; but like most anarchist-inspired plans which seek to solve all historic difficulties by means of the "will of nations" it has a defect, which is that in practice the plebiscite plan is even more difficult to implement than the autonomy of historical Georgia. The area specified in the Georgian plan would include scarcely 1,400,000 people, i.e., a figure corresponding to the population of a big modern city. This area, cut out quite arbitrarily from Georgia's traditional framework and present socioeconomic status, is not only an extremely small basis for autonomous life but moreover does not represent any organic entity, any sphere of material life and economic and cultural interests, besides the abstract interests of the Georgian nationality.

However, even in this area, the Georgians' nationality claims cannot be interpreted as an active expression of autonomous life, in view of the circumstance that their numerical preponderance is linked with their preeminently agrarian character.

In the very heart of Georgia, the former capital, Tiflis, and a number of smaller cities have an eminently international character, with the Armenians, who represent the bourgeois stratum, as the preponderant element. Out of Tiflis's population of 160,000 the Armenians constitute 55,000, the Georgians and Russians 20,000 each; the balance is composed of Tatars, Persians, Jews, Greeks, etc. The natural centers of political and administrative life as well as of education and spiritual culture are here, as in Lithuania, seats of foreign nationalities. This circumstance, which makes Georgia's nationality autonomy an insoluble problem, impinges simultaneously on another Caucasian problem: the question of the autonomy of the Armenians.

The exclusion of Tiflis and other cities from the autonomous Georgian territory is as impossible from the standpoint of Georgia's socioeconomic conditions as is their inclusion into that territory from the standpoint of the Armenian nationality. If we took as a basis the numerical preponderance of Armenians in the population, we would obtain a territory artificially patched together from a few fragments: two southern counties of Tiflis gubernia, the northern part of Erivan gubernia, and the northeastern part of Kars gubernia, i.e., a territory cut off from the main cities inhabited by the Armenians, which is senseless both from the historical standpoint and from the standpoint of the present economic conditions, while the size of the putative autonomous area would be limited to some 800,000. If we went beyond the counties having a numerical preponderance of Armenians we would find the Armenians inextricably mixed in the north with the Georgians; in the south—in the Baku and Elizabetpol gubernias—with the Tatars; and in the west, in the Kars gubernia, with the Turks. The Armenians play, in relation to the mostly agrarian Tatar population which lives in rather backward conditions, partly the role of a bourgeois element.

Thus, the drawing of a boundary between the main nationalities of the Caucasus is an insoluble task. But even more difficult is the problem of autonomy in relation to the remaining multiple nationalities of the Caucasian mountaineers. Both their territorial intermingling and the small numerical size of the respective nationalities, and finally the socioeconomic conditions which remain mostly on the level of largely nomadic pastoralism, or primitive farming, without an urban life of their own and with no intellectual creativity in their native language, make the functioning of modern autonomy entirely inapplicable.

Just as in Lithuania, the only method of settling the nationality question in the Caucasus, in the democratic spirit, securing to all nationalities freedom of cultural existence without any among them dominating the remaining ones, and at the same time meeting the recognized need for modern development, is to disregard ethnographic boundaries, and to introduce broad local self-government—communal, urban, district, and provincial—without a definite nationality character, that is, giving no privileges to any nationality. Only such a self-government will make it possible to unite various nationalities to jointly take care of the local economic and social interests, and on the other hand, to take into consideration in a natural way the different proportions of the nationalities in each county and each commune.

Communal, district, provincial self-government will make it possible for each nationality, by means of a majority decision in the organs of local administration, to establish its schools and cultural institutions in those districts or communes where it possesses numerical preponderance. At the same time a separate, empire-wide, linguistic law guarding the interests of the minority can establish a norm in virtue of which national minorities, beginning with a certain numerical minimum, can constitute a basis for the compulsory founding of schools in their national languages in the commune, district, or province; and their language can be established in local public and administrative institutions, courts, etc., at the side of the language of the preponderant nationality (the official language). Such a solution would be workable, if indeed any solution is possible within the framework of capitalism, and given the historical conditions. This solution would combine the general principle of local self-government with special legislative measures to guarantee cultural development and equality of rights of the nationalities through their close cooperation, and not their mutual separation by barriers of national autonomy.

IV

An interesting example of a purely formalistic settlement of the nationality question for the entire Russian empire is provided by the project of a certain K. Fortunatov published by the group "Trud i Borba" [Work and Struggle], an attempt at a practical solution of the problem in accordance with the principles of the Russian revolutionary socialists.* On the basis of the census, the author first arranges a map of the empire according to nationalities, taking as a basis the numerical preponderance of each nationality in the respective gubernias and counties. The numerically strongest nationality is the Great Russians who are preponderant in thirty gubernias of European Russia. They are followed by the Little Russians who have a majority in the Ukraine in the gubernias of Poltawa, Podolia, Kharkov, Kiev, and Volhynia, and are represented also in the gubernias of Ekaterinoslav, Chernigov, Kherson, Kuban, and Taurida, while in Bessarabia the Moldavians and in the Crimea the Tatars are preponderant. Apart from the Poles, the third nationality is the Byelorussians, who have a majority in five gubernias: Mogilev, Minsk, Vilna, Witebsk, and Grodno, with the exception of eight counties (Bialystok, inhabited mainly by Poles; Bielsk, Brzesc, and Kobryn, in which the Little Russians are preponderant; the Dzwinsk, Rezyca, and Lucin counties, where the Latvians are in the majority; and finally Troki, in which the Lithuanians prevail). On the other hand, the Krasne county of Smolensk gubernia has to be included in

* K. Fortunatov, *Natsonalniia Oblasti Rossii* (St. Petersburg: Knigoizdatelstvo Trud i Borba, 1906). The author is not the well-known statistician, Professor A. Fortunatov, as was erroneously surmised by the reviewer in *Humanity*, nos. 76 and 77, 1907.

Byelorussia because of the preponderance of that nationality. The Lithuanians and Samogitians prevail in the Kovno and Suwałki gubernias, with the exception of the Suwałki and Augustow counties in which the Poles are in the majority. The Latvians in Courland and the Estonians in Estonia have a decisive majority, and between them they divide Livonia into practically two equal parts, southern and northern. Including the Congress Kingdom, with the exception of the Suwałki gubernia, we obtain, in sixty-two gubernias of European Russia, the following picture of nationality relations:

Great Russians *preponderant in*	30 gubernias
Little Russians	10 gubernias
Byelorussians	5 gubernias
Poles	9 gubernias
Lithuanians	2 gubernias
Latvians	2 gubernias
Estonians	1 gubernia
Moldavians	1 gubernia
Tatars	2 gubernias

Having examined the territorial distribution of nationalities in the Caucasus according to gubernias and counties, the author in turn moves to Asiatic Russia. In Siberia, the Russian element is in a decisive majority, forming 80.9 percent of the population besides the Buriats, 5 percent; Yakuts, 4 percent; Tatars, 3.6 percent; other nationalities, 6.5 percent. Only in the Yakut gubernia do the Russians constitute a minority of 11.5 percent while the Yakuts form 82.2 percent of the whole. In Central Asia, the most numerous nationalities are the Kirgis, who are in a majority in all gubernias with the exception of the three southern ones: Trans-Caspia, in which the Turkomans number 65 percent, Samarkana, inhabited by the Uzbekhs (58.8 percent) and Tadzikhs (26.9 percent), and the Fergan Valley, in which the Sarts form half,

Districts	*Population of gubernia forming part of district with preponderance of given nationality*	*Population of all counties, with a majority of a given nationality*	*Over-all figure of persons in a given nationality in the empire*
			In Thousands
1. Great Russian	57,617	57,250	55,673
2. Little Russian	25,347	26,587	22,415
3. Byelorussian	8,517	7,328	5,886
4. Polish	8,819	8,696	7,931
5. Lithuanian-Latvian	4,101	4,088	3,094
6. Estonian	413	958	1,003
7. Moldavian	1,935	1,352	1,122
8. Kartvelian		1,503	1,352
9. Armenian		946	1,173
10. Caucasian Mountaineers	6,497	1,109	1,092
11. Caucasian Tatars		1,982	1,533
12. Other Caucasians		527	
13. Chuvashes, Bashkirs, Tatars, Mordvinians	4,367	3,673	
14. Kiris-Turkoman	5,515	5,642	4,365
15. Sarts, Uzbekhs, and Tatchiks (Tadzikhs)	2,232	2,232	2,046
16. Yakuts	270	234	227
17. Others		1,173	
Total:	125,640	125,640	

the Uzbekhs 9.7 percent, the Kirgis 12.8 percent of the population.

Thus, taking as a basis the gubernias and counties with a preponderance of one nationality or another, Mr. Fortunatov ranges the following scheme of nationality districts in the whole empire, as shown on the left.

In this scheme we are struck by great numerical differences, e.g., between the tremendous Great Russian and Little Russian districts and such tiny ones as the Lithuanian, Estonian, or individual Caucasian, let alone the Yakut. This circumstance apparently offends the sense of symmetry of the admirers of the principle of "Federation." It also evokes in them some doubts as to whether nationalities so unequal in strength and size could enter into idyllic coexistence as autonomous districts possessing equal rights. Therefore, our statistician, without much thought, obviates the evil with scissors and glue by combining several small districts into one and simultaneously dismembering two big ones into smaller ones. Apparently taking a population of six to nine million as a normal measure of a nationality district—although it is unknown on what basis—he considers that it is "easy" to split the Little Russian district into three and the Great Russian into seven, separating for instance the Don, Astrakhazan, Kuban, Stavropol, and Black Sea gubernias and two counties of Tersk with a population of 6.7 million as a "Cossack" district, and the Kazan, Ufa, Orenburg, Samar gubernias and two counties of Symbir gubernia with nine million population as a Tatar Bashkir district, finally simply dividing the remaining territory of twenty-five gubernias with forty-two million people into five more or less symmetrical parts with eight million people, with no regard to the nationality principle.

In this way we obtain the plan of the division of the whole of Russia into the following sixteen "states" or autonomous districts on the basis of nationalities:

1	Poland with a population of	8,696,000
1	Byelorussia with a population of	7,328,000
1	Baltic with a population of	5,046,000
3	Little Russia with a population of	27,228,000
	a. Southwestern (Podolia, Volhynia and Kiev, and 3 counties of Grodno) with a population of	10,133,000
	b. Little Russia Proper (Poltawa, Kharkov, Chernigov without the northern counties as well as the Little Russian counties of Kursk and Voronezh gubernia) with a population of	8,451,000
	c. New Russia (Bessarabia, Kherson, Taurida, Ekaternoslav and Taganrog county) with a population of	8,644,000
1	Caucasus (without the Russian counties)	6,157,000
1	Kirgis in Central Asia (without 2 counties of Akmolin province) with a population of	7,490,000
1	Siberia (with 2 counties of Akmolin province) with a population of	6,015,000
7	Great Russia with a population of	57,680,000

In setting up the above scheme the author was obviously not restrained by any historical or economic considerations, or by the divisions of production or commercial communication created by modern development and natural conditions. It is well known that such pedestrian considerations can only hamper the political concoctions of people professing the "Marxist" doctrine and a materialistic world view. They do not exist for the theorists and politicians of "truly revolutionary socialism," who have in mind only the "rights" of nations, freedom, equality, and other such lofty matters. The separation of two Lithuanian gubernias—Kovno and Suwałki—with the exclusion of the Polish counties—from the historico-cultural heart of Lithuania, the Vilna gubernia and other neighboring regions with which economic relations were of long standing, and on the other hand the joining of these two curtailed gubernias with Livonia, Courland, and Estonia, with which the historical links, as well as present-day economic ones, are quite loose, clearly demonstrates this point. Although the cutting up of the Ukraine for the sake of symmetry into various divisions, despite the continuity of its natural and economic character, and on the other hand, combining into one autonomous region of Siberia a country comprising 12.5 million square kilometers, i.e., by one-third bigger than the whole of Europe, a country representing the greatest natural economic and cultural contrasts, is a demonstration that that method is free of any "dogmas." At the same time, the nationality autonomy in this scheme is treated free of any connection with the economic and social structure of the given nationality. From this standpoint other peoples are equally prepared for regional autonomy—that is, they evince a certain permanent territory and administration, legislation, and cultural life centralized in that territory. There are, on the one hand, the Poles, and on the other the Kirgis, the Yakuts, and the Buriats, who are still partly nomadic and are still living according to the traditions of tribal organization, thwarting to this very day the efforts of the territorial administration of Russian absolutism. The autonomous regional construction, in accordance with the "socialist-revolutionary" views, is thus entirely "free," unconnected with any real bases in time and space, and all the existing historical, economic, and cultural conditions play only the role of material out of which, by means of "revolutionary" scissors, artful nationality plots are to be cut out.

What is the result of this solely and exclusively ethnographic method of the political dismemberment of Russia? Mr. Fortunatov's scheme reduces the principle of nationality to an absurdity. Although the Lithuanians are cut off from the Polish nationality with which they coalesce culturally, still they are linked on the basis of ethnographic affinity into one "Baltic" nationality with the Latvians and the Estonians, with whom they identify as little as with the Poles; thus they gravitate toward the completely Germanized cultural centers of Livonia and Estonia. Combining the Georgians, Armenians, Tatars, and a few dozen other tribes of the Caucasus into one "Caucasian" nationality smacks of a malicious satire against national autonomous aspirations. No greater regard for these aspirations is evidenced by the inclusion of the Moldavians, situated in Bessarabia, in the Little Russian nationality, of the Crimean Tatars in the very same nationality, and finally by the combining of Samoyeds, Ostiaks, Tunguz, Buriats, Yakuts, Chuckchees, Kamchadals, and many other tribes, each living an entirely separate life, differing among themselves in the level of cultural development, language, religion, even partly race, with the Russian population of Siberia into one mysterious "Siberian" nationality with common legislative, administrative, and cultural institutions. Fortunatov's scheme is basically a simple negation of the nationality principle. It is also interesting as an example of the anarchistic approach to nationalism, unrestricted as it is by any considerations of objective social development. Having thrown its weight around in that valley of tears, it eventually returns to the results, very much resembling the same ugly history of reality which it had undertaken "to correct," i.e., the systematic violations of the "nationality rights" and their equality. The whole difference consists in the fact that the trampling of the "rights" of nationalities imagined by the ideology of liberalism and anarchism is, in reality, the result of the process of historical development which has its inner sense and—what is more important—its revolutionary dialectic, while revolutionary-nationalistic bungling tends, in its zealous cutting up of what had grown together socially, and in its gluing of what socially cannot be glued together, to trample eventually the nationality "rights" celebrated by it, merely for the sake of schematic pedantry deprived of any sense and blown up with political buffoonery.

Notes

1. Karl Marx, *The Eighteenth Brumaire of Louis Bonaparte* (New York: International Publishers, 1969), pp. 121-23.
2. Karl Kautsky, "Partikularismus und Sozialdemokratie," in *Die Neue Zeit, 1898–1899*, Vol. I, pp. 505-06.

There Can be No Self-Determination Under Capitalism[1]

It is true that socialism recognizes for every people the right of independence and the freedom of independent control of its own destinies. But it is a veritable perversion of socialism to regard present-day capitalist society as the expression of this self-determination of nations. Where is there a nation in which the people have had the right to determine the form and conditions of their national, political, and social existence? In Germany, the determination of the people found concrete expression in the demands formulated by the German revolutionary democrats of 1848; the first fighters of the German proletariat, Marx, Engels, Lassalle, Bebel, and Liebknecht, proclaimed and fought for a united German republic. For this ideal the revolutionary forces in Berlin and in Vienna, in those tragic days of March, shed their heart's blood upon the barricades. To carry out this program, Marx and Engels demanded that Prussia take up arms against tsarism. The foremost demand made in the national program was for the liquidation of the "heap of organized decay, the Hapsburg Monarchy," as well as of two dozen other dwarf monarchies within Germany itself. The overthrow of the German revolution, the treachery of the German bourgeoisie to its own democratic ideals, led to the Bismarck regime and to its creature, present-day Greater Prussia, twenty-five fatherlands under one helm, the German empire. Modern Germany is built upon the grave of the March Revolution, upon the wreckage of the right of self-determination of the German people. The present war, supporting Turkey and the Hapsburg monarchy, and strengthening German military autocracy, is a second burial of the March revolutionists, and of the national program of the German people. It is a fiendish jest of history that the Social Democrats, the heirs of the German patriots of 1848, should go forth in this war with the banner of "self-determination of nations" held aloft in their hands. But, perhaps the Third French Republic, with its colonial possessions in four continents and its colonial horrors in two, is the expression of the self-determination of the French nation? Or the British nation, with its India, with its South African rule of a million whites over a population of five million colored people? Or perhaps Turkey, or the Empire of the Tsar?

Capitalist politicians, in whose eyes the rulers of the people and the ruling classes are the nation, can honestly speak of the "right of national self-determination" in connection with such colonial empires. To the socialist, no nation is free whose national existence is based upon the enslavement of another people, for to him colonial peoples, too, are human beings, and, as such, parts of the national state. International socialism recognizes the right of free independent nations, with equal rights. But socialism alone can create such nations, can bring self-determination of their peoples. This slogan of socialism is like all its others, not an apology for existing conditions, but a guidepost, a spur for the revolutionary, regenerative, active policy of the proletariat. So long as capitalist states exist, i.e., so long as imperialistic world policies determine and regulate the inner and the outer life of a nation, there can be no "national self-determination" either in war or in peace.

Notes

1. Excerpted from *The Crisis in German Social Democracy* (New York: 1969), pp. 94-95. The pamphlet was first published in German in Zurich in 1916, under the pseudonym "Junius."

The Nationalities Question in the Russian Revolution[1]

The Bolsheviks are in part responsible for the fact that the military defeat was transformed into the collapse and breakdown of Russia. Moreover, the Bolsheviks themselves have, to a great extent, sharpened the objective difficulties of this situation by a slogan which they placed in the foreground of their policies: the so-called right of self-determination of peoples, or—something which was really implicit in this slogan—the slogan of the disintegration of Russia.

The formula of the right of the various nationalities of the Russian Empire to determine their fate independently, "even to the point of the right of governmental separation from Russia," was proclaimed again with doctrinaire obstinacy as a special battle cry of Lenin and his comrades, during their opposition against Miliukovist, and then Kerenskyan imperialism. It also constituted the axis of their inner policy after the October Revolution. And it constituted the entire platform of the Bolsheviks at Brest-Litovsk, all they had to oppose to the display of force by German imperialism.

One is immediately struck with the obstinacy and rigid consistency with which Lenin and his comrades stuck to this slogan, a slogan which is in sharp contradiction to their otherwise outspoken centralism in politics as well as to the attitude they have assumed toward other democratic principles. While they showed a quite cool contempt for the Constituent

Assembly, universal suffrage, freedom of press and assembly, in short, for the whole apparatus of the basic democratic liberties of the people which, taken all together, constituted the "right of self-determination" inside Russia, they treated the right of self-determination of peoples as a jewel of democratic policy for the sake of which all practical considerations of real criticism had to be stilled. While they did not permit themselves to be imposed upon in the slightest by the plebiscite for the Constituent Assembly in Russia, a plebiscite on the basis of the most democratic suffrage in the world, carried out in the full freedom of a popular republic, and while they simply declared this plebiscite null and void on the basis of a very sober, critical evaluation of its results, still at Brest they championed the "popular vote" of the foreign nationalities of Russia on the question of which land they wanted to belong to, as the true palladium of all freedom and democracy, the unadulterated quintessence of the will of the people, and as the court of last resort in questions of the political fate of nations.

The contradiction that is so obvious here is all the harder to understand since the democratic forms of political life in each land, as we shall see, actually involve the most valuable and even indispensable foundations of socialist policy, whereas the famous "right of self-determination of nations" is nothing but hollow, bourgeois phraseology and humbug.

Indeed, what is this right supposed to signify? It belongs to the ABC of socialist policy that socialism opposes every form of oppression, including also that of one nation by another.

If, despite all this, such generally sober and critical politicians as Lenin and Trotsky and their friends, who have nothing but an ironical shrug for every sort of utopian phrase such as disarmament, league of nations, etc., have in this case made a hollow phrase of exactly the same kind into their special hobby, this arose, it seems to us, as a result of some opportunistic kind of policy. Lenin and his comrades clearly calculated that there was no surer method of binding the many foreign peoples within the Russian Empire to the cause of the revolution, to the cause of the socialist proletariat, than that of offering them, in the name of the revolution and of socialism, the most extreme and most unlimited freedom to determine their own fate. This was analogous to the policy of the Bolsheviks toward the Russian peasants, whose land hunger was satisfied by the slogan of direct seizure of the noble estates and who were supposed to be bound thereby to the banner of the revolution and the proletarian government. In both cases, unfortunately, the calculation was entirely wrong.

While Lenin and his comrades clearly expected that, as champions of national freedom even to the extent of "separation," they would turn Finland, the Ukraine, Poland, Lithuania, the Baltic countries, the Caucasus, etc., into so many faithful allies of the Russian Revolution, we have witnessed the opposite spectacle. One after another, these "nations" used the freshly granted freedom to ally themselves with German imperialism against the Russian Revolution as its mortal enemy, and, under German protection, to carry the banner of counter-revolution into Russia itself. The little game with the Ukraine at Brest, which caused a decisive turn of affairs in those negotiations and brought about the entire inner and outer political situation at present prevailing for the Bolsheviks, is a perfect case in point. The conduct of Finland, Poland, Lithuania, the Baltic lands, the nations of the Caucasus, shows most convincingly that we are dealing here not with an exceptional case, but with a typical phenomenon.

To be sure, in all these cases, it was really not the "people" who engaged in these reactionary policies, but only the bourgeois and petit bourgeois classes, who—in sharpest opposition to their own proletarian masses—perverted the "national right of self-determination" into an instrument of their counter-revolutionary class policies. But—and here we come to the very heart of the question—it is in this that the utopian, petit bourgeois character of this nationalistic slogan resides: that in the midst of the crude realities of class society, especially when class antagonisms are sharpened to the uttermost, it is simply converted into a means of bourgeois class rule. The Bolsheviks were to be taught, to their own great hurt and that of the revolution, that under the rule of capitalism there is no self-determination of peoples, that in a class society each class of the nation strives to "determine itself" in a different fashion; and that, for the bourgeois classes, the standpoint of national freedom is fully subordinated to that of class rule. The Finnish bourgeoisie, like the Ukrainian petite bourgeoisie, was unanimous in preferring the violent rule of Germany to national freedom, if the latter should be bound up with Bolshevism.

The hope of transforming these actual class relationships somehow into their opposite through "plebiscites," on which everything turned at Brest, and of getting a majority vote for union with the Russian Revolution by depending on the revolutionary masses—if it was seriously meant by Lenin and Trotsky—represented an incomprehensible degree of optimism. And if it was only meant as a tactical flourish in the duel with the German politics of force, then it represented dangerous playing with fire. Even without German military occupation, the famous "popular plebiscite," supposing that it had come to that in the border states, would have yielded a result, in all probability, which would have given the Bolsheviks little cause for rejoicing; for we must take into consideration the psychology of the peasant masses and of great sections of still indifferent proletarians, as well as the reactionary tendency of the petite bourgeoisie, and the thousand ways in which the bourgeoisie could have influenced the vote. Indeed, it can be taken as an unbreakable rule in these matters of plebiscites on the national question, that the ruling class will either know how to prevent them where it doesn't suit their purpose, or, where they somehow occur, will know how to influence their results by all sorts of means, big and little, the same means which make it impossible to introduce socialism by a popular vote.

The mere fact that the question of national aspirations and tendencies toward separation were injected at all into the midst of the revolutionary struggle, and were even pushed into the foreground and made into the shibboleth of socialist and revolutionary policy as a result of the Brest peace, has served to bring the greatest confusion into socialist ranks and has actually destroyed the position of the proletariat in the border countries.

In Finland, so long as the socialist proletariat fought as a part of the closed Russian revolutionary phalanx, it possessed a position of dominant power: it had the majority in the Finnish parliament, in the army; it had reduced its own bourgeoisie to complete impotence, and was master of the situation within its borders.

Or take the Ukraine. At the beginning of the century, before the tomfoolery of "Ukrainian nationalism" with its silver rubles and its "Universals"[2] and Lenin's hobby of an "independent Ukraine" had been invented, the Ukraine was the stronghold of the Russian revolutionary movement. From there, from Rostov, from Odessa, from the Donetz region, flowed out the first lava streams of the revolution (as early as 1902–1904), which kindled all South Russia into a sea of flame, thereby preparing the uprising of 1905. The same thing was repeated in the present revolution, in which the South Russian proletariat supplies the elite troops of the proletarian phalanx. Poland and the Baltic lands have been, since 1905, the mightiest and most dependable hearths of revolution, and in them the socialist proletariat has played an outstanding role.

How does it happen then, that in all these lands the

counter-revolution suddenly triumphs? The nationalist movement, just because it tore the proletariat loose from Russia, crippled it thereby, and delivered it into the hands of the bourgeoisie of the border countries.

Instead of acting in the same spirit of genuine, international, class policy which they represented in other matters, instead of working for the most compact union of the revolutionary forces throughout the area of the Empire, instead of defending tooth and nail the integrity of the Russian Empire as an area of revolution and opposing to all forms of separatism the solidarity and inseparability of the proletarians in all lands within the sphere of the Russian Revolution as the highest command of politics, the Bolsheviks, by their hollow nationalistic phraseology concerning the "right of self-determination to the point of separation," have accomplished quite the contrary and supplied the bourgeoisie in all border states with the finest, the most desirable pretext, the very banner of the counter-revolutionary efforts. Instead of warning the proletariat in the border countries against all forms of separatism as mere bourgeois traps, they did nothing but confuse the masses in all the border countries by their slogan and delivered them up to the demagogy of the bourgeois classes. By this nationalistic demand they brought on the disintegration of Russia itself, pressed into the enemy's hand the knife which it was to thrust into the heart of the Russian Revolution.

To be sure, without the help of German imperialism, without "the German rifle butts in German fists," as Kautsky's *Neue Zeit* put it, the Lubinskys and other little scoundrels of the Ukraine, the Erichs and Mannerheims of Finland, and the Baltic barons would never have gotten the better of the socialist masses of the workers in their respective lands. But national separatism was the Trojan horse inside which the German "comrades," bayonets in hand, made their entrance into all those lands. The real class antagonisms and relations of military force brought about German intervention. But the Bolsheviks provided the ideology which masked this campaign of counter-revolution; they strengthened the position of the bourgeoisie and weakened that of the proletariat.

The best proof is the Ukraine, which was to play such an unhappy role in the outcome of the Russian Revolution. Ukrainian nationalism in Russia was something quite different from, let us say, Czech, Polish, or Finnish nationalism, in that the former was a mere whim, a folly of a few dozen petit bourgeois intellectuals, without the slightest roots in the economic, political, or psychological relationships of the country; it was without any historical tradition, since the Ukraine never formed a nation or government, was without any national culture, except for the reactionary romantic poems of Shevschenko. It is exactly as if, one fine day, the people living in the *Wasserkante* should want to found a new Low-German [*Plattdeutsche*] nation and government! And this ridiculous pose of a few university professors and students was inflated into a political force by Lenin and his comrades through their doctrinaire agitation concerning the "right of self-determination including, etc." To what was at first a mere farce they lent such importance that the farce became a matter of the most deadly seriousness—not as a serious national movement for which, afterward as before, there are no roots at all, but as a shingle and rallying flag of counter-revolution! At Brest, out of this addled egg crept the German bayonets.

There are times when such phrases have a very real meaning in the history of class struggles. It is the unhappy lot of socialism that in this World War it was destined to supply the ideological screens for counter-revolutionary policy. At the outbreak of the war, German Social Democracy hastened to deck the predatory expedition of German imperialism with an ideological shield from the lumber room of Marxism by declaring it to be a liberating expedition against Russian Tsarism such as our old teachers [Marx and Engels] had longed for. And to the lot of the Bolsheviks, who were the very antipodes of our government socialists, did it fall to supply grist for the mill of counter-revolution with their phrases about self-determination of peoples; and thereby to supply an ideology, not alone for the strangling of the Russian Revolution itself, but even for the planned counter-revolutionary settlement of the entire World War.

We have good reason to examine very carefully the policies of the Bolsheviks in this regard. The "right of self-determination of nations," coupled with the League of Nations and disarmament by the grace of President Wilson, constitute the battle cry under which the coming reckoning of international socialism with the bourgeoisie is to be settled. It is obvious that the phrases concerning self-determination and the entire nationalist movement, which at present constitute the greatest danger for international socialism, have experienced an extraordinary strengthening from the Russian Revolution and the Brest negotiations. We shall yet have to go into this platform thoroughly. The tragic fate of these phrases in the Russian Revolution, on the thorns of which the Bolsheviks were themselves destined to be caught and bloodily scratched, must serve the international proletariat as a warning and lesson.

And from all this there followed the dictatorship of Germany from the time of the Brest treaty to the time of the "supplementary treaty." The two hundred expiatory sacrifices in Moscow. From this situation arose the terror and the suppression of democracy.[3]

Notes

1. This selection is published as Chapter II of the pamphlet, *The Russian Revolution,* which was constituted out of notes prepared by Rosa Luxemburg in prison in 1918, and published posthumously. There is more than one version of certain passages. We have followed, for the most part, the text of the German edition edited by Paul Levi (Frankfurt-am-Main: 1922), as corrected by Felix Weill—see Grünberg's *Archiv für die Geschichte des Sozialismus und der Arbeiterbewegung* (1928), pp. 285-98.
2. The manuscript speaks of *Karbowentzen,* which may be a Germanization of the Russian word for "silver ruble," probably referring to a special Ukrainian coinage, and of "*Universals,*" the name applied to certain manifestoes or declarations of the Ukrainian Rada (National Assembly).
3. Six weeks after the signing of the Brest–Litovsk treaty, there was a codicil or supplement signed. The "two hundred expiatory sacrifices" may refer to the execution of persons charged with complicity in the assassination of the German ambassador, Count von Mirbach, shot by terrorists of the Socialist Revolutionary Party.

Appendix

"Theses" of the Editors of Gazeta Robotnicza

Editor's Note

The theses here presented are the work of Radek, Stein-Krajewski, and M. Broński, who were then located in Switzerland; before the draft was published, it was submitted also to Hanecki in Copenhagen. This was the so-called Rostamowcy fraction of the old SDKPiL. Nationalism was not an issue between this group and the Zarzadowcy faction to which Rosa Luxemburg belonged, so these theses are intended as an expression and continuation of Rosa Luxemburg's position on the national question. Of course, Rosa Luxemburg herself had by this time modified her position slightly, as will be evident from a study of the "Junius" pamphlet, published at the same time as these theses; her position two years later, in the pamphlet, *The Russian Revolution* (a chapter of which is included in the present collection), is again not precisely the same. However, the theses do express her general point of view.

I. Imperialism and National Oppression[1]

1. Imperialism represents the tendency of finance capital to *outgrow the bounds of a national state,* to win for domestic capital overseas possessions, raw-material sources, opportunities for investment, and markets, and to create also *in Europe large state blocs* through the fusion of adjacent areas which are complementary to each other regardless of the nationality of their population. This latter tendency is based also on military grounds, since imperialism aggravates the contradictions between states and makes offensive and defensive measures necessary.

The imperialistic tendencies toward colonial and continental annexations mean an *increase and generalization of national oppression,* which up to now was experienced only in individual states where, due to historical and geographical reasons, one nation ruled over others.

2. This national oppression is *against the interests of the working class.* The same imperialist bureaucracy, which constitutes an agent of national oppression, becomes the agent of the *oppression of the proletariat of its own nation;* it applies in the battle against the proletariat of the ruling nationality all those means and measures which are used in the fight with oppressed nations. *As to the working class of the oppressed nation,* national oppression restrains it in the *class struggle,* not only by restricting its *liberty of organization* and lower-

ing its cultural level, but also by arousing in it a *feeling of solidarity with its national bourgeoisie.* Tied hand and foot, corrupted politically by nationalism, the proletariat of the oppressed nation turns into a *defenseless object of exploitation* and at the same time into a dangerous competitor (wage-cutters, strikebreakers) to the workers of the oppressing nation.

The compulsory incorporation of nationally strange areas into the victorious state creates a new peril of war, as the conquered state will try to win those areas back, either because they are indispensable to it from the economic and strategic point of view, or because nationalist slogans serve best to conceal the imperialist policy of the conquered state.

3. The Social Democratic Party must therefore *fight* with the greatest energy against the *annexation policy* of imperialism and the resulting *policy of national oppression.*

In reply to the statement of the imperialists, that the acquisition of colonies is indispensable for the development of capitalism, Social Democracy points to the fact that in Central and Western Europe, as in the United States of America, the time to convert capitalism into socialism has already come. Socialism does not need colonies, because it will offer to the backward nations unselfish cultural support, and will secure from them through normal trade whatever products it is not able, for geographic reasons, to produce itself.

Not the expansion, not the prolongation of capitalism, but its abolition, is the historic task of the proletariat, which it can now fulfill.

In reply to the statement that in Europe annexations are necessary to guarantee the safety of the victorious imperialist state and thus to guarantee peace—Social Democracy points to the fact that annexations sharpen the contradictions and thus increase the peril of war. But even if this were not the case, Social Democracy cannot participate in the conclusion of a peace based on the oppression of peoples. If it accepted such a peace it would be *digging a chasm between the proletariat of the ruling and that of the oppressed nationality.* The proletariat of the ruling nation, by the acceptance of the annexation, would take responsibility for the imperialist policy and would be committed to support it; thus it would turn into a *slave of imperialism.* The proletariat of the *oppressed nation would unite with its bourgeoisie and would regard the proletariat of the ruling nation as its enemy.* Instead of an *international class struggle of the proletariat against the international bourgeoisie, a split among the proletarians would take place, the ideology of the workers would be corrupted,* the working class would be completely paralyzed in its everyday struggle as well as in its fight for socialism and against imperialism.

4. The starting point of the fight of Social Democracy against annexation, against keeping the oppressed nationalities persistently within the bounds of the annexing state, is the rejection of any *defense of the native country,* which, in the epoch of imperialism, would mean the defense of the rights of its bourgeoisie to oppress and rob foreign nations. The task of Social Democracy is to *reveal national oppression* as a stroke directed against the interests of the proletariat of the ruling nationality. This task consists in the demand for *all democratic rights* for the oppressed, among others, also for the liberty to agitate for a political separation, because democratic principles stipulate that any agitation should be fought by means of intellectual weapons and not by force. Refusing thus to bear the responsibility for the imperialist policy of oppression, Social Democracy resolutely opposes the setting of new boundaries in Europe, and demands the restoration of the borders abolished by imperialism. Where capitalism has developed without an independent state, history has shown that an independent state by no means constitutes an indispensable condition for the development of productive forces and for the establishment of a socialist structure. In

some cases, the wheel of imperialism crumbles an already established capitalist state, and through the brutal forms of imperialist oppression, brings about the political and economic concentration which prepares the way for socialism. Social Democracy, basing itself on the rising indignation resulting from this national and economic oppression, should teach the masses of both the oppressed and the oppressing nationalities how to wage a joint struggle, which alone is capable of abolishing national oppression and economic exploitation, *leading mankind through imperialism to socialism.*

If, in the developed capitalist states, Social Democracy cannot see the possibility of overcoming imperialism by returning to old forms, by creating new states or restoring old ones; if, on the contrary, it must, under the motto, "Away with borders!" prepare the way for *socialism,* for which the economic conditions are already ripe, there results also from this task of Social Democracy the demand: "Away with colonies!", a slogan which signals the top achievement of our fight against imperialist national oppression. The colonies are the source of new profits for capital as it seeks to prolong its life. Capitalism tries to extract from the colonies even human military resources, forming armies of natives which it uses on occasion against the revolutionary proletariat and, as now, in the World War, leads them against its competitors. This international renunciation of colonial expansion, which can be attained by the proletariat only by means of a revolutionary battle, will by no means signalize for the undeveloped capitalist states a return to barbarism, as the Social Imperialists maintain. In the more important Eastern countries (Turkey, China, India), an increase of bourgeois elements has been taking place for years, and these elements are able to fulfill independently capitalism's task of developing the productive forces. When it demands that European capitalism abstain from colonial expansion, Social Democracy should use the struggle of the young colonial bourgeoisie against European imperialism, to *increase the revolutionary crisis in Europe.* Social Democracy will support the proletarian fight in the colonies against European and native capital in order to advance the moment when the hour of socialism will strike also outside Europe; it will simultaneously try to deepen among the colonial proletariat the conviction that the latter's long-term interests demand its solidarity, not with its national bourgeoisie, but with the European proletariat, fighting for socialism.

5. Just as it is impossible to transform imperialism on a capitalistic basis so as to accord with the interests of the working class and to stop the growth of armaments, it is also *impossible to free it from the tendency toward national oppression, to cause it to acknowledge the rights of the nations to self-determination.* Therefore, *it is necessary to carry on the fight against national oppression as a fight against imperialism, for socialism.*

In order to free the nationally oppressed masses, the fight of Social Democracy must *turn into a social-revolutionary fight* and must aim at the abolition of the capitalist reign. Because only by doing away with capitalist private property can the working class avoid having an interest in national oppression, which constitutes only a part of class domination. The socialist society will not have any oppression; it will grant to all nations the right to decide in common about their needs, and the liberty to each citizen to take part in the *determination* of what he has to carry out together with the others.

Bringing the fight against national oppression into the wide stream of the revolutionary struggle of the masses for socialism does not mean postponing this fight indefinitely, nor does it mean consoling the oppressed nations with hopes for the future. For the boisterous impact of the imperialist epoch, which upsets and revolutionizes all the old relations, turns it into an epoch of socialist revolutions, in which the proletariat breaks all its chains.

II. The So-Called Right of Self-Determination of Nations

The formula of the right of self-determination is an inheritance from the Second International. In the Second International it played a double role: on the one hand, it was supposed to express a protest against all national oppression, and on the other hand the readiness of Social Democracy to "defend the Fatherland." The slogan was applied to specific national questions only to avoid the necessity of investigating its concrete content and the tendencies of its development. While the consequences of the policy of defending the Fatherland in the era of imperialism showed the counter-revolutionary character of this formula with complete clarity, its erroneous character as a formula which should sum up our struggle against national oppression is still not clear to many people. Since the slogan sharply expresses the opposition to the oppressive tendencies of imperialism, even revolutionary Social Democrats (for instance those of Russia) find it a necessary part of our revolutionary agitation. While we fully endorse the proletarian revolutionary goals which they seek to advance with the slogan of the right of self-determination, we still cannot recognize this formulation as the right expression of our struggle against imperialism. Here are the reasons:

1. *The right of self-determination is not applicable in capitalist society.*

Modern nations constitute the political-cultural form of

the supremacy of the bourgeoisie over the masses of the people who speak the same language. Split into classes as they are, nations have no common interests and no general will. The "national" policy is that which corresponds to the interests of the ruling class. This proposition is not at all affected by the fact that the several capitalist countries may enjoy political democracy. The influence of the economic domination of capital over the masses of the people, the systematic and continuing exercise of this domination through all the organs of the capitalist state (church, school, press), permits the bourgeoisie to impose its own capitalist will on the majority of the people indirectly, and let the will of capital appear as that of the people. That is the way modern democracy works! In the relations of nations with one another, what is decisive is the interest of the stronger bourgeoisie or of a combination of several of their national groups. Capital in its expansion cannot wait to impose its will on the popular masses in the territory into which it seeks to expand, through economic and cultural influences. This process would take decades; often the contrary will of other capitalist groups stands in its way and makes it impossible. Therefore, in *questions of the annexation of foreign territories, the forms of political democracy are dispensed with, and brute force decides.* The referendum can be used here only as an open betrayal, to sanction the acts of power. Therefore, it is completely impossible to make the will of nations the deciding factor in changing boundaries under capitalist conditions, as the so-called right of self-determination demands.

If this demand is taken to mean that a single part of a nation should itself decide its affiliation with this or that state, it is not only unrealistic—because capital will never leave the decision about its boundaries to the people—but also particularistic, undemocratic. If the popular masses of a country had in their hands the decision about its boundaries, the decision would have to be made by the whole state, not by a province alone. Even where it is a question of points of contention between two countries, the principles of democracy would call for an agreement between their democratically elected representatives. For example: suppose the annexation of Alsace–Lorraine to France raised a national question there—the efforts of that part of the population seeking a return to Germany. If this issue raised the question of Germany seeking revenge, thus threatening France with new wars, it is clear that it would be in no sense democratic for all these consequences to befall the French people, who had no voice in the decision, merely on account of the desires of the Alsatians.

2. *The right of self-determination is inapplicable to socialist society.*

The so-called right of self-determination is also used with the proviso that it will become a reality for the first time under socialism and is thus an expression of our striving for socialism. This proposition is open to the following objections. We know that socialism will do away with all national oppression, because it removes the class interests that furnish the driving force of such oppression. We also have no reason to assume that the nation, in socialist society, will form a politicoeconomic unit. By all indications it will have the character of a cultural and linguistic unit; for the territorial division of the socialist cultural unit, insofar as this will survive at all, can only follow the needs of production, and this division would have to be determined, not by individual nations separately, from their own power (as the "right of self-determination" demands), but through the *joint action* of all interested citizens. The carrying over of the formula of "right of self-determination" into socialism arises from a complete misunderstanding of the nature of socialist society.

3. *The tactical consequences of the application of the slogan of the right of self-determination.*

This slogan, like all utopian slogans, must spread false conceptions of the character of capitalist as well as socialist society and confuse the proletariat in its fight against national oppression. The proletariat is always confronted with the danger that its fate will be arbitrarily determined, under capitalism, by the clash of contending military and economic interests. This slogan arouses a hope *that cannot be fulfilled:* the hope, namely, that the war danger can be set aside *without capitalism having been banished*—the hope that capitalism can somehow adapt itself to the national interests of the weak peoples. Thus, this slogan, even against the will of its defenders, sets up *in place of the social-revolutionary perspective* which has been a major result of the World War, a national-reformist perspective. In the program of the proletariat in the *oppressed nations,* the slogan of the right of self-determination could serve as a bridge to social patriotism. As is shown by the experience of the Polish, Ruthenian, and Alsatian labor movements, this slogan is used as an argument for the nationalist movements in the working class, whereby the international front of the proletariat is broken.

When this slogan is accepted in the program of the oppressing nations, and put forward as the solution of the national question, it gives the social imperialists the chance, by proving that the slogan is an illusion, to picture our whole struggle against national oppression as a piece of historically unjustified sentimentality, and so to undermine the faith of the proletariat in the scientific basis of the social-democratic program. The slogan could even awaken in the proletariat of the oppressing nation the illusion that it, in contrast to the proletariat of the oppressed nation, was already self-determined, and thus had the duty to work together with other parts of the nation to defend their "common" interests, their will. But if the slogan of the right of self-determination is used in our propaganda to refer to a condition that will be realized only under socialism, then quite aside from the impossibility of the *self-determination* of a separate national group of socialist citizens taking precedence over the general interest, the slogan is not sufficient. For our *tactical interest* demands, in the transition period, when socialism is already possible, economically speaking, but social-revolutionary class struggle has still not begun, that the slogan of *socialism, of the social revolution, be put forward sharply and clearly, not obscured by any other slogan; this must be the central, preeminent idea, taking precedence over every partial struggle.*

4. *How to judge the question historically.*

Any attempts to appeal to the position that Marx took on the national question in the period 1848–1871 have not the least value, for if Marx campaigned for the freedom of Ireland and for the independence of Poland, he also at the same time came out against the movements for autonomy on the part of the Czechs, the South Slavs, etc. On the contrary, the fact that Marx did take a position shows precisely that it is not the job of Marxism to develop an attitude to concrete questions on the basis of abstract "rights." The negative position taken by Social Democracy on all national oppression results, as we showed in the first part of our theses, from the fact that the interests of the proletariat cannot be reconciled with supporting the ruling classes. Taking a positive position on any concrete national problem (Alsace–Lorraine, the Polish question, the Balkans) can only follow on the basis of the concrete tendencies to development of this question itself in the framework of the whole imperialist epoch.

To call the criticism of the right of self-determination Proudhonist makes no sense. Proudhonism denied that there was a national question and sought to solve all social questions, not by way of the class struggle, but by lower-middle-class associationism. The Marxist opponents of the so-called right of self-determination do not deny that there is a national question, and they do not postpone the fight against national oppression until the victory of socialism. But while they cannot be accused of Proudhonism, the method of the partisans of the right of self-determination can be recognized as the mechanical use of democratic concepts.

5. *Polish Social Democracy and the question of the so-called right of self-determination.*

Russian-Polish Social Democracy took its position on the Polish question on the basis of the analysis of Poland's economic development that was made in year 1893. The following twenty years of Polish history have fully confirmed this analysis, especially as neither in the 1905–1906 revolution, nor in the World War, did any *serious* social strata undertake any *independence movements in Poland.* They rejected the slogan of the right of self-determination when the International Congress in London, in 1896, brought it up, in order to distinguish their position from that of the Polish social patriots who had written on their flag the fight for the independence of Poland. After the self-determination term became the motto of social patriotism, the representatives of Polish Social Democracy fought against its being included in the program of Russian Social Democracy in 1903. Although it was included, the Russian-Polish Social Democracy joined the Party of the Whole [*Gesamtpartei*] in 1906, when, on the one hand, our complete victory over social patriotism had lessened the danger that it would be appealed to by the Russian Social Democrats, and the revolutionary mass struggle made a closing of the ranks imperative in spite of all differences of opinion. It could take this step all the more easily because this point did not play the least role in the agitation of the Russian Social Democracy during the Revolution; we had our own representatives in the central organs of the Party, and enjoyed the widest autonomy in our agitation. When, in the era of the counter-revolution, national questions assumed great significance in Russia, and in that connection a discussion began on the position of Social Democracy in regard to it, the Russian–Polish Social Democrats gave a fundamental explanation of their attitude on the question.

In these theses of ours we have expounded and developed our position. In *September 1915* we explained its application to the Polish question in a special resolution, which we append herewith, in order to show concretely how, in our opinion, the agitation from the social-revolutionary point of view should be conducted among the workers of oppressed nations.

III. The Polish Question and Social Democracy

The attitude of the possessing classes during the World War showed with all clarity the justice of the claim of Russian-Polish Social Democracy, that capitalist development has split the interests of Polish capitalism into opposing parts and combined its interests with those of the partition powers. This *burying of the independence movement* found its expression in the conscious renunciation of the independence slogan on the part of the Polish bourgeoisie; all its war programs were to be realized not by the military power of one or the other of the imperialist camps, but by the strengthening of one of these camps through its coming to include the Polish territories. All the war programs of the Polish bourgeoisie are directed against the independence of Poland.

The World War has shown that the period of building national states in Europe has passed. In the imperialist phase of capitalism, every state strives to extend its boundaries by annexations and the oppression of foreign peoples. The attitude of the Polish bourgeoisie in all the partition states showed clearly that the ideal of the national state in the imperialist phase is an anachronism, and it confirms the rightness of the attitude of the Russian-Polish Social Democrats toward the efforts for independence.

1. *The Polish proletariat has never made national independence its goal.* It grew up on the basis of the capitalistic

fusion of all three parts of Poland with the partition powers, and carried on its fight for democracy, for the improvement of its economic conditions, for socialism, *in the framework of the historically given states together with the proletarians of all other nations.* It sought to destroy, *not the given state boundaries, but the character of the state itself as the organ of class and national oppression. Today,* in view of the experiences of the World War, to raise the slogan of *independence* as a means to struggle against national oppression would be not only a *harmful* utopia, but the *denial of the simplest fundamentals of socialism.* This slogan would mean trying to build a new imperialist power, a power which would likewise strive for the subjection and domination of foreign peoples. The only result of such a program would be the weakening of class consciousness, the sharpening of national antagonisms, splitting the forces of the proletariat and increasing the danger of new wars.

2. The program of uniting the Polish territories under the rule of one of the imperialist states or a coalition of these, a program such as that put forward by the Austrophiles and the Russophiles, has its origin in the desire of the Polish bourgeoisie to strengthen their position as against the bourgeoisie of the partition powers, to secure for themselves a greater share in the imperialist booty of these states.

In the partition states, the desire to include the Polish territories arises from strategic and general imperialist interests, which call for augmenting the national territory. Arising as it does from the imperialist interests of the Polish bourgeoisie and of the bourgeoisie in the partition states, the idea of uniting the Polish territories under the dominion of a Great Power or a coalition of Great Powers *could only be an instrument of imperialist policy.* Since these imperialist interests, the general and especially the economic interests, demand that the Polish territories should be maintained in complete subjection, they do not contemplate a democratic system in these territories. Thus, there can be no question of such a union giving even minimal guarantees of free cultural development, the only aspect of the national question that is tied up with the interests of the proletariat.

The question whether the war will lead to a union of the Polish territories into one organism joined to the victorious state will depend on the military result of the war and on the diplomatic situation which results. The war might also end with a *splitting up of the Polish territories* through new annexations, and a new carving up of the Polish map. Some fear that such new partitions and the consequent changes in market, customs, and legal conditions would shake up the capitalist development of Poland and therewith the socialist movement of Russian Poland. No doubt these fears are exaggerated. The relatively advanced level of economic development in Poland has already created the productive forces which could cope with new conditions, and the weakening of the socialist movement in one part of Poland would be compensated by its strengthening in another part. Nevertheless, the necessity of such an adaptation would cause a long economic *crisis,* whose whole weight would be laid on the backs of the proletariat.

What has been said refers also to the idea of an independent *buffer state,* which, be it said, is a hollow utopia of small, powerless groups. If this idea was put into operation, it would mean the creation of a little Polish rump state, which would be the military colony of one or another of the Great-Power groups, a plaything of their military and economic interests, an area for exploitation by foreign capital, and a battlefield of future wars.

3. From these considerations it follows that the interests of the proletariat—economic, cultural, and political—exclude *any support for the war programs of the Polish bourgeoisie.* The old proletarian policy, which was determined by the class interests of the proletariat, must remain unchanged, and

the working class has not the least reason to abandon it in the interests of the bourgeois war programs. Support for these programs would correspond to no real need, and would mean abandoning actions oriented to the advantage of their own class; it would mean entering an alliance with the bourgeoisie for the whole duration of the war, and would divert the proletariat for many years from its rightful course. On the other hand, the proletariat cannot undertake to *defend the borders of the partition states,* because in the present epoch every capitalist state would become a drag on development, to say nothing of the fact that the partition powers were, for the Polish proletariat, organs not only of class oppression but also of national oppression.

Without closing our eyes to all the dangers mentioned above, which would arise for the Polish proletariat in the event of a new splitting up of Poland, the Polish proletariat must take into account that it also has to *avoid being left on one side in the imperialist epoch,* just as one cannot leave on one side all other dangers of imperialism without the victory of socialism.

4. The fact that the general questions raised by the war are incapable of solution under capitalism, and the further fact that it is impossible to defend adequately the national-cultural interests of the proletariat in the epoch of imperialism, naturally does not mean that the proletariat should "wait" with folded arms for socialism, which would free it from the new dangers and burdens of the war and from the dangers of new national oppression. Imperialism is a policy of capitalism at one stage of its development, which makes possible the socialist organization of production. The sacrifices which the proletariat brings to the war, the increase of the pressure of taxes, the political reaction, the worsening of labor conditions, all the results of the war will drive the proletariat to revolutionary struggles for socialism, which will fill the next historical epoch. The struggle against the war is

opening this new epoch. We show how capitalism, purporting to act for the people's interests, leads them to the slaughter-house and tears the nations to pieces; how it treads under foot the nation's needs; how it treats the masses of the people like dumb cows. And while we protest against this waste of the people's blood, this arbitrary tearing to pieces of nations by the Great Powers, this multiplication of national oppressions, we are preparing the proletariat for the revolutionary struggle.

Whether the sharpening of the political crisis during the war permits the proletariat to play an active role, or whether it will only be possible later for such struggles to take place, the proletariat will not endorse *any separatist policy* (defense of the status quo, fight against union under a single dominion), nor will it follow the will-o'-the-wisp of Polish independence. It will *change its protest against the consequences of the war* (blood sacrifice, economic injuries, annexations, national oppression) into the *struggle against the causes of imperialism.* The Polish proletariat will carry on this struggle in the sense of a *striving for socialist revolution, hand in hand with the international proletariat in general, but particularly with that of the partition powers.* This social-revolutionary struggle *in no way excludes the struggle for the democratization of political institutions* even within the framework of capitalism, as, for example, in Russia for the overthrow of tsarism; it does not preclude the winning of national freedoms, as, for instance, the extension of local, provincial, and regional autonomy. On the contrary, the revolutionary prospects must strengthen the proletariat's drive for immediate victories; for the consciousness that only the social revolution will lead to the complete ending of class and national oppression will arm the proletariat against every policy of compromise which would diminish the fury of the class war.

Notes

1. From *Gazeta Robotnicza*, no. 6, October 1916, and *Vorbote*, no. 2, April 1916. See Lenin's *Gesammeltę Werke* (Leipzig: 1930), XIX, 528-38.